Christ the Conqueror of Hell

The Descent into Hades
from an Orthodox Perspective

ARCHBISHOP HILARION ALFEYEV

ST VLADIMIR'S SEMINARY PRESS
CRESTWOOD, NEW YORK

Library of Congress Cataloging-in-Publication Data

Ilarion, Hieromonk.
    Christ the conqueror of hell : the descent into Hades from an Orthodox
perspective / Archbishop Hilarion Alfeyev.
        p. cm.
    Includes bibliographical references.
    ISBN 978-0-88141-061-7
    1. Jesus Christ—Descent into hell—History of doctrines.   2. Orthodox Eastern
Church—Doctrines.   I. Title.

    BT470.I425 2009
    232.96'7—dc22

                                                                    2009035366

ST VLADIMIR'S SEMINARY PRESS
575 Scarsdale Rd, Crestwood, NY 10707
1-800-204-2665
www.svspress.com

ISBN 978-0-88141-061-7

PRINTED IN THE UNITED STATES OF AMERICA

"Hell reigns, but not forever,

over the race of mortals"

—*The Vespers of Holy Saturday*

Contents

Introduction

Ancient Byzantine and Russian icons of the Resurrection of Christ never depict the resurrection itself, i.e., Jesus coming out of the grave. Rather, they depict the descent of Christ into Hades, or, to be more precise, his rising out of it. Jesus Christ, sometimes with a cross in his hand, is depicted as raising Adam, Eve, and other personages of biblical history from Hades. Under the Savior's feet is the black abyss of the nether world; against its background are castles, and locks and debris of the gates that once barred the dead's way to resurrection. Other motifs have been used to create the image of the Resurrection of Christ in the last several centuries,[1] but the above-described iconographic type is considered to be canonical. It reflects the traditional teachings of Christ's descent into Hades, his victory over death, and his raising and delivering of the dead from hell where they were imprisoned before his Resurrection. The present study, with particular emphasis on the Orthodox tradition, is devoted to this teaching, which is an integral part of the dogmatic and liturgical tradition of the Christian church.

The descent of Christ into Hades is one of the most mysterious, enigmatic, and inexplicable events in New Testament history. In today's Christian world this event is understood in different ways. Most liberal Western theologians reject altogether any possibility of speaking of Christ's literal descent into Hades, arguing that the scriptural texts on this theme should be understood metaphorically. The traditional Catholic doctrine insists that after his death on the cross Christ did indeed descend into Hades, but only to deliver the Old

---

[1]In particular, the image of the risen Christ coming out of the grave and holding a victory banner, borrowed from the Western tradition. For more details concerning Christian iconography of the Resurrection see: J. Villette, *La Résurrection du Christ dans l'art chrétien du IIe au VIIe siècle* (Paris, 1957).

9

Testament righteous from it. A similar understanding is quite wide-spread among Orthodox Christians.

The New Testament, however, speaks of the preaching of Christ in hell as addressed to the unrepentant sinners:

> For Christ also died for sins once for all, the righteous for the unrighteous, that he might bring us to God, being put to death in the flesh but made alive in the spirit; in which he went and preached to the spirits in prison, who formerly did not obey, when God's patience waited.[2]

Moreover, many church fathers and liturgical texts of the Orthodox Church repeatedly underline that having descended into Hades, Christ opened the way to salvation for all people, not only for the Old Testament righteous. The descent of Christ into Hades is perceived as an event of cosmic significance involving all people without exception. They also speak about the victory of Christ over death, the full devastation of hell, and that after Christ's descent into Hades there was no one left there except for the devil and demons.

What was the original faith of the church? What do early Christian sources tell us about the descent into Hades? What is the Orthodox Church's position on this issue? And what is the soteriological significance of the descent of Christ into Hades from the Orthodox point of view? These and other related questions are dealt with in the present study.

Without attempting to be exhaustive, many texts devoted to the descent of Christ into Hades will be considered, beginning with the analysis of New Testament and apocryphal texts, as well as of early Christian poetry. This will be followed by a survey of passages from Eastern church fathers and an excursus into the Western theological tradition. Then the hymns by St Ephrem the Syrian and St Romanos the Melodist, which exerted great influence on liturgical poetry of the Orthodox Church, will be analyzed, followed by the Orthodox liturgical texts themselves. The study of the dogmatic content of these texts is of crucial importance for understanding Orthodox belief,

---

[2] 1 Pet 3.18–21.

since it is precisely these texts that form the nucleus of Orthodox dogmatic teaching.

A special note should be made concerning the use of the terms Hades and hell. Both terms are used throughout the book to render the Greek *haidēs*, which in many cases denotes "the underworld," the realm of death, equivalent to the Hebrew *sheol*.[3] It is the place where, according to Old Testament beliefs, the souls of all people, both righteous and sinners, descended after death. The term *haidēs*, however, is also used to refer to a place of seclusion or of torment. In the New Testament, apart from *haidēs* (Hades, hell),[4] we find several other terms referring to the underworld reality, such as *phylakē* (prison, cf. Latin *carcer*),[5] *geenna* (Gehenna),[6] and *katachthonia* (the underworld).[7] Each has a particular nuance, though at times this nuance is not easily discernible. In many Byzantine patristic writings as well as in church liturgical poetry, all these terms are used synonymously. Depending on the context, they refer either to the underworld or, more frequently, to the place of torment for sinners after their death.

The present study, originally written in Russian, has been translated into English by Deacon Basil (William) Bush, Irina Kukota, and Zinaida Nossova; and partly edited by Dimitri Conomos. To each of them the author owes a special debt of gratitude.

---

[3] In the Septuagint, the Hebrew *sheol* is normally rendered as *haidēs*.
[4] Cf. Matt 11.23; 16.18; Luke 10.15; 16.23; Acts 2.27 (Ps 16.10), 30; 1 Cor 15.55 (Hos 13.14); Rev 1.18; 3.7; 6.8; 20.13, 14.
[5] Cf. Luke 12.58; 1 Pet 3.19.
[6] Matt 5.22, 29, 39; 10.28; 18.9; 23.15, 33; Mark 9.43, 45, 47; Luke 12.5; Jas 3.6.
[7] Phil 2.10. Cf. *katotera* in Eph 4.9.

Abbreviations

CCSA	Corpus Christianorum: Series apocryphorum
CCSG	Corpus Christianorum: Series graeca
CCSL	Corpus Christianorum: Series latina
CSCO	Corpus scriptorum christianorum orientalium
CSEL	Corpus scriptorum ecclesiasticorum latinorum
GCS	Die griechische christliche Schriftsteller der ersten [drei] Jahrhunderte
LXX	Septuagint
NPNF	Nicene and Post-Nicene Fathers, 2 series
OrChrAn	Orientalia christiana analecta
PG	Patrologia graeca
PL	Patrologia latina
PTS	Patristische Texte und Studien
RSV	Revised Standard Version
SC	Sources chrétiennes
TU	Texte und Untersuchungen

PART ONE

THE DESCENT INTO HADES IN SCRIPTURE AND PATRISTIC TRADITION

CHAPTER ONE

The New Testament, Apocryphal Literature, and Early Christian Poetry

KEY NEW TESTAMENT TEXTS

The descent of Christ into Hades, while not mentioned directly in any of the canonical Gospels, is indirectly referred to in the Gospel of Matthew, in his account of the crucifixion: "The tombs also were opened, and many bodies of the saints who had fallen asleep were raised, and coming out of the tombs after his resurrection they went into the holy city and appeared to many."[1] These words of the Evangelist reflect that "paschal faith" in the resurrection of the dead that imbues all of early Christianity.[2] They are also the basis for the teaching on Christ's resurrecting the Old Testament righteous, who were later equated with the "saints" mentioned by St Matthew.

The same Gospel quotes Christ's words concerning his three-day burial in the depths of the earth: "For as Jonah was three days and three nights in the belly of the whale, so will the Son of man be three days and three nights in the heart of the earth."[3] In the Christian tradition this story of the prophet Jonah is seen as a foretelling of Christ's descent into Hades.[4]

---

[1]Matt 27.52–53. Here and below the RSV is used for biblical quotations, except for those biblical verses that are quoted by a Greek apocryphal, patristic, or liturgical source. In the latter case the translation from the Septuagint (LXX) is normally used.

[2]Cf. J. Jeremias, *New Testament Theology*, vol. I (London, 1972), p. 309.

[3]Matt 12.40.

[4]Among other types and texts of the Old Testament related to Christ's descent

Belief in Christ's descent into Hades following the crucifixion is clearly expressed in the Acts of the Apostles. Peter's speech, given after the Holy Spirit had descended on the apostles on the day of Pentecost, runs as follows:

> Men of Israel, hear these words: Jesus of Nazareth, a man attested to you by God with mighty works and wonders and signs which God did through him in your midst, as you yourselves know—this Jesus, delivered up according to the definite plan and foreknowledge of God, you crucified and killed by the hands of lawless men. But God raised him up, having loosed the pangs of death, because it was not possible for him to be held by it.... Brethren, I may say to you confidently of the patriarch David that he both died and was buried, and his tomb is with us to this day. Being therefore a prophet, and knowing that God had sworn with an oath to him that he would set one of his descendants upon his throne, he foresaw and spoke of the resurrection of the Christ, that he was not abandoned to Hades, nor did his flesh see corruption.[5] This Jesus God raised up, and of that we all are witnesses.[6]

The first Epistle of Peter is another important New Testament text, which directly mentions Christ's decent into hell. Here the theme is examined within the context of baptism. The apostle speaks not only of Christ being in the "prison" of hell but also of his preaching to the souls therein:

> For Christ also died for sins once for all, the righteous for the unrighteous, that he might bring us to God, being put to death in the flesh but made alive in the spirit; in which he went and preached to the spirits in prison, who formerly did not obey, when God's

---

into Hades we should mention two texts in the Septuagint translation: Job 38.17 ("And do the gates of death open to thee for fear; and did the porters of hell quake when they saw thee?") and Hos 13.14 ("I will deliver them out of the power of Hades, and will redeem them from death: where is thy penalty, O death? O Hades, where is thy sting?").

[5]Ps 15.10.

[6]Acts 2.22–24, 29–32. Cf. also Acts 13.34–37.

patience waited in the days of Noah, during the building of the ark, in which a few, that is, eight persons, were saved through water. Baptism, which corresponds to this, now saves you . . . through the resurrection of Jesus Christ.[7]

The Petrine connection between Christ's descent into Hades and baptism can also be found in later Christian writings on baptism.[8]

In the same epistle we read: "For this is why the gospel was preached even to the dead, that though judged in the flesh like men, they might live in the spirit like God."[9] These words serve as the basis for understanding Christ's suffering for the "unrighteous" and how his preaching in hell reached even those of whom the Old Testament speaks: "And the Lord saw that the wickedness of man was great in the earth, and that every imagination of the thoughts of his heart was only evil continually."[10] Those who were condemned earlier "according to men in the flesh" by God who, according to the biblical expression, "was sorry" that he had created them,[11] did not perish eternally. Christ descended into hell, granting them another chance of salvation by preaching to them the Gospel of the kingdom so that they might live "according to God in the spirit."

Among other New Testament texts related to our theme, mention should be made of St Paul's words that speak of how Christ "descended into the lower parts of the earth"[12] and of his victory over death and hell.[13]

---

[7]1 Pet 3.18–21.

[8]For details cf. W. Bieder, *Die Vorstellung von der Höllenschaft Jesu Christi* (Zürich, 1949), pp. 198–199; O. Rousseau, "La descente aux enfers, fondement sotériologique du baptême chrétien," *Recherches de science religieuse* 40 (1950–1951), pp. 283–297; K. McDonnell, *The Baptism of Jesus in the Jordan* (Collegeville, Minn., 1996), pp. 156–70. An exhaustive study of the exegesis of 1 Pet 3.18–21 in the Christian tradition can be found in: B. Reicke, *The Disobedient Spirits and Christian Baptism* (Copenhagen, 1946). Cf. also W. J. Dalton, *Christ's Proclamation to the Spirits* (Rome, 1965).

[9]1 Pet 4.6.

[10]Gen 6.5.

[11]Gen 6.6.

[12]Eph 4.9.

[13]Cf. 1 Cor 15.54–57; also Rom 10.7; Col 2.14–15.

Christ as the vanquisher of Hades, on his casting the devil, death, and hell into the "lake of fire," is one of the main themes in the Book of Revelation.[14] In it Christ speaks of himself as "the first and the last, and the living one," saying, "I died, and behold I am alive for evermore, and I have the keys of Death and Hades."[15] The image of the "keys of Hades" is later developed in both iconography and liturgical poetry.

Thus, already in the New Testament we encounter three themes which A. Grillmeier regards as fundamental to all early Christian literature: 1) Christ descending into hell and preaching to the souls of all those held there, not only to the righteous but also to the sinners (*theme of kerygma*); 2) there is a certain relationship between Christ's descent into Hades and the sacrament of baptism (*baptismal theme*); and 3) Christ, descending into Hades, vanquished hell and death (*theme of victory*).[16]

APOCRYPHAL LITERATURE

The subject of Christ's descent into Hades is given much more attention in early Christian apocryphal literature than in the canonical New Testament texts. Before examining the content of particular works, I would like to point out that apocryphal stories, widespread in the first centuries of Christianity, differed not only in origin but also in content. Their fate in the Christian church also varied. Some apocryphal gospels, including those of gnostic or heretical origin, were condemned by the church and removed from use. At the same

---

[14]Cf. for example, Rev 20.10, 14.

[15]Rev 1.17–18.

[16]Cf. A. Grillmeier, "Der Gottessohn im Totenreich: Soteriologische und christologische Motivierung der Descensuslehre in der älteren christlichen Überlieferung," *Zeitschrift für Katholische Theologie* 71 (Vienna, 1949), pp. 4–5; Idem, *Christ in Christian Tradition*, vol. 1 (Atlanta, 1975), p. 74. For more on Christ's descent into Hades in the Judeo-Christian tradition cf. J. Daniélou, *Théologie du Judéo-Christianisme* (Paris, 1958), pp. 257–273; English translation: *The Theology of Jewish Christianity* (London, s.a.), pp. 233–248.

time those apocryphal books whose content did not contradict church doctrine were kept in church tradition in an indirect way, even though they were not included in the canon of the New Testament. Many ideas contained in them entered liturgical texts and even hagiographic literature. Among the apocryphal writings that influenced the development of Christian liturgics are the "Protoevangelium of James," which tells of the birth, childhood, and youth of the Most Holy Virgin Mary, and "The Gospel of Nicodemus," which speaks of the last hours of the earthly life, the death, and the Resurrection of Christ. Neither work contains gnostic or other ideas foreign to Christianity, but both contain biblical materials that complete, as it were, the accounts mentioned only briefly in the New Testament. Apocryphal writings that influenced Christian hagiography include the "Acts of Thomas," "The Teaching of Addaius the Apostle," "The Story of the Apostle Johannan," and other deeds of the apostles. These are preserved in Greek, Syriac, and other ancient languages.

One apocryphal text that deals especially with Christ's descent into Hades is the so-called "Ascension of Isaiah," an early Christian reworking of a Jewish apocryphal work written in the second century BC. It is thought to have been originally written in Hebrew or Aramaic with a later interpolation of the Christian apocalypse.[17] Chapters one through five comprise the Jewish section of this work while chapters six through eleven were written by a Christian author. This work is preserved in its entirety only in Ethiopic, although chapters six through eleven are also to be found in Latin and Slavonic (Old Bulgarian) versions. A Greek version also exists only in fragments:[18]

---

[17] *Oxford Dictionary of the Christian Church*, 3rd ed. (Oxford, 1997), pp. 849–850.

[18] The first publication of the Ethiopian version is: E. Tisserant, *Ascension d'Isaie de la version éthiopienne* (Paris, 1909). Greek fragments: B. Grenfell and A. Hunt, *The Amherst Papyri* I (London, 1900). The latest critical edition of all versions of this work: P. Bettiolo, A. G. Kossova, C. Leonardi, E. Norelli, and L. Perrone, cura, *Ascensio Isaiae. Textus*, CCSA 7 (Tournhout, 1995). For translations and studies on the texts cf. E. Norelli, cura, *Ascensio Isaiae. Commentarius*, CCSA 8 (Tournhout, 1995). For an analysis of its theological content cf. A. Acerbi, *L'Ascensione di Isaia: Cristologia e profetismo in Siria nei primi decenni dei II Secolo* (Milano, 1989). Cf. also E. Schürer, *The History of the Jewish People in the Age of Jesus Christ*, vol. 3, part 1 (Edinburgh, 1986), pp. 335–341.

The Beloved will descend . . . into the world in the last days the Lord, who will be called Christ . . . And the god of that world will stretch forth his hand against the Son, and they will crucify him on a tree, and will slay him not knowing who he is. And thus his descent, as you will see, will be hidden even from the heavens, so that it will not be known who he is. And when he hath plundered the angel of death, he will ascend on the third day. . . . And then many of the righteous will ascend with him, whose spirits do not receive their garments till the Lord Christ ascends and they ascend with him.[19]

In the same writing the Eternal (God the Father) directs his Son, saying, "Go forth and descend through all the heavens, and thou wilt descend to the firmament and that world: to the angel in Sheol[20] thou wilt descend."[21]

Yet another Christian fragment of the second century is interpolated into "The Testament of Asher," a Jewish apocrypha of the second century BC. It tells of how the Most High One, appearing on Earth and descending into water (an indication of Jesus' baptism in the Jordan), smote the head of the dragon.[22] This is clearly a development of the New Testament's "baptismal theme": Christ's victory over the devil at his descent into Hades is symbolically depicted using material from the story of his baptism by John in the Jordan. Later on this theme is developed both in Byzantine iconography and in liturgical texts. We read, for example, in the prayer of the Great Blessing of the Waters: "Thou hast sanctified the streams of the Jordan, having sent down thy Holy Spirit from the heavens, and crushed the head of the snakes lurking there."

The descent into Hades is also mentioned a number of times in "The Testament of Twelve Patriarchs."[23] The main part of this Judaic apocryphal work is dated to the second half of the first century, but

---

[19]Donalds-Robertson, trans., *The Ascension of Isaiah* IX, pp. 12–17.

[20]Latin: "ad angelum qui est in infernum."

[21]Donalds-Robertson, trans., *The Ascension of Isaiah* X, p. 8.

[22]J. H. Charlesworth, *The Old Testament Pseudepigrapha*, vol. 1 (1985), p. 88.

[23]The Greek text: R. H. Charles, ed., *The Greek Versions of the Testament of the Twelve Patriarchs* (Oxford, 1908).

the surviving Greek version is its Christian adaptation. The victory over Hades is described in the following way: "Know that the Lord will execute judgment upon the sons of men; because when the rocks are rent, and the sun quenched, and the waters dried up, and the fire trembling, and all creation troubled, and the invisible spirits melting away, and the grave spoiled in the suffering of the Most High, men unbelieving will abide in their iniquity, therefore with punishment shall they be judged."[24] In another passage the focus turns to the victory of the Lord over Beliar: "He shall make war against Beliar, and he shall give the vengeance of victory to our coasts. And the captivity shall he take from Beliar, even the souls of the saints, and shall turn disobedient hearts unto the Lord, and shall give to them who call upon him everlasting peace; and the saints shall rest in Eden, and the righteous shall rejoice in the new Jerusalem, which shall be unto the glory of God for ever and ever."[25] Finally, in a third instance, the matter concerns Christ's ascent from Hades after his suffering and death: "And the veil of the temple shall be rent, and the Spirit of God shall descend upon the Gentiles as fire poured forth. And he shall arise from the grave, and shall ascend from earth into heaven: and I know how lowly he will be upon the earth, and how glorious in heaven."[26] Here we can clearly see the early Christian notion that after his death on the cross Christ descended into hell, conquered Beliar, liberated the souls of the saints, and ascended to heaven.[27]

In "The Gospel of Peter," most probably written in the first half of the second century,[28] we find a story about Christ leaving his tomb accompanied by two men, one to his right and one to his left. "And

---

[24] *Testament of Levi* 4.

[25] *Testament of Dan* 5.

[26] *Testament of Benjamin* 9.

[27] For a detailed analysis of the texts quoted see: J. Daniélou, *The Theology of Jewish Christianity*, pp. 239–242.

[28] The Greek text was discovered in 1886 in Egypt and critically edited in M. G. Mara, éd., *Evangile de Pierre*, SC 201 (Paris, 1973). "The Gospel ascribed to Peter" was known to Origen (*Commentary on Matthew* 10, 17). Eusebius mentions the "Gospel of Peter" among the heretical writings (*Ecclesiastical History* 3, 3; 3, 25; 6, 12). For a more detailed analysis see, e.g., H. B. Swete, *The Gospel of Peter* (New York, 1893); Th. Zahn, *Das Evangelium des Petrus* (Erlangen, 1893).

they heard a voice from the heavens, saying, Hast thou preached to them that sleep? And a response was heard from the cross, Yea."[29] With these words the "theme of the kerigma" (Christ's preaching in Hades) finds its continuation from its first mention in 1 Peter 3.18. It is further developed in "The Epistle of the Apostles," dated to the second century and which survives in its entirety only in Ethiopic.[30] This "epistle" also speaks of Christ preaching in Hades and of his baptizing the righteous who had descended into it:

> For to that end went I down unto the place of Lazarus, and preached unto the righteous and the prophets, that they might come out of the rest which is below and come up into that which is above; and I poured out upon them with my right hand the water of life and forgiveness and salvation from all evil, as I have done unto you and unto them that believe on me. But if any man believe on me and do not my commandments, although he have confessed my name, he hath no profit therefrom but runneth a vain race: for such will find themselves in perdition and destruction, because they have despised my commandments.[31]

The baptism of the Old Testament righteous is also mentioned in "The Shepherd" by Hermas, an apocryphal apocalypse dating from the second half of the second century.[32] The baptismal theme, in connection with the decent into Hades, is developed in the following way:

> Before a man bears the name of the Son of God he is dead; but when he receives the seal he lays aside his deadness, and obtains life. The seal, then, is the water: they descend into the water dead, and they arise alive. . . . These apostles and teachers who preached the name

---

[29]Donalds-Robertson, trans., *The Gospel of Peter*, pp. 39–42.

[30]L. Guerrier, *Le testament en Galilée de Notre-Séigneur Jésus-Christ: Texte éthiopien édité et traduit avec le concours de S. Grébaut* (Paris, 1913), 141–236. For a scholarly analysis see in particular M. Hornschuh, *Studien zur Epistula Apostolorum*, PTS 5 (Berlin, 1965).

[31]M. R. James, trans., *The Epistle of the Apostles*, p. 27.

[32]For the Greek text see, in particular, F. X. Funk and K. Bihlmeyer, *Die apostolischen Väter* (Tübingen, 1924).

of the Son of God, after falling asleep in the power and faith of the Son of God, preached it not only to those who were asleep, but themselves also gave them the seal of the preaching. Accordingly they descended with them into the water, and again ascended. [But these descended alive and rose up again alive; whereas they who had previously fallen asleep descended dead, but rose up again alive.] By these, then, were they quickened and made to know the name of the Son of God.[33]

The subject of the descent is also found in "The Teachings of Silvanus," one of the few texts found in the Nag Hammadi Library that is not primarily gnostic in origin.[34] Though originally written in Greek, the work, discovered in 1945, survives in a Coptic translation. Scholars date the composition of the "Teachings" from the second century to the second or third decade of the fourth century.

O soul, persistent one, in what ignorance you exist! For who is your guide into the darkness? How many likenesses did Christ take on because of you? Although he was God, he [was found] among men as a man. He descended to the underworld. He released the children of death. They were in travail, as the scripture of God has said. And he sealed up the [very] heart of it [the underworld]. And he broke its strong bars completely. And when all the powers had seen him, they fled so that he might bring you, wretched one, up from the

---

[33]Donalds-Robertson, trans., *The Shepherd, Similitudes* 9, 16. In this text some scholars see an allusion to the practice of "baptism for the dead," allegedly widespread in the early church (cf. 1 Cor 15.29). This practice existed in some Marcionite communities (see Epiphanius, *Panarion* 28, 6 in PG 41:384d), but it was denounced by later Orthodox writers, notably St John Chrysostom (*Homilies on the 1st Epistle to the Corinthians* 40, 1). On the "baptism for the dead," see an informative but very tendentious article by H. Nibley, "Baptism for the Dead in Ancient Times," *Improvement Era* 51 (1948), pp. 786–788, 836–838; 52 (1949), pp. 24–26, 60, 90–91, 109–110, 112, 146–148, 180–183, 212–214. Cf. the critique by B. M. Foschini in *Catholic Biblical Quarterly* 13 (1951), pp. 51–53, 70–73.

[34]For an English translation see M. L. Peel and J. Zandee, *The Nag Hammadi Library*, ed. James M. Robinson; rev. ed. (San Francisco, 1990). For the theme of the descent into Hades in "The Teachings" see: M. L. Peel, "The *Descensus ad Inferos* in the Teachings of Silvanus," *Numen* 26, no. 1 (1979), pp. 23–49.

abyss, and might die for you as a ransom for your sin. He saved you from the strong hand of the Underworld.[35]

In another passage from the same source Christ is described as conquering the Underworld by breaking the chains that bound him and by humiliating the devil:

> Know who Christ is, and acquire him as a friend, for this is the friend who is faithful. He is also God and Teacher. This one, being God, became man for your sake. It is this one who broke the iron bars of the Underworld and the bronze bolts. It is this one who attacked and cast down every haughty tyrant. It is he who loosened from himself the chains of which he had taken hold. He brought up the poor from the abyss and the mourners from the Underworld. It is he who humbled the haughty powers; he who put to shame haughtiness through humility; he who has cast down the strong and the boaster through weakness; he who in his contempt scorned that which is considered an honor so that humility for God's sake might be highly exalted; [and] he who has put on humanity.[36]

The theme of the descent into Hades plays a key role in "The Gospel of Bartholomew," which has been preserved in Greek, Coptic, Syriac, Latin, and Slavonic.[37] Scholars date the text to anywhere between the second and fourth centuries.[38] The first part contains a dialogue between the risen Christ and the apostle Bartholomew.

---

[35]M. L. Peel and J. Zandee, trans., Account A 103.28–4.14.

[36]M. L. Peel and J. Zandee, trans., Account B 110.14–11.4.

[37]For the Greek and Slavonic texts see N. Bonwetsch, "Die apokryphen Fragen des Bartolomäus," *Nachrichten der Gesellschaft der Wissenschaften zu Göttingen* (Göttingen, 1897), pp. 1–42. For the Greek and Latin versions see A. Wilmart and E. Tisserant, "Fragments grecs et latins de l'Évangile de Barthélemy," *Revue biblique* 10 (1913), pp. 185–190. Another edition of the Latin version: V. Moricca, "Un nuovo testo dell Evangelo di Bartolomeo," *Revue biblique* 18 (1921), pp. 481–516; 19 (1922), pp. 20–30. For the Coptic version see E. Revillout, "Les apocryphes coptes; Premiere partie, Les évangiles des douze apôtres et de Saint Barthélemy," *Patrologia Orientalis* 2 (fasc. 2; Paris, 1907). For a theological analysis of the text consult: J. Kroll, *Gott und Hölle: Der Mythos vom Descensuskampfe* (Leipzig, 1932), pp. 71–82; J.-D. Kaestli, "Où en est l'étude de l' 'Évangile de Barthélemy'?" *Revue biblique* 95 (Paris, 1988), pp. 5–33.

[38]See: J. K. Elliott, *The Apocryphal New Testament* (Oxford, 1993), p. 652.

Responding to his disciple, Christ describes in detail his descent into Hades and the conversations between Hades, Death, and Beliar:

After the resurrection from the dead of our Lord Jesus Christ, Bartholomew came unto the Lord and questioned him, saying: ". . . Lord, when thou wentest to be hanged upon the cross, I followed thee afar off and saw thee hung upon the cross, and the angels coming down from heaven and worshipping thee. And when there came darkness, I beheld, and I saw thee that thou wast vanished away from the cross and I heard only a voice in the parts under the earth, and great wailing and gnashing of teeth on a sudden. Tell me, Lord, whither wentest thou from the cross?" And Jesus answered and said: "Blessed art thou, Bartholomew, my beloved, because thou sawest this mystery, and now will I tell thee all things whatsoever thou askest me. For when I vanished away from the cross, then went I down into Hades that I might bring up Adam and all them that were with him, according to the supplication of Michael the archangel." Then said Bartholomew: "Lord, what was the voice which was heard?" Jesus saith unto him: "Hades said unto Beliar: 'As I perceive, a God cometh hither.' And Beliar said unto Hades: 'Look carefully who it is that, for it is Elias, or Enoch, or one of the prophets that this man seemeth to me to be.' But Hades answered Death and said: 'Not yet are six thousand years accomplished. And whence are these, O Beliar; for the sum of the number is in mine hands. Be not troubled, make safe thy gates and strengthen thy bars: consider, God cometh not down upon the earth.' Hades saith unto him: 'These be no good words that I hear from thee: my belly is rent, and mine inward parts are pained: it cannot be but that God cometh hither. Alas, whither shall I flee before the face of the power of the great king? Suffer me to enter into myself: for before thee was I formed.' Then did I enter in and scourged him and bound him with chains that cannot be loosed, and brought forth thence all the patriarchs and came again unto the cross."[39]

---

[39]M. R. James, trans. from Greek, *The Gospel of Bartholomew* 1–20.

This text reflects a tradition that would eventually exert immense influence on church hymnography. The dialogues between Death, Hades, and Beliar recur as one of the most widespread subjects in ecclesiastical poetry (notably in St Ephrem the Syrian and St Romanos the Melodist). Enoch and Elijah also become permanent heroes of the descent story. As far as the liberation of Adam and the Old Testament righteous is concerned this would also appear as a leitmotif in all similar writings. In "The Gospel of Bartholomew" it is developed in the following way:

> Bartholomew saith unto him: "Tell me, Lord, who was he whom the angels bare up in their hands, even that man that was very great of stature?" Jesus answered and said unto him: "It was Adam the first-formed, for whose sake I came down from heaven upon earth. And I said unto him: I was hung upon the cross for thee and for thy children's sake. And he, when he heard it, groaned and said: So was thy good pleasure, O Lord." Again Bartholomew said: "Lord, I saw the angels ascending before Adam and singing praises. But one of the angels which was very great, above the rest, would not ascend up with them: and there was in his hand a sword of fire, and he was looking steadfastly upon thee only." And when he had thus spoken, he said unto the apostles: "Tarry for me in this place, for today a sacrifice is offered in paradise." And Bartholomew answered and said unto Jesus: "Lord, what is the sacrifice which is offered in paradise?" And Jesus said: "There be souls of the righteous which to-day have departed out of the body and go unto paradise, and unless I be present they cannot enter into paradise." And Bartholomew said: "Lord, how many souls depart out of the world daily?" Jesus saith unto him: "Thirty thousand." Bartholomew saith unto him: "Lord, when thou wast with us teaching the word, didst thou receive the sacrifices in paradise?" Jesus answered and said unto him: "Verily I say unto thee, my beloved, that I both taught the word with you and continually sat with my Father, and received the sacrifices in paradise everyday."[40]

---

[40]M. R. James, trans., *The Gospel of Bartholomew* 21–31.

The notion of Christ's omnipresence will also become a cardinal theme in both patristic and liturgical texts dedicated to the descent. The part of "The Gospel of Bartholomew" that deals with this episode ends with Christ's response to the question of how many people enter paradise from among those who die every day. Different versions of the text give different figures: in most cases the response is about fifty-three righteous people. Of that number, three "enter into paradise or are laid up in Abraham's bosom" (thus Abraham's bosom is identified with paradise), while the remaining fifty "go into the place of the resurrection."[41]

The most detailed description of Christ's descent into Hades is found in "The Gospel of Nicodemus." It exerted decisive influence on the formation of church doctrine on the subject. This text is preserved in many versions: Greek, Syriac, Armenian, Coptic, Arabic, and Latin.[42] The first part (chapters one through eleven), called "The Acts of Pilate," describes the death and burial of Jesus Christ. The second (chapters twelve through sixteen) reports on the discussion concerning Christ's resurrection, which supposedly took place in the Sanhedrin. The third (chapters seventeen through twenty-seven), entitled "Christ's Descent into Hades" (Descensus Christi ad inferos), describes the testimony of Simeon the God-receiver's two sons. Having been resurrected by Christ, they informed the Sanhedrin of what

---

[41]M. R. James, trans., *The Gospel of Bartholomew* 32–33.

[42]Critical edition of the Greek text: C. Tischendorff, *Evangelia apocrypha* (Leipzig, 1876), pp. 210–332 (edition A: 210–286; edition B, containing "Christ's Descent into Hades": 287–332). The Syriac version (including the Latin translation): J. E. Rahmani, *Apocrypha hypomnemata Domini nostri seu Acta Pilati: Antiqua versio syriaca*, Studia syriaca II (Sharfa, Lebanon, 1908). For more information on the various editions see J. K. Elliott, *The Apocryphal New Testament*, pp. 164–169. Cf. J. Hennecke, *New Testament Apocrypha*, vol. 1 (London, 1963), pp. 444–449. A complete list of editions is included in M. Geerard, ed., *Clavis Apocryphorum Novi Testamenti* (Tournhout, 1992), pp. 43–46. For more on "Christ's Descent into Hades" cf. in particular A. M. Vitti, "Descensus Christi ad Inferos iuxta Apocrypha," *Verbum Domini* 7 (Rome, 1927), pp. 138–144, 171–181; R. J. Hoffmann, "Confluence in Early Christian and Gnostic Literature: The Descensus Christi ad Inferos; Acta Pilati xvii–xxviii," *Journal for the Study of the New Testament* 10 (1981), pp. 42–60. The following older work has not lost its significance: A. Lipsius, *Die Pilatenakten kritisch Untersucht* (Kiel, 1886). See also Z. Izydorczyk, ed., "The Medieval Gospel of Nicodemus: Texts, Intertexts and Contexts in Western Europe," *Medieval and Renaissance Texts and Studies* 158 (1997).

had happened in hell during the Savior's descent (we are already familiar with this element from "The Gospel of Bartholomew").

The existing recension of "The Gospel of Nicodemus" dates approximately to the beginning of the fifth century[43] (the earliest-known Greek manuscript of this text is from the twelfth century).[44] At the same time it is obvious that the work contains material that at least partially dates to apostolic times.[45] In any event, Justin the Philosopher (second century) and Tertullian (third century) already knew of the "Acts of Pilate."[46] With respect to Christ's descent into Hades, it clearly contains many ideas that are also found in the works of early Christian authors such as Hermas, Justin the Philosopher, Irenaeus of Lyons, and Theophilus of Antioch. Whatever the conclusions regarding the dating of "Christ's Descent into Hades" may be it is obvious that this work reflects a very ancient tradition, whose main tenets were formed no later than the middle of the third century.[47]

---

[43]Scholars assume that since the term *theotokos* is mentioned six times in "The Gospel of Nicodemus" it cannot have been written before the Council of Ephesus in 431 AD (Third Ecumenical Council): cf. J. Hennecke, *New Testament Apocrypha*, p. 448; P. Chrēstou, *Hellēnikē patrologia*, t. 2 (Thessalonikē, 1991), p. 243. We should note, however, that the term *theotokos* had already been used by authors of the third and fourth centuries, particularly Origen, Basil the Great, Gregory the Theologian, Gregory of Nyssa, and Didymus of Alexandria: cf. G. W. H. Lampe, *A Patristic Greek Lexicon* (Oxford, 1987), p. 639.

[44]Cf. C. N. Jefford, "Acts of Pilate," *The Anchor Bible Dictionary* (1992), pp. 371–372.

[45]For more on the dating of "The Gospel of Nicodemus" see G. C. O'Ceallaigh, "Dating the Commentaries of Nicodemus," *Harvard Theological Review* 56 (1963), pp. 21–58.

[46]Cf. Justin, ch. 25 and 48 in *First Apology* (in which the "Acts compiled during Pontius Pilate's time" are mentioned); Tertullian, *Apology* 26.

[47]For some scholars, "The Gospel of Nicodemus" belongs to a tradition that reflects mythological notions of the ancients on descent into a subterranean kingdom. There are many studies that draw parallels between the Christian teaching on Christ's descent into Hades and works of Egyptian, Babylonian, Iranian, Indian, ancient Greek, and ancient Roman mythology. The most exhaustive survey of these works is in J. Kroll, *Gott und Hölle*, pp. 205–315, 363–512. Cf. W. Maas, *Gott und die Hölle: Studien zum Descensus Christi* (Einsiedeln, 1979). Cf. also J. Chaine, "Descente du Christ aux enfers," *Dictionnaire de la Bible*, Supplément 2 (Paris, 1934), pp. 397–403. At the same time there are other scholars who, rejecting any kind of connection between Christian teaching and pagan mythology, locate the genesis of the doctrine

The part of "The Gospel of Nicodemus" that deals with the descent into Hades contains the story of the two sons of the righteous Symeon. They had been raised by Christ and brought to the Jerusalem synagogue for interrogation. Having "made the seal of the cross with their fingers upon their tongues,"[48] they wrote the following account:

> O Lord Jesus Christ, the life and resurrection of the dead, suffer us to speak of the mysteries of thy majesty which thou didst perform after thy death upon the cross, inasmuch as we have been adjured by thy Name. For thou didst command us thy servants to tell no man the secrets of thy divine majesty which thou wroughtest in hell. Now when we were set together with all our fathers in the deep, in obscurity of darkness, on a sudden there came a golden heat of the sun and a purple and royal light shining upon us. And immediately the father of the whole race of men, together with all the patriarchs and prophets, rejoiced, saying: This light is the beginning [author] of everlasting light which did promise to send unto us his co-eternal light. And Isaiah cried out and said: This is the light of the Father, even the Son of God, according as I prophesied when I lived upon the earth: The land of Zabulon and the land of Nephthalim beyond Jordan, of Galilee of the Gentiles, the people that walked in darkness have seen a great light, and they that dwell in the land of the shadow of death, upon them did the light shine. And now hath it come and shone upon us that sit in death . . . And after that there came one as it were a dweller in the wilderness, and he was inquired of by all: Who art thou? And he answered them and said: I am John, the voice and the prophet of the most High, which came before the face of his advent to prepare his ways,[49] to give knowledge of salvation unto his people, for the remission of their sins.[50]

---

of Christ's descent into Hades in Jewish tradition. See, in particular, J.A. MacCulloch, *The Harrowing of Hell* (Edinburgh, 1930), pp. 318–319. An analysis of these scholarly opinions falls beyond the scope of this study.

[48]The sign of the cross is mentioned in the second and third centuries in the *Epistle of Barnabas* (chapter 12), Justin (*First Apology* 55), and Tertullian (*Apology* 23).

[49]Cf. Mark 1.2–3; Isa 40.3; Mal 3.1.

[50]M. R. James, trans., "The Gospel of Nicodemus," in *The Apocryphal New Testament* (Oxford, 1950), pp. 123–125. Cf. Mark 16.16.

There follows a dialogue between Satan and Hades in which various acts and miracles performed by Jesus Christ are discussed. Satan tries to convince Hades to accept the Son of God, while Hades, being in terror, refuses to do so:

> While all the saints were rejoicing, behold Satan the prince and chief of death said unto Hell: Make thyself ready to receive Jesus who boasteth himself that he is the Son of God, whereas he is a man that feareth death.... Hell answered and said unto Satan the prince: who is he that is so mighty, if he be a man that feareth death? For all the mighty ones of the earth are held in subjection by my power, even they whom thou hast brought me subdued by thy power. If, then, thou art mighty, what manner of man is this Jesus who, though he fear death, resisteth thy power? ... But Satan the prince of Tartarus said: Why doubtest thou and fearest to receive this Jesus which is thine adversary and mine? ... Hell answered and said: Thou hast told me that it is he that hath taken away dead men from me.... Satan the prince of death answered and said: It is that same Jesus. When Hell heard that he said unto him: I adjure thee by thy strength and mine own that thou bring him not unto me.[51]

All of a sudden a voice as of thunder and a cry are heard: "Lift, O princes, your gates, and be ye lifted up, ye everlasting doors, and the King of Glory shall come in."[52] Hades continues to resist the coming Christ and orders its demons to "shut the hard gates of brass and put on them the bars of iron and withstand stoutly," however, the forefathers and prophets protest and demand that the gates be opened. Again the voice is heard: "Lift, O princes, your gates, and be ye lifted up ye doors of hell, and the King of Glory shall come in," after which the King of Glory himself appears in the realm of death. "We are overcome by thee," cry Satan and Hell. "Who art thou that art so great and so small, both humble and exalted, both soldier and commander, a marvellous warrior in the shape of a bondsman, and a King of Glory dead and living, whom the cross bare slain upon it?" With-

---

[51]M. R. James, trans., *The Gospel of Nicodemus*, p. 20.
[52]Ps 24.7 (LXX).

out responding to them, the King of Glory "trampled upon death, and laid hold on Satan the prince and delivered him unto the power of Hell, and drew Adam to him unto his own brightness."[53] Having received Satan, Hell reproaches him by saying: "Behold now, this Jesus putteth to flight by the brightness of his majesty all the darkness of death, and hath broken the strong depths of the prisons, and let out the prisoners and loosed them that were bound. And all that were sighing in our torments do rejoice against us, and at their prayers our dominions are vanquished and our realms conquered."[54]

The liberation of the dead from Hades by the incarnate Lord is described in "The Gospel of Nicodemus" in the following way:

> And the Lord stretching forth his hand, said: "Come unto me, all ye my saints which bear mine image and my likeness. Ye that by the tree and the devil and death were condemned, behold now the devil and death condemned by the tree." And forthwith all the saints were gathered in one under the hand of the Lord. And the Lord holding the right hand of Adam, said unto him: Peace be unto thee with all thy children that are my righteous ones." . . . And the Lord stretched forth his hand and made the sign of the cross over Adam and over all his saints, and he took the right hand of Adam and went up out of hell, and all the saints followed him. . . . And the Lord holding the hand of Adam delivered him unto Michael the archangel, and all the saints followed Michael the archangel, and he brought them all into the glory and beauty of paradise.[55]

At the gates of paradise all the saints meet Enoch and Elijah and the good thief, who await Adam and the other righteous at the entrance. "The Gospel of Nicodemus" ends with Symeon's sons becoming invisible after delivering their story to the archpriests.[56]

"The Gospel of Nicodemus" contains the entire array of ideas and images used in Christian literature of subsequent centuries to depict what some contemporary scholars refer to as the Höllensturm (liter-

---

[53]M. R. James, trans., *The Gospel of Nicodemus*, p. 21.

[54]M. R. James, trans., *The Gospel of Nicodemus*, pp. 22–23.

[55]M. R. James, trans., *The Gospel of Nicodemus*, pp. 24–25.

[56]M. R. James, trans., *The Gospel of Nicodemus*, pp. 26–27.

ally, "the storming of hell").[57] Christ does not merely descend into the depths of hell—He invades it, vanquishing the devil and demons, smashing the gates, and breaking their locks and bolts. All of these images are intended to illustrate one fundamental idea: Christ descends not as a victim of hell but as the victor over death and Hades. Before him the powers of hell are powerless. It is precisely such an understanding of this event that characterizes works of liturgical poetry on this theme.

The main ideas of "The Gospel of Nicodemus," as mentioned above, were formulated no later than the third century. This will be confirmed below by the analysis of early Christian poetic works as well as by a survey of patristic testimonies from the second and third centuries.

EARLY CHRISTIAN POETRY

The themes of Christ's descent into Hades and his victory over hell and death are treated extensively in surviving early Christian poetry. We do not know precisely when the short hymn known as the Easter troparion was composed. It is likely, however, that it was already written in the second century (similar hymns, or "tropes,"[58] which were paraphrases of texts from Scripture, were an inseparable part of early Christian services)[59] and it continues to be used in the services of the Orthodox Church:

> Christ is risen from the dead, trampling down death by death, and upon those in the tombs bestowing life.

This hymn reflects a theological idea formed in the second century by St Irenaeus of Lyons, that the redemptory sacrifice of Christ, the second Adam, is a "recapitulation" (i.e., a backward reproduction) of the life of the first-created Adam, who personifies all mankind. In

---

[57]Cf. in particular: J. Kroll, *Gott und Hölle*, p. 529.

[58]From the Greek *tropos*, "paraphrase."

[59]This hymn is a paraphrase of St Paul's words in 1 Cor 15.20–23.

order to "restore in himself all people who came from Adam, all nations and mankind along with Adam himself," Christ systematically goes through all the main stages of human life so that the effects of the fall of Adam might be corrected in each of them. By his becoming the "first-born from the dead,"[60] Christ renews people for the divine life, "having himself become the first of the living, just as Adam became the first of the dying."[61] Christ's death therefore becomes a victory over death, and his resurrection brings life and resurrection to the dead. The doctrine on Christ's descent into Hades is later developed in works of liturgical poetry precisely in this vein.

Of all the works of early Christian poetry, which can be more or less exactly dated, first mention should be made of "On Easter," a liturgical poem by St Melito of Sardis. The complete text of this poem, written in Greek around the middle of the second century, was discovered as recently as 1940. Until then only fragments in the original Greek, as well as in Latin, Syriac, Coptic, and Georgian, were known.[62] The poem is a paschal sermon intended to be read on Good Friday after the Old Testament readings. In Melito's work the teachings on Christ's raising the dead and on his victory over the devil, death, and hell are quite fully expounded:

> The Lord, when he had clothed himself with man . . .
> arose from the dead and uttered this cry:
> ". . . I am the one that destroyed death
> and triumphed over the enemy
> and trod down Hades
> and bound the strong one
> I carried off man to the heights of heaven;
> I am the one," says the Christ.
> "Come then, all you families of men who are

---

[60]Col 1.18.

[61]Irenaeus of Lyons, *Against Heresies* 3, 20, 3.

[62]Cf. the critical text of Méliton de Sardes, *Sur la Pâque et fragments*, SC 123, introduction, texte critique, traduction et notes par Othmar Perler (Paris, 1966). A more recent (but not necessarily more reliable) edition is Melito of Sardis, *On Pascha and Fragments*, texts and trans., ed. Stuart George Hall (Oxford, 1979).

compounded with sins,
and receive forgiveness of sins.
For I am your forgiveness,
I am the Pascha of salvation,
I am the lamb slain for you;
I am your ransom,
I am your life,
I am your light,
I am your salvation,
I am your resurrection,
I am your king.
I will raise you up by my right hand;
I am leading you up to the heights of heaven;
There I will show you the Father from ages past."[63]

First of all, this text indicates that in the second century the subject of Christ's descent into Hades was an inseparable part of the paschal divine services. Secondly, it shows that, already in second century Christian hymnography, Christ's redemptive sacrifice was viewed as pertinent for all people without exception. Thus it speaks not of Christ saving the righteous but of his forgiving all "those who sullied themselves with sin." After destroying death, vanquishing the enemy, trampling down hell, and binding the devil, he calls them to himself in order to grant them forgiveness of sins and to lead them up to God the Father.

In an early Christian apocryphal writing known under the name of the "Sybilline Oracles," Christ's preaching in Hades is also mentioned:

When the Eternal came himself on earth
And into Hades shall he come announcing

---

[63]Melito of Sardis, *On Pascha and Fragments*, SC 123, 120, text and trans., ed. Stuart George Hall (Oxford, 1979), pp. 57–59, 100–103. For a more recent translation see: Melito of Sardis, *On Pascha: With the Fragments of Melito and Other Material Related to the Quartodecimans*, trans., introduced, and annotated, Alistair Stewart-Sykes (Crestwood, New York, 2001). For more information on Melito's approach to the descent see A. Grillmeier, *Der Gottessohn im Totenreich*, pp. 5–14.

> Hope unto all the saints, the end of ages
> And the last day, and having fallen asleep
> The third day he shall end the lot of death;
> Then from the dead departing he shall come
> To light, the first to show forth to the elect
> Beginning of resurrection, and wash off
> By means of waters of immortal spring.[64]

The descent of Christ into Hades is also reflected in hymns inter-polated in the apocryphal "Acts of Thomas," dated to the first half of the third century and preserved in Syriac, Greek, Armenian, Ethiopic, and two Latin versions.[65] The Syriac version of the "Acts," which is believed to be the original, contains a hymn called the "Song of Praise of Thomas the Apostle."[66] It is a narrative about Christ putting the devil to death and bringing the hope of resurrection into Sheol:

> Praised be you, the Son, the adored Fruit,
> Who rose upon all in mercy,
> And put on our humanity, and slew our adversary. . . .
>
> Glorified be you, the Father omnipotent,
> Who has sent to us your living and life-giving fruit,
> And he reconciled by the blood of his cross
> your mercy with your creatures. . . .

---

[64]Milton S. Terry, trans., *The Sybilline Oracles* 13, pp. 410–418. For the Greek original see J. Geffcken, ed., *Oracula Sibyllina*, GCS 8 (Leipzig, 1902), p. 162. The "Sybilline Oracles" contain didactic poems, most of which were composed in the second century on the basis of earlier Judaic and Hellenistic material.

[65]For the Syriac cf. W. Wright, *Apocryphal Acts of the Apostles*, vol. 1 (London, 1981), pp. 171–333. For the Greek text see R. A. Lipsius and M. Bonnet, eds., *Acta Apostolorum Apocrypha*, Part 2 (Hildesheim, 1959). For a scholarly analysis of the "Acts" cf. G. Bornkamm, *Mythos und Legende in den apokryphen Thomas-Akten* (Göttingen, 1933). On the descent in the Book of Acts see J. Kroll, *Gott und Hölle*, pp. 30–34; W. Bousset, *Kyrios Christos: Geschichte des Christusglaubens von den Anfängen des Christentums bis Irenaeus* (Göttingen, 1921), p. 29; A. A. Bevan, *The Hymn of the Soul, Contained in the Syriac Acts of St Thomas* (Cambridge, 1897).

[66]See W. Wright, *The Apocryphal Acts of the Apostles*, vol. 2, pp. 246–251. The Russian translation renders some passages in the Syriac text more accurately than W. Wright: E. Mescherskaya, trans., *Apokrificheskie Deyaniya Apostolov*, pp. 229–231.

> The angels glorify you on high through your Messiah,
> Who became peace and hope to the dead in Sheol,
> who came to life and were raised. . . .

The same subject also occurs in another passage when Judas Thomas is forced by the king to pray for his daughter at the marriage feast. He addresses himself to Christ in this fashion:

> Our Lord, companion of his servants . . .
> You have shown the glory of your Godhead,
> In your longsuffering towards our manhood,
> When you hurled the evil one from his power,
> And called with your voice to the dead and they became
>   alive . . .
> And you descended into Sheol and went to its uttermost
>   end;
> And opened its gates and brought out its prisoners,
> And trod for them the path [leading] above by the nature
>   of your Godhead.[67]

In the Greek version of "The Acts of Thomas," which is significantly different from the Syriac original, there is the following prayer:

> Jesus Christ, Son of compassion and perfect saviour, Christ, Son of the living God, the undaunted power that hast overthrown the enemy, and the voice that was heard of the rulers, and made all their powers to quake, the ambassador that wast sent from the height and camest down even unto hell, who didst open the doors and bring up thence them that for many ages were shut up in the treasury of darkness.[68]

Though in this text the liberation of all people from Hades would seem to be implied, in the following one the question exclusively concerns those who "fled unto" Christ:

---

[67]See A. F. J. Klijn, *The Acts of Thomas* (Leiden: Brill, 1962), p. 70.

[68]R. M. James, trans. from Greek, *The Acts of Thomas*, p. 10. For the Greek original see: R. A. Lipius and M. Bonnet, eds., *Acta Apostolorum Apocrypha*, p. 115.

O companion and defender and hope of the weak and confidence of the poor, refuge, and lodging of the weary: voice that came forth of the height, comforter dwelling in the midst: port and harbor of them that pass through the regions of the rulers, physician that healest without payment, who among men wast crucified for many: who didst go down into hell with great might: the sight of whom the princes of death endured not; thou camest up with great glory, and gathering all them that fled unto thee didst prepare a way, and in thy footsteps all they journeyed whom thou didst redeem; and thou broughtest them into thine own fold and didst join them with thy sheep.[69]

The subject of the descent into Hades is also treated in the "Odes of Solomon." The origin of this book, composed of forty-two odes and preserved in Syriac,[70] is still unclear. Most likely it appeared in the second century among Christian communities in Syria (possibly in Edessa),[71] but scholars do not agree on the original language. Several of them consider it to be Syriac,[72] while others think that it was Greek.[73] The hypothesis that the "Odes" were originally written in Greek is mostly based on the fact that one of the odes has been preserved in Greek in a third-century papyrus. Also, the Syriac text of the odes contains many Greek words. Five odes were included in the gnostic treatise "Pistis Sophia" (third century),[74] a fact that brought some

---

[69]R. M. James, trans. from Greek, *The Acts of Thomas*, p. 156. For the Greek original see: *Acta Apostolorum Apocrypha*, p. 265.

[70]Edition of the Syriac text: J. H. Charlesworth, ed. and trans., *The Odes of Solomon* (Oxford, 1973). An analysis of the poetical structure of the "Odes" can be found in M. Franzmann, *The Odes of Solomon: An Analysis of the Poetical Structure and Form* (Göttingen, 1991).

[71]J. de Zwaan, "The Edessene Origin of the Odes of Solomon," *Quantalacunque: Studies Presented to K. Lake* (London, 1937), pp. 285–302.

[72]E. A. Abbot, "The Original Language of the Odes of Solomon," *Journal of Theological Studies* 14 (1913), pp. 313ff.; S. A. Emerton, "Some Problems of Text and Language in the Odes of Solomon," *Journal of Theological Studies* 18 (1967), pp. 372–406.

[73]Cf. R. H. Connolly, "Greek the Original Language of the Odes of Solomon," *Journal of Theological Studies* 14 (1913), pp. 530ff.

[74]This work has been preserved in Coptic.

scholars to associate the "Odes" with the gnostic movements of the second century.[75] Other scholars reject the gnostic character of this work.[76] In any case, there is nothing in the "Odes" that contradicts church doctrine. There is no gnostic dualism, there are many references to baptism, and one of the odes ends with a Trinitarian doxology.

The "Odes of Solomon" were well known among early Christian authors. Lactantius (circa 250–325) quotes the nineteenth Ode,[77] which testifies to the existence of a Latin translation around the end of the third or beginning of the fourth centuries. Parallels with the "Odes" can be found in the works of St Ephrem the Syrian (fourth century) and other Syrian church writers.[78] The "Odes of Solomon" are also mentioned in the "Synopsis of Holy Scripture," a work epigraphically attributed to St Athanasius of Alexandria[79] but currently thought to have been compiled at the beginning of the fifth century.[80] In this work the "Odes" are mentioned among the "disputed" (*antilegomena*) books of the Old Testament, recommended for reading by catechumens.[81]

The theme of the descent occupies a prominent place in the "Odes."[82] The most interesting in this respect are Odes 15, 17, 22, 24, and 42. In the concluding verses of Ode 15, a reference is made to the abolition of death and Hades by the risen Christ:

---

[75]For more on gnostic parallels with the "Odes" cf. W. Stölten, "Gnostische Parallelen zu den Oden Salomos," *Zeitschrift für die neutestamentliche Wissenschaft und die Kunde der älteren Kirche* 13 (Giessen, 1912), pp. 29–58.

[76]J. H. Charlesworth, "The Odes of Solomon, Not Gnostic," *Catholic Biblical Quarterly* 31 (1969), pp. 357–369; H. Chadwick, "Some Reflections on the Character and Theology of the Odes of Solomon," *Kyriakon: Festschrift Johannes Quasten*, vol. 1 (Münster, 1970), p. 267.

[77]Cf. Lactantius, *The Divine Institutes* 4, 12, 3.

[78]Cf. A. J. Wensinck, "Ephrem's Hymns on Epiphany and the Odes of Solomon," *The Expositor*, ser. 8, vol. 3 (1912), pp. 108–112; J. R. Harris, "Ephrem's Use of the Odes of Solomon," *The Expositor*, ser. 8, vol. 3 (1912), pp. 113–119.

[79]*Synopsis Scripturae Sacrae*, PG 28:283–438.

[80]P. Chrēstou, *Hellēnikē patrologia*, vol. 3 (Thessalonica, 1987), p. 518.

[81]The complete list of these books comprises Wisdom, Sirach, Esther, Judith, Tobit, the four Maccabees, the Ptolemaic Books, the Psalms and Odes of Solomon, and the Book of Susanna.

[82]See in particular R. Newbold, "The Descent of Christ in the Odes of Solomon," *Journal of Biblical Literature* 31 (1912), pp. 168–209.

> I put on immortality through his name,
> and took off corruption by his grace.
> Death has been destroyed before my face,
> and Sheol has been vanquished by my word.
> And eternal life has arisen in the Lord's land,
> and it has been declared to his faithful ones,
> and has been given without limit to all that trust in him.[83]

Ode 17 speaks of Christ demolishing the iron locks of Hades and descending to its depths in order to liberate those detained there.[84] Their liberation is also mentioned in Ode 22. In it the themes of Christ's descent into Hades and of his victory over the powers of evil are intertwined with the subject of a Christian's descent into the water of baptism and the subsequent liberation from the pangs of death.[85] Christ's opening and shutting of the abyss of Hades is mentioned in Ode 24,[86] and in Ode 42 a magnificent picture of Christ's preaching in Hades and of his resurrecting the dead is unfolded:

> Sheol saw me and was shattered,
> and Death ejected me and many with me.
> I have been vinegar and bitterness to it,
> and I went down with it as far as its depth. . . .
> And I made a congregation of living among his dead;
> and I spoke with them by living lips;
> in order that my word may not be unprofitable.
> And those who had died ran towards me;
> and they cried out and said, Son of God, have pity on us.
> And deal with us according to your kindness,
> and bring us out from the bonds of darkness.
> And open for us the door by which we may come out to you;
> for we perceive that our death does not touch you.
> May we also be saved with you, because you are our Savior.

---

[83]Ode 15, 8–11 (trans. J. H. Charlesworth).
[84]Ode 17, 9–11.
[85]Ode 22, 1–7; cf. J. Daniélou, *The Theology of Jewish Christianity*, pp. 245–246.
[86]Ode 24, 5–7.

Then I heard their voice, and placed their faith in my heart.

And I placed my name upon their head,

because they are free and they are mine.[87]

Works of early Christian hymnography bear considerable significance since their many and varied motifs are later developed in medieval liturgical poetry. In particular, numerous ideas from St Melito of Sardis' "On Easter" were later incorporated into the liturgical texts for Good Friday and Great Saturday. The diverse themes from the "Odes of Solomon" were expanded upon in poems by St Ephrem the Syrian and then by St Romanos the Melodist and his Byzantine disciples. The theme of the descent into Hades, found in the writings of the second century, never disappears from Christian poetry but goes from one work to another, from one generation of hymnographers to the next, until it becomes firmly established in the liturgical life of the Orthodox Church.

---

[87]Ode 42, 11–20 (trans. J. H. Charlesworth).

CHAPTER TWO

The Patristic Tradition

I n the previous chapter the cardinal New Testament and apocryphal texts devoted to Christ's descent into Hades were considered, as well as some pieces of ancient Christian poetry. We may now survey, though by no means exhaustively, the relevant patristic references. Reflection upon these references will help in better understanding the origins of theological thought, reinforcing the liturgical texts on this subject that are preserved by the Orthodox Church in its worship.

EASTERN FATHERS OF THE SECOND AND THIRD CENTURIES

Eastern Christian authors of the second and third centuries—including Polycarp of Smyrna, Ignatius of Antioch, Hermas, Justin, Melito of Sardis, Hyppolitus of Rome, Irenaeus of Lyons, Clement of Alexandria, and Origen—make reference to the descent of Christ into Hades and to his raising the dead.

St Polycarp of Smyrna, disciple of St John the Evangelist, speaks of Jesus Christ, "who for our sins suffered even unto death, but whom God raised from the dead, having loosed the pangs of the grave."[1]

St Ignatius of Antioch states repeatedly that when Jesus Christ came to earth he raised from the dead those "most divine prophets" who "no longer observed the Sabbath, but lived in the observance of the Lord's Day."[2] In another passage the same author states that Christ saved the prophets who "proclaimed the Gospel, and hoped in

---

[1] *Letter to the Philippians* 1, 2. Cf. Acts 2.24.
[2] *Letter to the Magnesians* 8–9.

Him, and waited for Him, in whom also, believing, they were saved."[3]
Christ is called "the Door of the Father, by which Abraham, Isaac,
Jacob, and the prophets and the apostles and the Church enter in."[4]
These are the earliest patristic references to the raising of the
prophets by the risen Christ.[5]

Belief in Christ's victory over Hades and death is also found in St
Melito of Sardis' poem "On Pascha," cited in chapter one. In other
extant fragments, Melito also refers to Christ who "appeared to the
dead in Hades and to the mortals in the world."[6]

The writings of St Irenaeus of Lyons make a number of references
to the descent.[7] In the "Demonstration of the Apostolic Preaching,"
which has survived in Armenian, he asserts that Christ's descent into
Hades "was for the salvation of the dead."[8] Again in the treatise
"Against the Heresies" he argues:

> It was for this reason, too, that the Lord descended into the regions
> beneath the earth,[9] preaching his advent there also, and [declaring]
> the remission of sins received by those who believe in Him. Now all
> those believed in him who had hope towards Him, that is, those who
> proclaimed his advent, and submitted to his dispensations, the
> righteous men, the prophets, and the patriarchs, to whom he remit-
> ted sins in the same way as he did to us.[10]

The particular stress that Irenaeus puts on the salvation of the Old
Testament righteous, prophets, and patriarchs is explained by the fact

---

[3]*Letter to the Philadelphians* 5.

[4]*Letter to the Philadelphians* 9.

[5]Cf. also Tertullian, *On the Soul* 55 ("Christ . . . descended into the underworld
in order to make patriarchs and prophets his companions").

[6]*On Baptism*, frag. 8b, 4 (SC 123, 232–233). Cf. *On the Soul and Body*, frag. 2, 12 (in:
M. van Esbroek, "Nouveaux fragments de Méliton de Sardes," *Analecta Bollandiana*
90 [1972], pp. 78–79); *On Baptism*, frag. VIIIb, 44 (SC 123, 232–233).

[7]On Irenaeus' interpretation of the descent see, in particular, J. A. MacCulloch,
The Harrowing of Hell, pp. 87–93.

[8]*The Demonstration of the Apostolic Preaching* 78 (SC 406, 192–193).

[9]Cf. *Against the Heresies* 5, 31, 2 (SC 153, 392–393): the Lord "tarried until the third
day in the lower parts of the earth (*in inferioribus terrae*)."

[10]*Against the Heresies* 4, 27, 2 (SC 100/2, 738–741).

that a significant part of his treatise is directed against the teachings of Marcion. The latter, according to Irenaeus, taught that Christ abandoned the prophets and the patriarchs in hell while saving the "unrighteous" of the Old Testament.[11] It was Marcion's corruption of Orthodox doctrine that prompted Irenaeus and some subsequent authors to specifically mention the Old Testament righteous as those who profited from Christ's descent into Hades.

In his anti-heretical treatise, Irenaeus refers to what he believes to be a passage from the prophet Isaiah: "And the holy Lord remembered his dead Israel, who had slept in the land of sepulture; and he came down to preach his salvation to them, that he might save them."[12] Elsewhere Irenaeus ascribes this *logion* to Jeremiah;[13] however, this passage can be found in neither Isaiah nor Jeremiah. St Justin the Martyr, who also ascribes the passage to Jeremiah, accuses the Jews of deleting it from the Old Testament and thereby corrupting the Scriptures.[14]

St Hyppolitus of Rome suggests that when Christ rose from Hades he brought Adam back.[15] Hyppolitus also was one of the first to speak of John the Baptist's preaching in Hades before Christ's descent therein: "He also first preached to those in Hades, becoming a forerunner there when he was put to death by Herod, that there too he might intimate that the Savior would descend to ransom the souls of the saints from the hand of death."[16] This theme, developed by other authors of the second and third centuries,[17] came to occupy a prominent place in church hymnography.[18] One text that survives in

---

[11]*Against the Heresies* I, 27, 3 (SC 264, 352–353). Cf. Theodoret of Cyrus, *Compendium of Heretical Fables* I, 24 (PG 83:376); Epiphanius of Cyprus, *Panarion* 42, 4 (GCS 31bis, 99–100).

[12]*Against the Heresies* 3, 20, 4 (SC 211, 394–397).

[13]*Against the Heresies* 4, 22, 1 (SC 100/2, 684–689).

[14]*Dialogue with Trypho* 72, 4, in Justin, *Dialogue avec Tryphon*, I, éd. et trad. G. Archambault (Paris, 1909), pp. 348–351. On the *logion* by Jeremiah see J. Daniélou, *The Theology of Jewish Christianity*, pp. 235–237.

[15]*On the Song of Moses* (PG 10:612a).

[16]*On Christ and Antichrist* 45 (PG 10:764b).

[17]See, in particular, Clement of Alexandria, *Stromateis* 6, 6; Origen, *Second Homily on the Book of Kings* (PG 12:1024a); et al.

[18]See chapter four.

Greek under the name of Hyppolitus raises the question of Christ's soul descending into Hades while his body remained in the tomb:

> For this reason the warders of Hades trembled when they saw Him;[19] and the gates of brass and the bolts of iron were broken. For, lo, the Only-begotten entered, a soul among souls, God the Word with a (human) soul. For his body lay in the tomb, not emptied of divinity; but as, while in Hades, he was in essential being with his Father, so was he also in the body and in Hades. For the Son, just as the Father, is not contained in space and he comprehends all things in himself. But of his own will he dwelt in a body animated by a soul, in order that with his soul he might enter Hades, and not with his pure divinity.[20]

Hyppolitus' name is further connected with the so-called Apostolic Tradition, which survives in Coptic, Arabic, Ethiopic, and Latin.[21] Dated approximately to AD 218, this text has special significance for the study of ancient Christian liturgy because it contains the following words at the eucharistic anaphora:

> We give thanks to you O God, through your beloved son Jesus Christ, whom you sent to us in former times as Saviour, Redeemer, and Messenger of your Will. . . . It is he who . . . when he was delivered to voluntary suffering, in order to dissolve death, and break the chains of the devil, and tread down hell, and bring the just to the light, and set the limit, and manifest the resurrection, taking the bread, and giving thanks to you, said, "Take, eat, for this is my body which is broken for you." Likewise the chalice, saying, "This is my

[19]Job 38.17 (according to LXX).

[20]Frag. III cited by Nicetas the Deacon in *Hyppolitus Werke*, GCS 1 (Leipzig, 1897), p. 268.

[21]The Greek original is lost. Scholars differ in their opinion regarding the authorship of the "Apostolic Tradition." E. Schwartz, R. Connolly, G. Dix, and many others regard it as an authentic writing by Hyppolitus: E. Schwartz, *Über die pseudo-apostolischen Kirchenordnungen* (Strassburg, 1910); R. H. Connolly, *The So-called Egyptian Church Order and Derived Documents* (Cambridge, 1916); G. Dix, *The Apostolic Tradition of St Hyppolitus* (London, 1937). G. Magne, on the contrary, argues against the authorship of Hyppolitus: G. Magne, *Tradition Apostolique sur les Charismes et Diataxeis des saints Apôtres* (Paris, 1975).

blood which is shed for you. Whenever you do this, do this in memory of me."[22]

It is the earliest Christian anaphora that mentions Christ's descent into Hades in the context of the eucharistic commemoration of the Last Supper. It is noteworthy that many later anaphoras also mention the descent into Hades, including that which is used in the Orthodox Church under the name of St Basil the Great.[23]

The teaching on Christ's descent into Hades is developed quite fully by Clement of Alexandria in his "Stromateis." He argues that Christ preached in hell not only to the Old Testament righteous but also to the Gentiles who lived outside the true faith. Commenting on 1 Peter 3.18–21, Clement expresses the conviction that the preaching of Christ was addressed to all in hell who were able to believe in Christ:

> Do not [the Scriptures] show that the Lord preached the Gospel to those that perished in the flood, or rather had been chained, and to those detained "in ward and guard"? . . . And, as I think, the Saviour also exerts his might because it is his work to save; which accordingly he also did by drawing to salvation those who became willing, by the preaching [of the Gospel], to believe on Him, wherever they were. If, then, the Lord descended to Hades for no other end but to preach the Gospel, as he did descend, it was either to preach the Gospel to all or to the Hebrews only. If, accordingly, to all, then all who believe shall be saved,[24] although they may be of the Gentiles, on making their profession there.[25]

Clement emphasizes that there are righteous people both among those who have the true faith and among the Gentiles, that it is possible for those who did not accept him while alive to turn to God. Their virtuous lives opened their hearts to accept the message of Christ and the apostles after death:

---

[22] *The Apostolic Tradition* 4.
[23] See the quotation in the conclusion of our book. On the descent in eucharistic anaphoras see: J. A. MacCulloch, *The Harrowing of Hell* (1930), pp. 75–82.
[24] I.e., those who came to believe while in hell.
[25] *Stromateis* 6, 6 (GCS 62bis, 454–455).

A righteous man, then, differs not, as righteous, from another righteous man, whether he be of the Law [Jew] or a Greek. For God is
not only Lord of the Jews, but of all men. . . .[26] So I think it is
demonstrated that God, being good, and the Lord powerful, saves
with a righteousness and equality which extend to all that turn to
Him, whether here or elsewhere.[27]

According to Clement, righteousness is of value not only for those
who live in true faith but also for those outside it. On this basis it
appears that Christ preached in hell to all but saved only those who
came to believe in him. In any event, Clement assumes that this
preaching did not prove to be salutary for all in hell who heard it: "Did
not the same dispensation obtain in Hades, so that even there, all the
souls, on hearing the proclamation, might either exhibit repentance,
or confess that their punishment was just, because they believed
not?"[28] Thus for Clement, hell sheltered also those who, hearing
Christ's preaching, neither believed in nor followed him.

From Clement's writings we understand that God's punishment
of sinners is not for retribution but for reformation, that souls released
from their corporal shells are better able to understand the meaning
of such punishment.[29] In these words lies the nucleus of the teaching
on the purifying and saving nature of the torment of hell developed
by some later authors.[30] In our discussion of Maximus the Confessor's views on Christ's descent into Hades, we shall return to the question of whether the pains of hell can be salutary. An exhaustive
examination of this question, however, is beyond the scope of this
book.

Origen, another great Alexandrian teacher, makes frequent mention of Christ's descent into Hades. In his main apologetic treatise,
"Against Celsus," we read:

---

[26]Cf. Rom 3.29; 10.12.
[27]Stromateis 6, 6 (GCS 62bis, 455–456).
[28]Stromateis 6, 6 (GCS 62bis, 456).
[29]Stromateis 6, 6 (GCS 62bis, 455).
[30]In the East it was developed by Gregory of Nyssa and Isaac the Syrian. In the
West it gradually led to the formation of the doctrine on purgatory.

Celsus next addresses to us the following remark: "You will not, I suppose, say of him, that, after failing to gain over those who were in this world, he went to Hades to gain over those who were there." But whether he likes it or not, we assert that not only while Jesus was in the body did he win over not a few persons merely, but so great a number, that a conspiracy was formed against him on account of the multitude of his followers; but also, that when he became a soul, without the covering of the body, he dwelt among those souls which were without bodily covering, converting such of them to himself as were willing, or those whom he saw, for reasons known to him alone, to be better adapted to such a course.[31]

In other writings Origen claims that "the Son of God, for the salvation of the world, descended even into Hades and called the first-born from it"[32] and that Christ's descent and subsequent resurrection made it possible for the good thief to enter paradise.[33] Origen believes that both the Old Testament prophets[34] and John the Baptist[35] descended into hell in order to preach Christ. The words of John the Baptist about Christ, whose shoes he was not worthy to untie,[36] are treated by Origen as an allegorical reference to Christ's descent into Hades:

If the passage about the shoes possesses a hidden meaning we ought not pass over it. I think, therefore, that the Incarnation, when the Son of God takes up flesh and bones, is one of the shoes; and the descent into Hades, whoever Hades is, and the journey into prison with the spirit is the other. It is said in Psalm 15 of the descent into Hades: "You will not leave my soul in Hades."[37] And Peter, in the Catholic Epistle, says of the journey into prison with the spirit,

---

[31]*Against Celsus* 2, 43 (SC 132, 382–383, trans. Donalds-Robinson).
[32]*Homilies on Genesis* 15, 5 (SC 7bis, 368–369). Cf. *Dialogue with Heracleides* 8 (SC 67, 72–73).
[33]*Homilies on Matthew* 12, 13 (PG 13:980c); *Homilies on Leviticus* 9, 5 (PG 12:514a).
[34]*2nd Homily of the Book of Kings* (PG 12:1021c).
[35]*Commentary on Luke* 4 (ΒΕΠ 15, 18); *2nd Homily of the Book of Kings* (PG 12:1024a).
[36]John 1.27.
[37]Ps 16.10 (LXX).

"Having been put to death in the flesh, but enlivened in the spirit, in which also he went and preached to the spirits in prison which were once disobedient when God's patience waited in the days of Noah while the ark was being built."[38]

Here Origen uses the terms "Hades/hell" (*ha̦dēs*) and "prison" (*phylakē*) synonymously.[39] In the introduction, the coexistence of the two different notions of Hades—one referring to the Old Testament underworld (*sheol*), and another referring to the *phylakē*, a place of torment—was mentioned. According to certain early Greek fathers, the souls of the Old Testament righteous before the coming of Christ remained not in a place of torment but in the nether world, where they awaited the Messiah's descent. There, neither patriarchs nor prophets were able to enjoy the fullness of the beatitude;[40] they all remained in "Abraham's bosom"[41] awaiting Christ. Sinners, meanwhile, such as those that perished in the flood, remained in the "prison." Therefore Christ's descent into Hades adumbrated his preaching to all the dead, regardless of their righteousness or sinfulness. However, as Clement of Alexandria emphasizes, this evangelism may not necessarily have been salutary for all. The final outcome for each person would depend on whether he responded to this preaching.

Origen also mentions the descent in the existing Latin recensions of his works. In the "Commentary on Romans" he describes what befell the devil after Christ's victory over him:

The realm of death is truly destroyed and the captivity that it held is abducted. However, because the enemy and tyrant must be destroyed anew at the end of times (*in fine saeculi*), we now see him not so much reigning as plundering (*non tam regnari, quam latrocinari*) and exiled from his realm, wandering in deserts and along roads in order to find the unbelievers for himself.[42]

---

[38] *Commentary on John* 6, 174–175 (SC 157, 260–262). Cf. 1 Peter 3.18–20.

[39] C. Schmidt, *Der descensus ad inferos in der alten Kirche*, TU 43 (Leipzig, 1919), p. 546.

[40] C. Schmidt, *Der descensus ad inferos in der alten Kirche*, pp. 490–494.

[41] Luke 16.22.

[42] *Commentary on Romans* 5, 1 (PG 14:1019bc).

With Christ in Hades, the devil is vanquished and deprived of his power, nevertheless he continues to act until his power is annihilated totally at Christ's second coming. The victory over the devil is described also in the following text, which contains an allegorical interpretation of Matthew 12.29:

> Christ emptied himself . . . and took upon himself the form of a servant, suffered the dominance of the tyrant and became obedient unto death.[43] By this death he destroyed him who possessed the power of death (*mortem imperiam*), that is the devil, in order to liberate those held by death. For, having bound the strong man and having conquered him by the cross, he entered into his house, which is the house of death, or Hades, and spoiled his goods, that is, liberated the souls which death held. It is precisely this that the Gospel enigmatically refers to when saying: "How can one enter a strong man's house and plunder his goods, unless he first binds the strong man?"[44] He first bound him on the cross and then entered his house, that is, Hades, and from there "ascended on high" and "led a host of captives,"[45] namely, those who were risen with him and entered the heavenly Jerusalem. This is why the Apostle rightly says: "Death no longer has dominion over him."[46]

Our survey of references to the descent in the writings of early Christian authors shows that by the third century[47] a tradition had developed that contained the following elements: 1) Christ descended into hell after his death on the cross; 2) John the Baptist preached in hell before Christ's descent; 3) having descended into hell Christ brought Adam and other Old Testament patriarchs and righteous back from it; 4) owing to Christ's resurrection and descent the good thief entered paradise; and 5) by his descent Christ conquered the devil, hell, and death. All of these themes are developed by subsequent church writers.

---

[43]Cf. Phil 2.7–9.
[44]Matt 12.29.
[45]Eph 4.8.
[46]*Commentary on Romans* 5, 10 (PG 14:1051c–1052b). Cf. Rom 6.9.
[47]Cf. also Methodius of Olympos, *Fragment on Job 38, 16* (GCS 27, 517).

EASTERN FATHERS OF THE FOURTH CENTURY

Every major writer from the "golden age of Eastern Christian literature" touches, in one way or another, on the theme of Christ's descent into Hades. As their predecessors before them, the fathers of the fourth century developed this subject primarily in the context of the doctrine of redemption. Let us look at some characteristic texts.

St Athanasius of Alexandria mentions the descent several times,[48] particularly in his polemics against Arianism. In his attempt to prove the divinity of the Son of God to his opponents while simultaneously emphasizing the unity between the Father and the Son, Athanasius writes: "Neither can the Lord be forsaken by the Father . . . nor is it lawful to say that the Lord was in terror, at whom the keepers of hell's gates shuddered and set open hell, and the graves did gape, and many bodies of the saints arose and appeared to their own people."[49] Elsewhere Athanasius speaks about God who "redeemed all of us, or rather the whole race of humans, from death, and brought them up from the grave."[50]

Apart from the Arians, those opposed to Athanasius claimed that the Divine Logos (Word) was transformed into flesh at the incarnation. Arguing against this view, Athanasius speaks of the descent of the Logos into hell:

> This Body it was that was laid in a grave, when the Word had left it, yet was not parted from it, to preach, as Peter says, also to the spirits in prison.[51] And this above all shows the foolishness of those who say that the Word was changed into bones and flesh. For if this had

---

[48]Cf., e.g., *Against the Arians* 3, 54–56 (PG 26:437–441); *Discourse on the Incarnation of the Word* 20, 4–5 (SC 199, 338–341); 27, 4 (SC 199, 364–365); 29, 4 (SC 199, 370–371); *On the Synods* 8, 5 (*Athanasius Werke* II, 1, hrsg. H.-G. Opitz, p. 236); 30, 5 (*Athanasius Werke* II, 1, hrsg. H.-G. Opitz, p. 259); *Exposition on Psalm* 68 (67), 34 (PG 27:304c). Cf. also Pseudo-Athanasius, *On the Incarnation of Our Lord Jesus Christ, against Apollinarius* 1, 7 (PG 26:1005a); 1, 12–17 (PG 26:1113–1125); 2, 14–19 (PG 26:1155c–1164c); *On Virginity* 10–20 (TU 29/2a, 51); et al.

[49]*Against the Arians* 3, 56 (PG 26:441a). Cf. Matt 27.52–53.

[50]*Festal Letter* 10, 10 (PG 26:1402cd).

[51]Cf. 1 Pet 3.19.

been so, then there would have been no need of a tomb. For the body would have gone by itself to preach to the spirits in Hades. But as it was, he himself went to preach, while Joseph wrapped the body in a linen cloth and laid it away at Golgotha. And so it is shown to all that the body was not the Word, but the body of the Word.[52]

As A. Grillmeier mentions, nowhere in his authentic writings does Athanasius speak of the descent of Christ's soul into Hades while his body remained in the tomb; the question is always about the descent of the Divine Logos.[53] However, in an apparently non-authentic writing ascribed to Athanasius, directed against the teachings of Apollinarius,[54] the question is precisely about the descent of Christ's soul into Hades: "The divinity [of Christ] neither left his body in the tomb nor separated itself from his soul in Hades. . . . The realm of death was destroyed and the resurrection from Hades was accomplished and preached to souls by God's soul, while corruption was abolished and incorruption was shown from the tomb by Christ's body."[55]

The homily "On the Soul, Body, and Passions of Our Lord,"[56] ascribed to St Athanasius survives in Coptic and Syriac and has a direct genetic link with the poem of St Melito of Sardis "On Pascha." Scholarly opinion on the authorship of the homily diverges, and

---

[52]*The Letter to Epictetus* 5–6 (PG 26:1060ab).

[53]A. Grillmeier, *Christ in Christian Tradition*, vol. 1, pp. 316–317.

[54]The authenticity of this work is questioned. The teaching that is criticized in it was proclaimed by Apollinarius only in AD 373, i.e., in the year of Athanasius' death. The style of the treatise is also different from that of Athanasius and rather betrays the hand of an Antiochene or Cappadocian theologian. See: P. Chrēstou, *Hellenikē patrologia*, t. 3 (Thessalonikē, 1987), pp. 526–527 (with relevant bibliography).

[55]*On the Incarnation of Our Lord Jesus Christ, against Apollinarius* 1, 14–15 (PG 26:1156c–1157a).

[56]The Coptic text and the English translation is found in the *Coptic Homilies in the Dialect of Upper Egypt*, edited from the Papyrus Codex Oriental 5001 in the British Museum by E. A. Budge (London, 1910). The Syriac text was published by A. Mai, *Nova Patrum Bibliotheca* (Roma, 1844), pp. 529–539. The most recent translation into German, supplied with a scholarly analysis of the homily: D. Bumazhnov, *Der Mensch als Gottes Bild im christlichen Ägypten*, Studien und Texte zu Antike und Christentum 34 (Tübingen, 2006).

among its possible composers mentioned is St Alexander of Alexandria. In this text the descent into Sheol is presented in expressions redolent of particular liturgical texts from the ancient church: similar motifs may be found in the Syriac hymns of St Ephrem[57] and in the antiphons of the Holy Friday services. In spite of its title, the homily narrates Christ's vanquishing of Hades and death:

> The light of the day took to flight, the world was shrouded in darkness, the darkness of the blackest night. All these things happened before Christ closed his eyes.
>
> And his Light made haste to rise in Amente.[58] And Amente was perturbed when the Lord went down into it, not in flesh, but in spirit, for he had power over all creation, and he could destroy it before his last hour. He poured out his Blood on the earth, and it protected the earth and those who were therein.
>
> His body continued to hang upon the tree for the sake of the elements, and his Spirit went down into Amente, and saved those who were in that region. He despoiled Amente, and made himself Master of all of it.
>
> His body raised up those who were dead on the earth, and his spirit set free the souls that were in Amente. For in that hour in which our Lord was hanging on the cross, in that very same hour, the sepulchres opened, and the gatekeepers of Amente saw Him, and they shook with fear and took to flight. He burst open the gates of brass, he broke through the bolts of iron, and he took the souls that were in Amente and carried them to his Father. When the Lord had broken up Amente, and had gained the victory over death, he set the enemy under restraint. Now the souls he brought out of Amente, but the bodies he raised up on the earth.[59]

The author of the homily continues to say that if the foundations of the world could not sustain the body of Christ hanging on the wood, Hades was even more unable to withstand his spirit. Resurrected from the dead, the Lord "trampled death, bound the tyrant and

---

[57]See the chapter below.
[58]*Amente* is a Coptic word analogous to the Greek *ha;dēs*.
[59]*Coptic Homilies in the Dialect of Upper Egypt*, pp. 271–272.

released the man." Victory over death and Hades is vividly described in the following passage:

> Moreover, Death fell down to the feet of Christ, and Christ carried him away, and the Devil who had been a rebel became a captive. Christ made Amente to quake and the power of the Devil he turned backwards. Death heard the voice of the Lord as he cried unto all souls: "Come forth, O ye who are bound in fetters, O ye who sit in the darkness and shadow of death, on you hath the light risen.[60] I preach unto you life, for I am Christ, the Son of God." Then he set free the souls of the saints, and he raised them up with Him.
>
> And earth itself cried out, saying: "Spare me, O Lord. Free Thou me from the curse that is on me. Remove from me the wickedness of the Devil. Thou hast held me to be worthy of having Thy Body buried in me, in the place of the Blood, which was poured out upon me, in order that Thou mightest raise men from the dead. Thy glorious image is spread abroad in every place. Except Thyself, when Thou utterest Thy words, no one shall resist Thy commands; but it was Thy love which compelled Thee to come to the beings whom Thou has fashioned. For behold, Thou didst stand on the earth, and didst seek after the members of the beings whom Thou hast made. Take Thou, then, man, the deposit. Take Thou Thine image, which Thou hast committed as a pledge to me.[61] Take Thou Adam, being complete in his likeness."
>
> Then Christ rose from the dead in the third hour of the day, and he took the saints with him to his Father; now all mankind shall receive salvation through the death of Christ.
>
> For one was judged instead of all men, and salvation and mercy [came] into the whole world. Moreover, one died in order that all might rise from the dead. And the Lord died on behalf of every one, in order that every one should rise from the dead with Him. For having died, he put man on himself like a garment, and took him with him into the heavens, and man became one of one with him. He took him as a gift to his Father.[62]

---

[60]Cf. Isa 49.9; Luke 1.78–79.

[61]Cf. St Ephrem's *Carmina Nisibena* 36, 15–17.

[62]*Coptic Homilies in the Dialect of Upper Egypt*, pp. 273–274.

Unlike Melito's "On Pascha," in which Christ's descent into Hades is mentioned only in passing, this text develops the theme substantially. For example, it depicts the Höllensturm ("storming of hell") with all its attributes: the destruction of iron gates, the breaking of locks, the flight of death from the Lord, the disarmament of the enemy, the captivity of death, and the liberation of holy souls from Hades. What was only briefly referred to in second-century liturgical poetry was fully developed in the third and fourth centuries.

Eusebius of Caesarea, a church historian and collector of various "traditions of the fathers," writes about the preaching of the Apostle Thaddeus to Prince Abgarus of Edessa after Christ's ascension into heaven.[63] In his address to the prince the Apostle speaks

> concerning the coming of Jesus, how he was born; and concerning his mission, for what purpose he was sent by the Father; and concerning the power of his works, and the mysteries which he proclaimed in the world, and by what power he did these things; and concerning his new preaching, and his abasement and humiliation, and how he humbled himself, and died and debased his divinity and was crucified, and descended into Hades, and burst the bars which from eternity had not been broken, and raised the dead; for he descended alone, but rose with many, and thus ascended to his Father.[64]

In the writings of the Cappadocian fathers, references to the descent are quite frequent. St Basil the Great, in his exposition of Psalm 49 (48), speaks of Christ's descent into Hades as a continuation of his pastoral ministry on earth:

> "They are laid in hell like sheep: death shall feed upon them."[65] He, who carries away into captivity those who are beastlike and who are

---

[63]"The Acts of Thaddeus," quoted earlier (see chapter one), served as a source for this story.

[64]Eusebius, *Church History* I, 13, 20 (SC 31, 45). Cf. also *Demonstration of the Gospel* 4, 12, 3 (GCS 23, 169); 5, 20, 5 (GCS 23, 243–244); 9, 12, 5 (GCS 23, 431); 10, 8, 501–502 (GCS 23, 482–484); 10, 8, 507 (GCS 23, 488–489); *Commentaries on Psalms* 63 (62), 10 (PG 23:612bc); 69 (68), 2–3 (PG 23:728ab); 71 (70), 20 (PG 23:785d); 88 (87), 4–13 (PG 23:1053d–1064b); *Prophetic Eulogy* 3, 8 (PG 22:1133a).

[65]Ps 49/48.14 (LXX).

compared to senseless herds, like the sheep, which have neither the intelligence nor the ability to defend themselves, since he is an enemy, has already cast them down into his own prison and has handed them over to death to feed. For, death tended them from the time of Adam until the administration of Moses,[66] until the true Shepherd came, who laid down his own life for his sheep and who thus, making them rise together and leading them out[67] from the prison of hell to the early morning of the Resurrection, handed them over to the righteous, that is to say, to his holy angels, to tend them.[68]

St Gregory Nazianzen refers to the descent both in his orations and in his theological poetry. In his famous "Discourse 45," which for many centuries had been an inseparable part of the Byzantine paschal service, St Gregory develops the tradition. He derives from early Christian paschal *egkomia*, such as the aforementioned "On Pascha" by Melito of Sardis, and describes the "paschal mystery" in an elevated and highly poetic tone:

Today is salvation come unto the world, to that which is visible, and to that which is invisible. Christ is risen from the dead, rise ye with Him. Christ is returned again to himself, return ye. Christ is freed from the tomb, be ye freed from the bond of sin. The gates of hell are opened, and death is destroyed, and the old Adam is put aside, and the New is fulfilled; if any man be in Christ he is a new creature; be ye renewed. ... The Lord's Passover, the Passover, and again I say the Passover to the honour of the Trinity. This is to us a Feast of feasts and a Solemnity of solemnities.[69]

Continuing along the same lines, Gregory addresses his listeners: "If he descends into Hell, descend with Him. Learn to know the mysteries of Christ there also: what is the providential purpose of the twofold descent, to save all humans absolutely by his manifestation,

---

[66]Cf. Rom 5.14.

[67]Cf. John 10.3–18.

[68]Basil, *Homily on Psalm* 48 (49), 9 (PG 29:451–454). Cf. also *Homily on Psalm* 45 (44), 9 (PG 29:408); *On the Holy Spirit* 14, 32 (SC 17bis, 358–359); 15, 35 (SC 17bis, 356–357).

[69]*Discourse* 45, 1–2 (PG 36:624ac).

or there, too, only them that believe?"[70] When speaking of the "twofold descent" Gregory means the *katabasis* of the Son of God on earth (the incarnation) and his *katabasis* into Hades. Both themes were intertwined in early Christian literature.[71]

It is noteworthy that the question raised by Gregory, namely, whether all humans or only those who believed in Christ will be saved, is left unanswered. Gregory Nazianzen is very cautious when speaking about eschatological questions and, unlike Gregory of Nyssa, he abstained from definitive conclusions regarding issues for which there was no clear response from Christian tradition. But not every church father took this approach; a number of subsequent authors were much less cautious when discussing the same issue. Theophilactus of Bulgaria (twelfth century), for example, refers to Gregory Nazianzen but modifies his words in the following way: "Having appeared to those in Hades, Christ saves not all humans, but only those that believe."[72] In the same manner, Gregory's words are modified in the spurious "Oration for Great Saturday," which survives under the name of Epiphanius of Cyprus (to this work we shall return later). What Gregory Nazianzen considers to be a mystery surpassing the boundary of human reason, Theophilactus and Pseudo-Epiphanius treat as a commonly accepted teaching requiring no special clarification.

In his poem "Hymn to Christ after Silence, on Easter" (from the collection of hymns under the common title "On Himself"), Gregory speaks of Christ's victory over Hades:

> Today the great Christ rose from the dead, with whom he had been mixed,
> And dissipated the sting of death
> And destroyed the dark gates of doleful Hades
> And gave freedom to the souls.
> Today, having risen from the tomb, he appeared to the people

---

[70]*Discourse* 45, 24 (PG 36:657a).
[71]See J. Daniélou, *The Theology of Jewish Christianity*, p. 233.
[72]Theophilactus of Bulgaria, *The Exposition of the 1st Epistle of St Peter* 3, 19 (PG 125:1232d).

For whose sake he had been born, for whose sake he had died,
and for whose sake he had risen from the dead,
In order that we, being regenerated and having escaped death,
Ascended [to heaven] together with him who ascends [there].[73]

Insofar as its style, vocabulary, and meter are concerned, this poem stands apart from those pieces of Christian poetry past and present that are used at paschal services. Gregory's poetry, apparently not intended for liturgical use, was written primarily for didactic purposes. In it he uses an obsolete, artificial language that imitates Homer, Euripides, and other ancient Greek poets.

Written also "in the style of Euripides" (*kat'Euripidēn*) is the tragedy (*hypothesis dramatikē*—literally, "dramatic performance") that survives under the name "Christus patiens" ("The Suffering Christ") and is ascribed in the manuscript tradition to Gregory Nazianzen. Scholars held different opinions regarding its authorship and date; many ascribe the work to an unknown twelfth-century author. There are, nevertheless, sufficient grounds to assume that the work is authentic.[74] In particular, its style is similar to that of Gregory's poetry, which is also characterized by numerous allusions to ancient Greek authors.[75] The uniqueness of this work lies in the fact that, unlike most Christian poetry, it is written for the theater, not for the church.[76] Though there is no evidence that it was ever performed in the Byzantine period, its popularity is confirmed by the fact that it was translated into other languages, Syriac in particular.[77]

---

[73] *On Himself* 38 (PG 37:1328a).

[74] For a fuller discussion of the authorship of "Christus patiens" see the introduction by A. Tuilier to Grégoire de Nazianze, *La passion du Christ. Tragédie*, SC 149, 11–121. See also: F. Trisoglio, *San Gregorio di Nazianzo e il Christus patiens. Il problema dell'autenticità gregoriana del drama*, Filologia, Testi e Studi 7 (Firenze, 1996). Both authors, while examining a wide range of opinions regarding the authenticity of the drama, come to the conclusion that it is very likely authentic.

[75] Another fourth-century author who imitates ancient Greek poets is Synesius. His references to the descent into Hades are analyzed in: J. Kroll, *Gott und Hölle*, p. 113.

[76] See A. Tuilier, "Introduction," SC 149, p. 40.

[77] "Liber tragediae" by Gregory Nazianzen is mentioned in the late thirteenth- and early fourteenth-century catalogue of church books compiled by the East Syrian writer Ebed-Jeshu. See J. S. Assemani, *Bibliotheca orientalis* III, 1 (Rome, 1725),

The main hero of the tragedy is Mary the Theotokos. Others include Christ, an angel, an anonymous theologian, Joseph of Arimathea, Nicodemus, Mary Magdalene, and Pontius Pilate. The discourse is centered on the end of time; the crucifixion; and the death, interment, and resurrection of Christ. The descent into Hades also serves as one of the leitmotifs. It appears in different contexts and is commented on by different characters. Addressing Christ, the Theotokos asks: "O Son of the King of all, how is it that the death of the forefathers now leads you into the abodes of Hades (*eis haidou domous*)?"[78] Again the Theotokos exclaims: "O Child of the Most High, how much suffering you brought to me both when you were alive and when you descended to Hades."[79] The Theotokos also utters the following monologue:

> You descend, O beloved Child, into the abodes of Hades,
> In order to hide yourself in a refuge where you choose to be
>   hidden.
> However, descending into the darkest cave of Hades,
> You introduce to Hades the bitterest sting.[80]
> You descend into the valley of the dead and to the gates of
>   darkness
> Desiring to illuminate and shine upon the [human] race,
> To raise Adam, the father of mortals,
> For whose sake you assumed and carried the image of the
>   mortal.[81]
> You descend into a deep and gloomy darkness of Hades,

---

pp. 23–24. Most translations from Greek into Syriac were made in the fifth and sixth centuries. The fact that "Christus patiens" was translated into Syriac may well indicate that it was written no later than the sixth century.

[78] *Christus patiens* 878–879 (SC 149, 198). The expression "the abodes of Hades" is found in Homer, where it means "the nether world." See H. G. Liddell and R. Scott, *A Greek-English Lexicon* (Oxford, 1989), p. 21.

[79] *Christus patiens* 1338–1339 (SC 149, 236).

[80] Gregory uses both the Doric form that had been used by tragic poets (*haidas*) and the Attic form (*haidēs*). We translate both as "Hades."

[81] Cf. 1 Cor 15.49.

Having accepted death from enemies and having left your
    Mother sorrowful.
But the good will of the Father will slay you
In order to bring salvation to others.
It was the Father's goodness that brought you to death.
O bitter mourning! The earth receives you, O Child,
When you descend to the dark gates of Hades
In order to pierce Hades by the sharpest arrow.
For you descend there alone
In order to take the dead [with you] and not in order to be
    taken by the dead
And in order to liberate all, for you alone are free.
For you are the only man who dares to do this,
You alone suffer for human nature.
But the feats which you accomplished have now finished,
And you win victory over the enemies,
Having put to flight Hades, the serpent and death. . . .
Having seized the [human] race, you will immediately
depart [from Hades] with glory,
O King, immortal King, remaining God,
But uniting human nature with your image.
And now you descend into the abodes of Hades,
Desiring to illuminate and shine upon darkness.[82]

The theme of the descent is also developed by another hero in the tragedy, the theologian (his role is to comment on events and to give theological explanations):

The light of one sun is sufficient for Christ
In order to annihilate the abodes of Hades and
    tomorrow again
Return to earth, having quenched the pain of mortals.
For it is for this reason that, having put on poor
    clothes,

---

[82]*Christus patiens* 1505–1538 (SC 149, 250–252).

You descended into Hades and, having seized many arms
[of the enemy],
You became the overseer of those in the nether world
(*nerterōn episkopos*).
Having slain the custodians and the gatekeepers,
He will return from there in order that everybody should
recognize Him
As Helper, Self-Rooted (*autorizos*)[83] and Benefactor,
Who was slain by his own people out of jealousy.[84]

It is clear from the passages quoted above that the author of
"Christus patiens" regards the descent into Hades as a redemptive
feat, accomplished by Christ for the salvation of all humanity and not
only for a particular group of people. By his descent Christ destroys
Hades, illumines the human race and raises Adam, who personifies
all of humanity. Ascending from Hades, he returns to earth[85] in order
to announce his own resurrection to his mother, to the myrrh-bearing women, and to the apostles.

We find references to the descent also in the writings of St Gregory of Nyssa. He often entwines this theme with the theory of
"divine deception." With respect to the latter, he builds on his own
teaching on the redemption. According to this theory Christ, being
God incarnate, deliberately concealed his divine nature from the devil
so that the devil, mistaking Christ for an ordinary man, would not be
terrified at the sight of an overwhelming power approaching him.
When Christ descended into hell the devil supposed him to be a
human being. Christ was a divine "hook" and the devil swallowed the
"bait."[86] By admitting God incarnate into his domain the devil himself signed his own death warrant: Incapable of enduring the divine
presence, he was overcome and defeated, and hell was destroyed.

This is precisely the idea that Gregory of Nyssa develops in one
of his Easter sermons, "The Three-Day Period of the Resurrection of

---

[83]Or "Self-Founded."
[84]*Christus patiens* 1731–1740 (SC 149, 266).
[85]*Christus patiens* 2188–2189 (SC 149, 306).
[86]*The Great Catechetical Oration* 23–24.

Christ." Judging by its contents, this homily was intended for Holy Saturday,[87] and in it Gregory poses the question of why Christ spent three days "in the heart of the earth."[88] This period was necessary and sufficient, he argues, for Christ to "expose the foolishness" (*mōranai*) of the devil;[89] that is to outwit, ridicule, and deceive him.[90] How did Christ manage to "outwit" the devil? Gregory gives the following reply to this question:

> As the ruler of darkness could not approach the presence of the Light unimpeded, had he not seen in him something of flesh, then, as soon as he saw the God-bearing flesh and saw the miracle performed through it by the Deity, he hoped that if he came to take hold of the flesh through death, then he would take hold of all the power contained in it. Therefore, having swallowed the bait of the flesh, he was pierced by the hook of the Deity and thus the dragon was transfixed by the hook.[91]

The theme of the descent is also present in St Amphilochius of Iconium who, in one of his sermons, describes the destruction Hades' graves upon Christ's descent. Together with the theologians of the Alexandrian tradition Amphilochius understands the descent as an event whose result is the liberation of all those detained in Hades:

> When [Christ] appeared to Hades, he destroyed its graves and emptied its tombs. He emptied them not by visibly contesting [Hades], but by invisibly granting resurrection. He did not unloose anybody, but all (*pantes*) were released. He did not talk to anybody, but freedom was announced. He did not call anybody, but all (*pantes*) ran after Him. For when he appeared as King, the tyrant was humiliated, the light shone and the darkness faded away. For one could see

---

[87] *The Homily on the Three-Day Period* (pp. 444–446). For the text of this sermon, see *Grēgoriou Nyssis hapantata erga*, t. 10, Hellēnes pateres tēs ekklēsias 103 (Thessalonikē, 1990), pp. 444–487. Since in this edition the text is not divided into chapters, we indicate only page numbers.

[88] Cf. Matt 12.40.

[89] Lit. "to make a fool of somebody" (from *mōros*, fool).

[90] *The Homily on the Three-Day Period* (pp. 452–454).

[91] *The Homily on the Three-Day Period* (pp. 452–454). Cf. 1 Cor 15.26.

every (*panta*) prisoner free and every (*panta*) captive rejoicing in the resurrection.[92]

Foremost among the fourth-century authors is St John Chrysostom, who in many of his writings speaks of Christ's descent into Hades. In the "Homily on the Cemetery and the Cross" Chrysostom comments on the "gates of brass" and describes the transformation of Hades into Heaven after Christ descended into it and illumined its regions with his light:

> Today our Lord goes around all the places of Hades; today he "broke in pieces the doors of bronze and cut asunder the bars of iron."[93] Note the exactness of expression. He did not say "opened the gates of bronze," but "broke in pieces the gates of bronze," in order that the whole prison become useless. He did not open the bars of iron, but cut them asunder, in order that the guard becomes powerless. Where there is neither door, nor lock, there whoever enters will not be guarded. So, if Christ breaks in pieces, who else can repair it? . . . He broke in pieces the gates of bronze in order to show that death is finite. They are called "of bronze" not because they were made of bronze, but in order to demonstrate the cruelty and mercilessness of death. . . . Do you want to know how harsh, inexorable and unconquerable it was? In so long a time nobody convinced her to release anyone of those it possessed until the Lord of angels himself descended and forced it to do so. He first bound the strong man and then plundered his goods.[94] This is why the prophet adds: "treasures of darkness, which are invisible."[95] . . . This place of Hades, dark and joyless, had bean eternally deprived of light; this is why the [gates] are called dark and invisible. They were truly dark until the Sun of righteousness descended [into Hades], illumined it and made Hades Heaven. For where Christ is, there also is Heaven.[96]

---

[92] *Homily 6, Against the Heretics.* Translated from: *Amphilochii Iconiensis Opera*, ed. C. Datema, CCSG 3 (Louvain, 1978), p. 152. Cf. also *Homily* 5, 1 in the same edition.

[93] Isa 45.2.

[94] Matt 12.29.

[95] Isa 45.3 (LXX).

[96] *Homily on the Cemetery and the Cross* (PG 49:394–395).

Chrysostom further affirms that Christ, having descended into Hades freed the entire human race from hell and bound and conquered Death:

> He calls Hades "treasures of darkness." This is accurate, because great riches were detained there. The entire human nature, which is God's treasure, was robbed by the devil, who deceived the first man, and was subjected to death ... Like a certain king, having found a chief of robbers, who assaulted towns, robbed everywhere, who hid himself in caves and there concealed his treasures, binds this chief of robbers and condemns him to death, transferring the treasures to the royal treasury. So Christ, by his death bound the chief of robbers and the jailer, that is, the devil and death, and transferred his treasures, that is, the entire human race, to the royal treasury. ... The King himself came to the prisoners . . . broke gates, destroyed locks, appeared to Hades, left its entire guard deserted, bound the jailer, captured him, and then ascended to us. The tyrant is captured, the strong is bound; death itself, having thrown away its arms, ran naked to the King's feet.[97]

Developing the same theme in another homily Chrysostom uses a "gastronomic" analogy, which is also to be found in the Syriac tradition (see the quotation from Aphrahat below) and in liturgical texts. Hades, Chrysostom affirms, swallowed Christ but, unable to "digest" him, vomited him up:

> When [Christ's Body] was crucified, then were the dead raised up, then was that prison burst, and the gates of brass were broken, and the dead were loosed, and the keepers of hell-gate all cowered in fear. And yet, had he been one of the many, death on the contrary should have become more mighty; but it was not so. For he was not one of the many. Therefore was death dissolved. And as they who take food which they are unable to retain, on account of that vomit up also what was before lodged in them; so also it happened unto death. That Body, which he could not digest, he received: and therefore had to cast forth that which he had within him. Yea, he travailed in pain,

---

[97] *Homily on the Cemetery and the Cross* (PG 49:395–396).

whilst he held Him, and was straitened until he vomited him up. Wherefore says the Apostle, "Having loosed the pangs of death."[98] For never woman labouring of child was so full of anguish as he was torn and racked in sunder, while he held the Body of the Lord. And that which happened to the Babylonian dragon, when, having taken the food it burst asunder in the midst this also happened unto him. For Christ came not forth again by the mouth of death, but having burst asunder and ripped up in the very midst, the belly of the dragon, thus from his secret chambers[99] right gloriously he issued forth and flung abroad his beams not to this heaven alone, but to the very throne most high.[100]

In his "Homilies on Matthew" the same church father reproduces traditional teachings on Christ's victory over the devil and on death's destruction by his death:

Consider what a thing it is to hear, how on the one side God from Heaven, arising out of the royal thrones, leaped down unto the earth, and even unto Hades itself, and stood in the battle array; and how the devil on the other hand set himself in array against Him; or rather not against God unveiled, but God hidden in man's nature. And what is marvellous, you will see death destroyed by death, and curse extinguished by curse, and the dominion of the devil put down by those very things whereby he did prevail.[101]

In the same work Chrysostom turns to the question: Who was liberated by Christ from Hades? In the "Homily on the Cemetery and the Cross" he speaks of the salvation of all the departed, whereas in the "Homilies on Matthew" he claims that only those who believed in the true God were freed. Here he specifies that, although through Christ's descent into Hades the power of death was destroyed, not every single person was automatically liberated from the responsibility of his sins:

[98] Acts 2.24.
[99] Cf. Ps 19.5 (LXX).
[100] *Homilies on the First Epistle of St Paul to the Corinthians* 24, 7 (NPNF 1 12:142–143).
[101] *Homilies on Matthew* 2, 1 (NPNF 1 10:9).

The present life indeed is the season for right conversation, but after death is judgment and punishment. "For in hell," it is said, "who will confess unto thee?"[102] How then were "the gates of brass burst, and the bars of iron broken asunder"? By his body; for then first was a body shown, immortal, and destroying the tyranny of death. And besides, this indicates the destruction of the might of death, not the loosing of the sins of those who had died before his coming. And if this were not so, but he have delivered all that were before him from hell, how says He, "It shall be more tolerable for the land of Sodom and Gomorrah?"[103] For this saying supposes that those are also to be punished; more mildly indeed, yet still that they are to be punished. And yet they did also suffer here the most extreme punishment, nevertheless not even this will deliver them. And if it is so with them, much more with such as have suffered nothing.[104]

Chrysostom then argues that in Old Testament times "men might be saved, even though they had not confessed Christ . . . this was not required of them, but not to worship idols, and to know the true God." Chrysostom contests the opinion according to which it would be unjust to condemn to hell those who had not even heard of its existence. Even if they had, he argues, they would have lived in the same way as we live today, because we hear daily the sayings about hell but give no heed at all. "And besides, there is this also to be said: that he who is not restrained by the judgments in sight, much less will he be restrained by those others."[105] Thus the question of the salvation of those in hell is totally transferred to the realm of morality. Christ's descent into Hades is used here by Chrysostom as a pretext for a moral lesson which he gives to his flock: one must not count on salvation after death if one does not do good deeds while on earth. This is more a pedagogical than a theological approach to the problem.

---

[102]Ps 6.5 (LXX).
[103]Cf. Matt 11.24.
[104]*Homilies on Matthew* 36, 3 (NPNF 1 10:236).
[105]*Homilies on Matthew* 36, 3–4 (NPNF 1 10:236–237).

Chrysostom refers to the descent also in other writings.[106] It is central to the "Catechetical Oration on Easter," which the Orthodox tradition ascribes to him and which is solemnly read at Easter matins. We shall return to this sermon below in the discussion on liturgical texts. For the moment we shall confine ourselves to noting that, like the "Homily on the Cemetery and the Cross," the Catechetical Oration stresses the universal character of Christ's descent into Hades: after his resurrection, not a single dead person is left in Hades but all, whether they came at the sixth, ninth, or eleventh hour, partake at the "banquet of faith."

St Epiphanius of Cyprus develops the theme of the descent in his anti-heretical compendium "Panarion," where it is touched on a number of times.[107] In the "Exposition of Faith," which is the final section of the "Panarion," Epiphanius argues in particular that Christ's soul descended into Hades together with his divinity:

> [Christ] suffered by his flesh and died in his flesh, but by his divinity he was always alive and raised the dead. His body was truly buried and for three days remained without soul, breathless and motionless; it was wrapped by a shroud, put into a grave, covered by a stone and sealed. His divinity, however, was neither sealed nor buried. Together with his holy soul it descended into the nether world and liberated captive souls from there; it destroyed the sting of death, demolished bars and locks of steel, but its power unloosed the pains of Hades and ascended from it with the soul. His soul was not left in hell and his flesh did not see corruption,[108] because the divinity raised it; or rather, the Lord God himself, the Word and the Son of God was risen, together with his soul, body and all members.[109]

---

[106]See, for example, *Against the Jews and the Pagans, That Christ Is God* 4 (PG 48:819–820); *Homilies on the Book of Genesis* 45, 2 (PG 53:416); *Homilies on the Epistle of St Paul to the Ephesians* 11, 2 (PG 62:81–82); *Homilies on the First Epistle to the Corinthians* 40, 1 (PG 61:348); *Homilies on the Epistle of St Paul to the Hebrews* 4, 2 (PG 63:39).

[107]For a more detailed discussion see R. Gounelle, *La descente du Christ aux Enfers. Institutionalisation d'une croyance*, Etudes augustiniennes, Série antiquité 162 (Paris, 2000), pp. 109–113.

[108]Cf. Ps 16.10 (LXX).

[109]*Exposition of Faith* 17 (PG 42:814c–816a).

The theme of the descent into Hades is also central to the Syriac theological tradition.[110] Among the authors that develop it, one should first mention Jacob Aphrahat,[111] "the Persian sage," for his book of instructions known as the "Demonstrations." Aphrahat devoted the following characteristic text in which a personification of death enters into dialogue with Christ:

> When Jesus, the slayer of Death, came and put on a body (*lbesh pagra*)[112] from the seed of Adam, and was crucified in the body and tasted death; and as soon as Death perceived that he descended to him,[113] he quivered in his place and became agitated at the sight of Jesus. He shut up the doors and did not want to receive Him. However, he shattered the doors and entered to him [Death] and began to rob him of his possessions. As the dead saw light shining in darkness, they raised up their heads from the bondage of death and looked forth and saw the brightness of Christ, the King. Then the powers of darkness sat lamenting, for Death was destroyed and stripped of his authority. And Death has tasted deadly poison (*sam mauta*)[114] and his hands slackened and he realised that the dead will revive and escape his tyranny. As he [Christ] conquered Death by spoiling him of his possessions, Death cried out and wept bitterly and said: "Go out of my place and do not come back. Who is that who dared to enter my home alive?" And then Death cried out, as he saw darkness starting to disperse and some among the righteous ones who were lying down there, rose up to ascend with him

---

[110]Cf. R. Gounelle, *La descente du Christ aux Enfers*, pp. 39–47.

[111]Syriac text: *The Homilies of Aphraates, the Persian Sage*, ed. W. Wright (London–Edinburgh, 1869). There is also a later edition: *Aphraatis sapientis persae demonstrationes*, Textum syriacum vocalium signit instruxit, latine vertit, notis illustravit D. Joannes Parisot, Patrologia Syriaca 1–2 (Paris, 1894–1907).

[112]The idiom "to put on the body" is one of the most characteristic expressions in the Eastern Syriac Christological tradition and serves to express the teaching on the Incarnation. See, in particular, S. Brock, *The Luminous Eye: The Spiritual World Vision of St Ephrem* (Kalamazoo, Michigan, 1992), pp. 39, 85–98; H. Alfeyev, *The Spiritual World of Isaac the Syrian* (Kalamazoo, Michigan, 1985), pp. 20, 54.

[113]In Syriac the word "death" (*mautha*) is masculine, which to a great extent defines the symbolism connected with it. Sheol, on the contrary, is feminine.

[114]This point about vinegar and poison is also found in the *Odes of Solomon* 42.12.

[Christ]. And he said [to Death] that he will return at the end of time, and will release all captives from his authority, and will draw them to himself, so that they could see light. Thus, as Christ had completed his ministry (*teshmeshta*) among the dead, Death let him escape out of his region, for he could not endure his presence there. For it was not sweet for him to swallow Christ up as [it was with] the rest of the dead. And Death did not prevail over the Holy One and he was not subjected to corruption.[115]

Thus in Aphrahat's way of thinking, some of the righteous were resurrected with Christ after his descent into Hades, but the rest imprisoned there will be liberated at his second coming. His release of the righteous from Hades is seen as a pledge of the general resurrection, which is expected at the end of time. Nevertheless, Death has already been conquered by Christ; his days have been numbered from the very moment of Christ's descent. To enhance this statement Aphrahat presents the image of poison gradually affecting all organs of the body:

And when Death indeed had let him escape and he went out of his region, he left him the promise of life, as poison, which little by little would bring to nought his authority. Likely, as someone who has taken a deadly poison with food, and he disgorges from his stomach the nourishment to which the venom has admixtured itself, but the poison continues to spread in the members of his body. Gradually, the structure of the body is being destroyed and corrupted. In the same way the dead Jesus became the destroyer of Death, for in him reigns life. For he made Death perish, as it was said to him: "Where is your victory, O Death?"[116]

St Ephrem the Syrian also pays special attention to the theme of the descent into Hades. His poetry will be the subject of a separate discussion. As for his prose works, however, mention should first and

---

[115]*Demonstration* 22, 4. Translation from the Syriac text published in: *The Homilies of Aphraates, the Persian Sage*, ed. W. Wright, pp. 420–421.

[116]*Demonstration* 22, 5. Translation from the Syriac text published in: *The Homilies of Aphraates, the Persian Sage*, ed. W. Wright, p. 421

foremost be made of the "Commentary on the Diatessaron," which survives in the Syriac original and in Armenian translation. Here Ephrem produces a narrative on the death of the Savior on the cross as the cause of the resurrection for the multitude of the dead. He also refers to Christ's victory over death and the final annihilation of hell.

But [the Lord] in his turn vanquished death through his great cry when he had gone up on the cross. Whereas death was binding one person on the cross, all those who had been bound in Sheol were being delivered because of the chains of one person . . . his hands, which delivered us from the bonds of death, were transfixed by nails, his hands which broke our chains and tied those which were binding us.

It was an amazing thing that the dead were killing the living one, [whereas] the slain one was raising the dead to life. They directed their fury more intensely towards heaven, whereas he humbled his greatness even further down into the depths. . . .

[Death] stole him, took him away and put him in the tomb while he was asleep, but, on awaking and standing up, he stole his stealer. This is the cross which crucifies those who crucified [the Lord], and this is the captive who leads into captivity those who had led him into captivity. The cross, through your death, has become a fountain of life for our mortal life . . . death used his body to taste and devour the life hidden in mortal bodies. What it had hastened to gulp down while famished it was forced to restore very quickly . . . he commanded the stones and they were split in two. [He commanded] death and it did not prevent the just from going forth at his voice. He trained the lower regions to his voice to prepare them for hearing it on the last day, when this voice will empty [the lower regions].[117]

---

[117]Syriac version. Translated into English by Carmel McCarthy in *Saint Ephrem's Commentary on Tatian's Diatessaron: An English Translation of Chester Beatty Syriac MS 709 with Introduction and Notes*, Journal of Semitic Studies, Supplement 2 (Oxford, 1993), pp. 309–312. Armenian version: Saint Ephrem, *Commentaire de l'Evangile concordant*, éd. par L. Leloir, CSCO 137, Scr. armeniaci 1 (Louvain, 1953).

St Ephrem also deals with the theme of the descent into Hades in his "Homily on Our Lord," written in metrical prose.[118] Here the author juxtaposes the events of the incarnation of God and his exodus from Sheol:

> The Only Begotten proceeded from the Being [of the Father] and dwelled in the Virgin, so that through his bodily birth the Only Begotten became a brother of many.
>
> And he went forth out of Sheol and settled in the Kingdom so that he could tread a path from Sheol, which deceives everyone, to the Kingdom that rewards everyone.
>
> For our Lord made his Resurrection a pledge to the mortal ones, that he could liberate them from Sheol that receives the dead without discernment, [and to lead them] to Kingdom receiving the invited with discernment [between the sinners and the righteous].[119]

Clearly the Old Testament notion of Sheol as a place where all the dead go regardless of their moral state ("without discernment") remained in the Syriac tradition for much longer than in the Greek. Moreover, it is considered to be a peculiarity of the Syriac tradition to parallel (and sometimes to equate) the descent of Christ into Sheol with his descent into the waters of the Jordan at his baptism by John the Forerunner. This is reflected in the following stanzas from the "Homily on Our Lord," where St Ephrem advances the notion of Christ's three births. Each is a stage of the incarnation: divinity, humanity, and baptism. The last is paralleled to the descent into Sheol:

> The Father begat him and through him created the whole Creation.
> Flesh begat him and through him mortified passions.
> Baptism begat him to wash away the stains [of our sin].

---

[118]A critical edition of the text is in *Des heiligen Ephraem des Syrers Sermo de Domino nostro*, hrsg. von. E. Beck, CSCO 270, Scriptores Syri 116 (Louvain, 1966).

[119]*Des heiligen Ephraem des Syrers Sermo de Domino nostro* (CSCO 270, Scriptores Syri 116, 1).

> Sheol begat him so that through him her treasures would be plundered.[120]

Parallelism between Christ's baptism and his descent into Sheol is discernible already in the "Odes of Solomon."[121] It will later be developed in the works of St Ephrem's follower, Jacob of Serugh (AD 451–521), who also describes Christ's baptism in terms of descent into the muddy waters of Sheol for the purpose of recovering from their depths a pearl—fallen Adam.[122]

A very original approach to the subject of Christ's descent into Hades may be found in a book entitled "Spiritual Homilies," which survives under the name of Macarius of Egypt. In it, the liberation of Adam is seen as the prototype of the mystical resurrection, which the soul experiences in its encounter with the Lord:

> When you hear that the Lord in the old days delivered souls from hell and prison and that he descended into hell and performed a glorious deed, do not think that all these events are far from your soul. . . . So the Lord comes into the souls that seek Him, into the depth of the heart's hell, and there commands death, saying: "Release the imprisoned souls which have sought Me and which you hold by force." And he shatters the heavy stones weighing on the soul, opens graves, raises the true dead from death, brings the imprisoned soul from the dark prison. . . . Is it difficult for God to enter death and, even more, into the depth of the heart and to call out dead Adam from there? . . . If the sun, being created, passes everywhere through windows and doors, even to the caves of lions and the holes of creeping creatures, and comes out without any harm, the more so does God and the Lord of everything enter caves and abodes in which death has settled, and also souls, and, having released Adam from there, [remains] unfettered by death. Similarly, rain coming down from the sky reaches the nethermost parts of the

---

[120]*Des heiligen Ephraem des Syrers Sermo de Domino nostro* (CSCO 270, Scriptores Syri 116, 2). Cf. *Nisibene Hymns* 37, 4 (on the birth of Christ from the Virgin's womb and on Chrst's sojourn in the womb of Sheol).

[121]See Odes 22 and 24.

[122]*Homily* IV, v.193–198 (CSCO 508, Scriptores Syri 214, 98–99).

earth, moistens and renews the roots there and gives birth to new shoots.[123]

This text is significant principally because the author regards Christ's descent as a commonly accepted and undisputed doctrine—one that serves as a solid foundation on which to build his mystical and typological construction. By employing the images of the sun rising over both good and evil, and of rain that falls on both the just and the unjust,[124] the author of the "Homilies" clearly sees the descent as a reality that affects not only the Old Testament righteous but also all of humanity. Moreover, it affects the inner processes that take place within every human soul. The descent into Hades is not an abstract truth, nor is it an event of olden times that affects only those from that age. For Macarius it is something that is forever relevant. It is not only one of the fundamental Christian doctrines, nor simply a subject of faith and confession, it is, rather, to be associated with the mystical life of the Christian; a mystery to be experienced in the depth of one's heart.

We may sum up the teaching of the fourth-century Eastern fathers on the descent into Hades as follows: first, as a commonly accepted and indisputably integral part of the church's *kerygma*;[125] second, as an event of universal significance with all the dead included in salvation; third, as an event of limited significance, with only particular categories of the dead included in salvation; fourth, as the accomplishment of the Savior's "economy," the crowning feat he performed in order to save all people; fifth, as the victory of Christ over the devil, hell, and death; and sixth, as the prototype of the resurrection of the human soul—the mystical dimension of the teaching.

---

[123] *Spiritual Homilies* 11, 11–13 (PG 34:552d–556a).
[124] Cf. Matt 5.45.
[125] Cf. R. Gounelle, *La descente du Christ aux Enfers*, p. 107.

EASTERN FATHERS OF THE FIFTH TO EIGHTH CENTURIES

From the fifth to the eighth centuries a large number of authors refer to Christ's descent into Hades, but without making detailed commentary. Thus it became commonplace for paschal homilies only to mention that Christ conquered death and destroyed the power of the devil by his death.[126]

There exist a number of pseudepigraphal writings dedicated specifically to the descent, such as the four homilies that have come down under the name of Eusebius of Alexandria but which belong most probably to a certain John the Notarius believed to have lived in Syria[127] in the sixth or seventh century.[128] All four texts contain reworking of material from the first Christian centuries, which have formed the basis of many authentic writings. These include the "Nisibian Hymns" by Ephrem the Syrian and the *kontakia* by Romanos the Melodist (to which the third chapter of this study is dedicated). The first homily, "On John's Descent into Hades and on Those in It,"[129] consists of two parts. In the first part the prophets, overjoyed by John the Baptist's presence among them, repeat their prophecies about Christ. In the second there is a dialogue between Hades and Satan. The second homily is dedicated to Judas,[130] while the third, entitled "On the Devil and Hades,"[131] resembles the first in that it

---

[126]See, for example, the paschal homilies of Hesychius of Jerusalem, Basil of Seleucia, and Leontius of Constantinople in SC 187. Cf. also Mark the Ascetic, "Letter to Nicholas the Solitary," in *The Philokalia: The Complete Text*, compiled by St Nikodimos of the Holy Mountain and St Makarios of Corinth, trans. from the Greek and ed. by G. E. H. Palmer, Philip Sherrard, and Kallistos Ware, vol. 1 (London–Boston, 1979), p. 156. ("[Remember] the sufferings which he patiently accepted for us: crucifixion; death; the three-day burial; the descent into Hades. Then keep in mind all that has come from these sufferings: the resurrection from the dead; the liberation from hell and from death of those who were raised with the Lord; the ascension to the heavens . . .")

[127]See F. Nau, "Notes sur diverses homélies pseudépigraphiques," *Revue de l'Orient chrétien* 13 (1908), pp. 433–434.

[128]See H. G. Beck, *Kirche und theologische Literatur im byzantinischen Reich* (München, 1959), pp. 400–401.

[129]PG 86:509–526.

[130]PG 86:525–536.

[131]PG 86:384–406 (three different versions).

includes a dialogue between the two, who discuss the miracles, death, and resurrection of Jesus Christ. The fourth homily, "On Holy and Great Friday and on the Holy Passion of the Lord," also found among the spurious works by John Chrysostom[132] and dedicated to Christ's descent into Hades, is essentially a reworking of the "Gospel of Nicodemus."[133]

Another pseudepigraphal writing in this genre is the "Homily on Great Saturday," ascribed to St Epiphanius of Cyprus and preserved in a large number of copies in Greek, Syrian, Coptic, Armenian, Georgian, Arabic, and Slavonic. Most scholars date this oration to the seventh or eighth century.[134] It contains a significant number of passages taken directly from other church writers, notably Gregory Nazianzen, as well as many expressions and images from the "Gospel of Nicodemus." The narrative of the descent resembles that of the latter except for the fact that Pseudo-Epiphanius clearly divides the inhabitants of hell into two groups: those who recognize Christ as King and Savior and thus follow him, and those who, as Christ approaches them, run away from him into the depths of the nether world. This is not the kind of imagery normally found in the authentic writings of the church fathers. The latter either limit the circle of the saved to the Old Testament righteous or speak about the salvation of all humanity; they leave open the question of who could possibly remain in Hades after Christ's ascent from it.[135]

Returning to the authentic patristic writings, it can be seen that only a few fifth- to eighth-century authors have enriched our understanding of the descent with new insights. In what follows we shall limit ourselves to passages by the three most significant writers of the period, St Cyril of Alexandria, St Maximus the Confessor, and St John Damascene.

---

[132]PG 62:721–724.

[133]For a fuller analysis of these homilies see: J. A. MacCulloch, *The Harrowing of Hell*, pp. 174–191.

[134]See *Clavis patrum graecorum*, vol. II, ed. M. Geerard (Louvain, 1974), pp. 333–334 (No. 3768). See also: A. Vaillant, "L'homélie d'Épiphane sur l'ensevelissement du Christ," *Radovi staroslovenskog instituta* 3 (Zagreb, 1958), pp. 5–100.

[135]For a fuller analysis of these homilies see: J. A. MacCulloch, *The Harrowing of Hell*, pp. 192–198.

The doctrine of the descent of Christ into Hades occupies a vital place in the works of St Cyril of Alexandria. In his "Paschal Homilies" he repeatedly mentions that, as a consequence of Christ's descent, the devil was left entirely alone, while hell was devastated: "For having destroyed hell and opened the impassable gates for the departed spirits, he left the devil there abandoned and lonely."[136]

In his "Festive Letters" Cyril of Alexandria elaborates on the theme of the preaching of Christ in Hades, popular in the Alexandrian tradition since Clement.[137] He views this preaching as the fulfilment of the "history of salvation," which had begun with the Incarnation:

> He showed the way to salvation not only to us, but also to the spirits in hell; having descended, he preached to those once disobedient, as Peter says.[138] For it did not befit for love of man to be partial, but the manifestation of [this] gift should have been extended to all nature. . . . Having preached to the spirits in hell and having said "go forth" to the prisoners, and "show yourselves"[139] to those in prison on the third day, he resurrected his temple and again opened up to our nature the ascent to heaven, bringing himself to the Father as the beginning of humanity, pledging to those on earth the grace of communion in the Spirit.[140]

Cyril clearly emphasises the universality of the salvation given by Christ to humanity. Perceiving the descent of Christ into Hades as salvific for the entire human race, he avoids limiting salvation to one part of humanity, such as the Old Testament righteous. Salvation is likened to rain sent by God on both the just and the unjust.[141] Putting

---

[136] *Seventh Paschal Homily* 2 (PG 77:552a).

[137] Cf. *Festive Letters* 2, 8 (SC 372, 230); 5, 1 (SC 372, 284); 6, 12 (SC 372, 396–397); 11, 8 (SC 392, 308–309); 14, 2 (SC 334, 162–163); 20, 4 (PG 77:848–849); 21, 3 (PG 77:856a); 28, 4 (PG 77:956b). Cf. also *On the Incarnation of the Only-Begotten One* 692d–693d (SC 97, 234–237); *Commentary on Luke*, Homily 37 (CSCO 70, Scriptores Syri 27, 77); et al.

[138] Cf. 1 Pet 3.19–20.

[139] Isa 49.9 (LXX).

[140] *2nd Festive Letter* 8, 52–89 (SC 372, 228–232)

[141] Cf. Matt 5.45. See the same comparison in "Spiritual Homilies" by Macarius of Egypt.

emphasis on the universality of the saving feat of Christ, Cyril follows in the steps of other Alexandrian theologians, beginning with Clement, Origen, and Athanasius the Great.[142] Christ's descent, according to Cyril's teaching, signifies victory over that which previously appeared unconquerable, and it ensures the salvation of all humanity:

> Death unwilling to be defeated is defeated; corruption is transformed; unconquerable passion is destroyed. While hell, diseased with excessive insatiability and never satisfied with the dead, is taught, even if against its will, that which it could not learn previously. For it not only ceases to claim those who are still to fall [in the future], but also sets free those already captured, being subjected to splendid devastation by the power of our Saviour. . . . Having preached to the spirits in hell, once disobedient, he came out as conqueror by resurrecting his temple like a beginning of our hope and by showing to [our] nature the manner of the raising from the dead, and giving us along with it other blessings as well.[143]

Clearly, Cyril perceives the victory of Christ over hell and death as complete and definitive. For him, hell loses authority both over those who are in its power and those who are to become its prey in the future. Thus the descent into Hades, a single and unique action, is perceived as a timeless event. The raised body of Christ becomes the guarantee of universal salvation, the beginning of the way leading human nature to ultimate deification.

A more elaborate teaching of the descent of Christ into Hades is found in St Maximus the Confessor. In his analysis Maximus takes the words of St Peter as a starting point: "This is why the gospel was preached even to the dead, that though judged in the flesh like men, they might live in the spirit like God."[144] In Maximus' view, St Peter does not refer to the Old Testament righteous but to those sinners who, during their lifetime, were punished for their evil deeds:

---

[142]See above quotations from these authors.
[143]*Fifth Festive Letter* 1, 29–40 (SC 372, 284).
[144]1 Pet 4.6.

Some say that Scriptures call "dead" those who died before the coming of Christ, for instance, those who were at the time of the flood, at Babel, in Sodom, in Egypt, as well as others who in various times and in various ways received various punishments and the terrible misfortune of divine damnation. These people were punished not so much for their ignorance of God as for the offences they imposed on one another. It was to them, according to [St Peter] that the great message of salvation was preached when they were already damned as men in the flesh, that is, when they received, through life in the flesh, punishment for crimes against one another, so that they could live according to God by the spirit, that is, being in hell, they accepted the preaching of the knowledge of God, believing in the Saviour who descended into hell to save the dead. So, in order to understand [this] passage in [Holy Scripture] let us take it in this way: the dead, damned in the human flesh, were preached to precisely for the purpose that they may live according to God by the spirit.[145]

Thus, according to Maximus, punishments endured by sinners "in the human flesh" were necessary so that they might live "according to God by the spirit." These punishments, therefore, whether they were troubles and misfortunes in their lifetime or pains in hell, were of pedagogical and reforming significance. Maximus stresses that in damning them, God used not so much a religious as a moral criterion. People were punished "not so much for their ignorance of God as for the offences they imposed on one another." In other words, one's religious or ideological convictions were not decisive, but rather one's actions with respect to one's neighbours.

In St John Damascene we find lines that encapsulate the discussion on the theme of Christ's descent into Hades in Eastern patristic writings from the second through eighth centuries:

The soul [of Christ] when it is deified descended into Hades, in order that, just as the Sun of Righteousness rose for those upon the earth, so likewise he might bring light[146] to those who sit under the

---

[145] *Questions-Answers to Thalassius* 7 (PG 90:284bc).
[146] Cf. Isa 9.2.

earth in darkness and the shadow of death: in order that just as he
brought the message of peace to those upon the earth, and of release
to the prisoners, and of sight to the blind,[147] and became to those
who believed the Author of everlasting salvation and to those who
did not believe, a denunciation of their unbelief, so he might become
the same to those in Hades: "That every knee should bow, in heaven
and on earth and under the earth."[148] And thus after he had freed
those who had been bound for ages, straightway he rose again from
the dead, showing us the way of resurrection.[149]

According to John Damascene, although Christ preached to
those in hell his preaching did not prove salutary for all, since not
everyone was capable of responding to it. For some it could be only
"a denunciation of their disbelief," not the cause of salvation. In this
judgment John actually repeats the teaching on salvation articulated
not long before him by Maximus the Confessor. According to Maximus, human history will be accomplished when all without exception unite with God and God will become "everything to every
one."[150] For some this unity will mean eternal bliss, while for others
it will become the source of suffering and torment, as each will be
united with God "according to the quality of his disposition" toward
God.[151] In other words, all will be united with God, but each will have
his own, subjective, feeling of this unity, according to the measure of
the closeness to God he has achieved. Following a similar line, John
Damascene also understands the teaching on the descent to Hades to
mean that Christ opens the way to paradise for all and calls all to salvation. The response to Christ's call, however, may lie either in con-
senting to follow him or the voluntary rejection of salvation.
Ultimately it depends on the person, on free choice. God does not
save anyone by force, but calls all to salvation: "Behold, I stand at the

---

[147]Cf. Luke 4.18–19; cf. Isa 61.1–2.

[148]Cf. Phil 2.10.

[149]*An Exact Exposition of Orthodox Faith* 3, 29 (PG 94:1101a).

[150]1 Cor 15.28.

[151]Maximus the Confessor, *Questions-Answers to Thalassius* 59 (PG 90:609c). For
more on this teaching, see J.-C. Larchet, *La divinisation de l'homme selon Maxime le
Confesseur* (Paris, 1996), pp. 647–652.

door and knock; if any one hears my voice and opens the door, I will come in to him."[152] God knocks at the door of the human heart; he does not break into it.

Within the history of Christianity one idea that has repeatedly cropped up is that God predestines some people for salvation and others to perdition. This idea is based on a literal interpretation of the words of St Paul about predestination, calling, and justifica-tion[153] and became the cornerstone of the Reformation, preached with particular consistency by John Calvin.[154] Eleven centuries before Calvin, the Eastern Christian tradition in the person of John Chrysostom expressed a different view of predestination and calling. "Why are not all saved?" Chrysostom asks. "Because ... not only the call [of God] but also the will of those called is the cause of their sal-vation. This call is not coercive or forcible. Everyone is called, but not all follow the call."[155] Later fathers, including Maximus and John Damascene, speak in the same spirit. According to their teaching, God does not save certain people while ruining others; rather, some people follow the call of God to salvation while others do not. Like-wise, God does not lead some people from hell and leave others behind; rather, there are some people who wish and others who do not wish to believe in him.

This examination of John Damascene's teaching on Christ's descent into Hades completes our survey of the passages from the Eastern church fathers. After him, nothing essentially new has been added to the subject in question in the Eastern patristic tradition. Moreover, precisely after the eighth century the writing of church hymnography reached its acme. (This will be the principal object of attention in chapter four.) The liturgical texts composed in this period, and which continue to be used in worship in the Orthodox Church, fully absorbed the doctrinal tradition whose formation was

---

[152]Rev 3.20.

[153]Rom 8.29–30.

[154]See John Calvin, *Instruction in Christian Faith,* V. II, Book III ("Concerning the pre-eternal election whereby God predestined some for salvation while others for condemnation").

[155]*Homilies on the Epistle to the Romans* 16.

more or less completed by the fourth century, though further eluci-
dated by fifth- through eighth-century authors.

WESTERN CHURCH WRITERS

The development of the doctrine of the descent in the Christian West
falls beyond the scope of this book but is a topic that is well represented in modern patristic scholarship. We shall confine ourselves,
therefore, to a survey of the views of only the most significant Western authors on the descent in order to compare the difference of
approaches to this theme in the East and West.

References to the descent are numerous in treatises by third-century authors such as Tertullian, St Cyprian, and Lactantius.[156] Writing in the fourth century, St Hilarius repeatedly refers to the descent.
He states, in particular, that by his death Christ "destroys the gates of
brass (*portas aereas confringit*), demolishes the bars of iron (*vectes ferreos
conterit*). . . . redeems him whom he created after his image, returns to
him the sweetness of paradise."[157] According to Hilarius, having
descended into hell, Christ continued to be present in paradise.[158]

At Christ's descent into Hades, death and corruption are obliter-
ated: "He it is . . . that slays death in hell (*mortem in inferno perimens*),
that strengthens the assurance of our hope by his resurrection, that
destroys the corruption of human flesh by the glory of his body."[159]
Christ's victory over death has a universal character: "The Son of God
is nailed to the cross; but on the cross God conquers human death.
Christ, the Son of God, dies; but all flesh (*omnis caro*) is made alive in
Christ. The Son of God is in hell; but man is carried back to
heaven."[160]

---

[156]See, e.g., Tertullian, *On the Soul* 55 (CCSL 2, 861–863); *On the Resurrection of
Flesh* 43; Cyprian, *Testimony against the Jews* 2, 24–27; Lactantius, *Divine Instructions*
4, 12 (PL 6, 481 AB); 4, 27 (PL 535 A); et al.

[157]*On Psalm* 138, 25 (PL 9, 805 C).

[158]*On the Trinity* 10, 34 (PL 10, 370 B).

[159]*On the Trinity* 4, 42 (PL 10, 128 A).

[160]*On the Trinity* 3, 15 (PL 10, 84 B).

St Jerome comments on the descent when interpreting the Book of Jonah. In the patristic tradition the story of Jonah is understood as typifying Christ's burial and his three-day and three-night stay in the heart of the earth.[161] In one of his letters Jerome uses the imagery of the "bait," which we remember from St Gregory of Nyssa:

O death that dividest brothers knit together in love, how cruel, how ruthless thou art so to sunder them! "The Lord hath fetched a burning wind that cometh up from the wilderness: which hath dried thy veins and hath made thy well spring desolate." Thou didst swallow up our Jonah, but even in thy belly he still lived. Thou didst carry him as one dead, that the world's storm might be stilled and our Nineveh saved by his preaching. He, yes He, conquered thee, he slew thee, that fugitive prophet who left his home, gave up his inheritance and surrendered his dear life into the hands of those who sought it. He it was who of old threatened thee in Hosea: "O death, I will be thy plagues; O grave, I will be thy destruction."[162] By his death thou art dead; by his death we live. Thou hast swallowed up and thou art swallowed up. Whilst thou art smitten with a longing for the body assumed by Him, and whilst thy greedy jaws fancy it a prey, thy inward parts are wounded with hooked fangs.[163]

In the same letter Jerome ponders the fate of the righteous people who died before the coming of Christ. He identifies "Abraham's bosom" with hell and argues that it was only after Christ's resurrection that the Old Testament righteous were delivered from hell and granted the bliss of paradise:

If Abraham, Isaac, and Jacob be in hell, who can be in the kingdom of heaven? . . . Even if Lazarus is seen in Abraham's bosom and in a place of refreshment, still the lower regions cannot be compared with the kingdom of heaven. Before Christ's coming Abraham is in the lower regions: after Christ's coming the robber is in paradise. And therefore at his rising again "many bodies of the saints which

---

[161]Cf. Matt 12.40.
[162]Cf. Hos 13.14.
[163]*Letter* 60, *to Heliodorus*, 2.

slept arose, and were seen in the heavenly Jerusalem." Then was fulfilled the saying: "Awake thou that sleepest, and arise from the dead,
and Christ shall give thee light."[164]

We do not find in St Jerome a clear answer to who was saved from
hell by Christ's descent into it. In his "Interpretation of the Book of
Jonah" Jerome claims that Christ descended into hell "in order to liberate *all* those who were locked there" (*ut omnes qui clausi fuerant, lib-
eraret*).[165] However, in another passage from the same book, he speaks
of Christ who "brought to life *many* people with Him" (*secum plurimus
educat ad vitam*)."[166] In his "Interpretation of the Epistle to the Ephesians" Jerome states that the Savior descended to hell in order to
bring out "the souls of *saints* who were locked there."[167] We note the
same interplay of "all," "many," and "saints" in the Eastern church
fathers of the same period.

Another notable fourth-century author is St Ambrose, who spoke
of the descent on many occasions.[168] As far as Latin hymnography is
concerned, St Ambrose seems to be the first author who explicitly
refers to the descent in one of his poems.[169]

However, it was another fourth-century poet, Prudentius, who
spoke of the descent much more extensively. In one poem from the
"Book of Every Day Hymns," Prudentius argues that Christ's descent
brought relief to the sinners in hell:

---

[164]*Letter* 60, *to Heliodorus*, 3. Cf. Eph 5.4.

[165]*Interpretation of the Book of Jonah* 2, 6. Cited from: *S. Hieronymi Presbyteri
Opera*, pars I, 6, CCSL 76 (Louvain, 1969), pp. 399–400.

[166]*Interpretation of the Book of Jonah* 2, 11. Cited from: *S. Hieronymi Presbyteri
Opera*, pars I, 6, CCSL 76 (Louvain, 1969), p. 403.

[167]*Interpretation of the Epistle to the Ephesians*, book 2.

[168]Cf. *Explanation of Psalms* 44 (43), 85–86 (CSEL 64, 322–323); 49 (48), 22
(CSEL 64, 322–323); 119 (118), 13, 19, 2 (CSEL 62, 293); 119 (118), 19, 37, 2 (CSEL 62,
441); 119 (118), 20, 3, 3 (CSEL 62, 446); *On Faith to Gratian* 3, 4, 27–28 (CSEL 78,
117–118); 3, 14, 111–112 (CSEL 78, 147–148); 4, 1, 3 (CSEL 78, 259); *On Interpellation of
Job and David* 1, 8, 26 (CSEL 32/3, 227); *On the Repose of His Friend Satyrus* 2, 102–104
(CSEL 73, 305–307); et al.

[169]See *Hymn* 5, v. 21–24 in Ambroise de Milan, *Hymnes*, édition et traduction par
J. Fontaine et al. (Paris, 1992), pp. 274–275. Cf. R. Gounelle, *La descente du Christ aux
Enfers*, pp. 232–233.

Even souls of the lost suffering in the depth of Hell
have some respite from pain, holding glad holiday
on that night when the Lord came to the world above
up from Acheron's pool, rising to life again,

Not as Lucifer bright, springing from Ocean's bed,
with his glimmering ray tinges the sombre night,
but more vast than the sun, shedding the light anew
on the world that had grown dark at the Saviour's cross

Hell's fierce torments subside, bringing surcease from pain
to the spirits that live ever in penal fires;
calm and joy for a while reign in that prison house
and the sulphurous streams burn not with wonted rage.[170]

In another hymn Prudentius speaks of the resurrection of the righteous, who before Christ's descent had bean detained in hell. In this hymn we find clear echoes of the tradition deriving from the "Gospel of Nicodemus":

That the dead might know salvation, who in limbo long
 had dwelt,
into Hell with love he entered; to him yield the broken
 gates,
as the bolts and massive hinges fall asunder at his word.

Now the door of ready entrance, but forbidding all return,
Outward swings as bars are loosened and sends forth the
 prisoned souls,
by reversal of the mandate, treading its threshold once
 more.

But while God with golden splendour lighted up the halls
 of Death,

---

[170]*Hymn* 5, "A Hymn for the Lighting of the Lamp," in *The Poems of Prudentius*, trans. sister M. Clement Eagan, The Fathers of the Church 43 (Washington, D.C., 1962), pp. 36–37. For the Latin text see: *Aurelii Prudentii Clementis Carmina*, cura et studio M. P. Cunningham, CCSL 126 (Louvain, 1966), p. 27.

while he shed the dawn's refulgence on the startled shades
   of night,
radiant stars grew pale with sorrow in the lurid ashen sky,

And the sun took flight from heaven, clad in dusky
   mourning robes,
left behind his fiery chariot, hid himself in anxious grief,

For a while salvation's Leader gave himself to realms of
   Death,
that he might the dead, long buried, guide in their return
   to light,
when the chains that had been welded by that primal sin
   were loosed.

Then, in steps of their Creator, many saints and
   patriarchs,
putting on their fleshly garments and arising from their
   tombs,
followed Him, at length returning on the third day to the
   earth.[171]

From the fourth century come the first references to the descent
into Hades in Western baptismal creeds. Rufinus, for example, mentions that this clause existed in the creed at Aquileia.[172] In the early

---

[171]*Hymn* 9, "A Hymn for Every Hour," in *The Poems of Prudentius*, trans. by M.
Clement Eagan, pp. 65–66. For the Latin text see: *Aurelii Prudentii Clementis
Carmina*, pp. 50–51.

[172]*Commentary on the Apostolic Creed* 18 (CCSL 20, 154). Rufinus also adds that
neither the Roman creed nor Eastern creeds contain the words about the descent into
Hades. The latter statement may be accurate with regard to baptismal creeds but not
with regard to the various definitions of faith produced in the East in the fourth century. Thus the Council in Sirmium (AD 359) confessed Christ, "who died and
descended in the lower world and accomplished his economy there, and the gate-
keepers of Hades, seeing Him, were terrified" (cf. Athanasius, *Epistle on the Councils*
1, 9). The Council of Nicea (AD 359) professed Christ, "who died and was buried,
and descended in the lower world, and before whom Hades itself trembled" (cf.
Socrates, *Church History* 2, 30). An identical formula was produced by the 359 Council of Constantinople (cf. Athanasius, *Epistle on the Councils* 2, 31). For the texts of the
359 Sirmian formula, as well as of the Nicene and Constantinopolitan creeds of the

fifth century the clause *descendit ad inferos* (or *ad inferna*) appears in the so-called Athanasian creed (known as *Quiqunque vult*), also of Western provenance. In later centuries the words *descendit ad inferos* are found in various local forms of the so-called Apostles' Creed until they become, no later than the eighth century, its universally accepted part.[173]

The greatest father of the Western Church, whose influence on the formation of its theological doctrine was decisive, St Augustine, wrote extensively on the descent. Following Jerome, he turned to the story of the prophet Jonah, in which he also saw the prototype of Christ's descent into the depths of hell:

> The prophet Jonah not so much by speech as by his own painful experience prophesied Christ's death and resurrection much more clearly than if he had proclaimed them with his voice. For why was he taken into the whale's belly and restored on the third day, but that he might be a sign that Christ should return from the depths of hell (*de profundo inferi*) on the third day?[174]

Augustine's teaching on the descent is rather contradictory. Sometimes he admits that the Old Testament righteous people, those

---

same year see A. Hahn and G. L. Hahn, *Bibliothek der Symbole und Glaubensregeln der Alten Kirche* (Breslau, 1897), nos. 163, 164, 167. On Rufinus as a commentator of the Apostolic Creed see: M. Villain, "Rufin d'Aquilée, Commentateur du Symbole des Apôtres," *Recherches de science religieuse* 31 (1944), pp. 129–156.

[173]The literature on the symbols and creeds of the early church is immense. Among the classical studies see F. J. Bradcock, *The History of the Creeds* (London, 1930); A. E. Burn, *The Apostles' Creed* (London, 1906); Idem., *The Athanasian Creed and Its Early Commentaries*, Texts and Studies 4 (Cambridge, 1896); J. N. D. Kelly, *Early Christian Creeds* (Essex, 1950); Idem., *The Athanasian Creed* (London, 1964); H. B. Swete, *The Apostles Creed. Its Relation to Primitive Christianity* (Cambridge, 1894); Th. Zahn, *Das apostolische Symbolum. Eine Skizze seiner Geschichte und eine Prüfung seines Inhalts* (Erlangen-Leipzig, 1893). For the discussion of the descent in early Christian Creeds see, in particular: R. Gounelle, *La descente du Christ aux Enfers*, pp. 257–367. See also: J. A. MacCulloch, *The Harrowing of Hell*, pp. 71ff.

[174]*The City of God* 18, 30. The Latin text in: *Sancti Aurelii Augustini De civitate Dei*, libri XI–XXII, CCSL 48 (Louvain, 1955), p. 621. Cf. also *The City of God* 18, 44 ("when it happened that the prophet himself was three days in the whale's belly, it signified besides, that he who is Lord of all the prophets should be three days in the depths of hell").

awaiting Christ's coming, were detained in hell: "It does not seem absurd to believe that the ancient saints who believed in Christ and his then future coming, were detained in places far removed indeed from the torments of the wicked, but yet in hell, until Christ's blood and his descent into these places delivered them."[175] In other instances, however, notably in his "Literal Meaning of the Book of Genesis," Augustine claims that the ancient saints were preserved in the bosom of Abraham, which he, unlike Jerome, does not identify with hell:

> I admit that I have not yet found the term "hell" applied to the place where the souls of the just are at rest. . . . I have not found any passage in Scripture, at least in the canonical books, where the term "hell" is to be taken in a good sense. I am still looking for such a passage and can think of none, but I doubt whether anybody could tolerate an interpretation of Abraham's bosom and the resting place to which the angels carried the devoted poor man in anything but a good sense, and so I do not see how we may believe that that resting place is in hell.[176]

On the contrary, Augustine is ready to admit that the "bosom of Abraham" is nothing other than a third heaven or paradise, where the souls of the just find their repose.[177] Both Abraham and the poor man in his bosom were separated from hell by a great gulf, "but they are not said to be in hell," insists Augustine.[178]

In his "Literal Meaning of Genesis" Augustine attempts to answer the question: Who was saved by Christ when he descended into hell? "The soul of Christ," he says, "went to that very region where sinners are tormented (*ad ea loca in quibus peccatores cruciantur*) in order to release from their suffering *those whom he decreed should be*

---

[175] *The City of God* 20, 15. For the Latin text see: *De civitate Dei*, pp. 725–726. Cf. also Pseudo-Augustine's paschal homily, in which he speaks of Christ saving the righteous who were detained in hell on account of original sin: *Paschal Homily* 160 (PL 39, 2060).

[176] *The Literal Meaning of Genesis* 12, 33 (PL 34, 481).

[177] *The Literal Meaning of Genesis* 12, 34 (PL 34, 482).

[178] *The Literal Meaning of Genesis* 12, 33 (PL 34, 481).

released according to the inscrutable ways of his justice."[179] Elsewhere he claims that Christ "did not disdain to visit this part of the world," that is, hell, because "He could not have been ignorant of the fact that *some were to be delivered from there in accordance with the mysteries of God's justice*, and there he went to deliver them."[180] These formulations clearly reflect Augustine's rather ambiguous idea of predestination, of which so much has been written from the time of Pelagius up to the Reformation and modern times. According to Augustine's views, which are based on a literal interpretation of Romans 8.29–30,[181] salvation will be granted by God to those who were predestined to it, while others will be damned. Thus the salvific effect of Christ's descent into Hades does not extend to those who were not predestined to salvation. Indeed, in one instance Augustine even explicitly refers to the "heresy" of those who claimed that, when Christ descended into hell, the unbelievers believed in him and were liberated.[182]

The Augustinian teaching on Christ's descent into Hades is expounded more fully in a letter addressed to Evodius. This letter, which contains a comprehensive interpretation of 1 Peter 3.18–21, suggests that the teaching on the evacuation of all in hell and the complete devastation of hell by the risen Christ was widespread in his time. Augustine begins with the question of whether Christ preached only to those who perished in the days of Noah or to all who were imprisoned. In answering it, Augustine begins by refuting the opin-

---

[179] *The Literal Meaning of Genesis* 12, 33 (PL 34, 481).

[180] *The Literal Meaning of Genesis* 12, 34 (PL 34, 482).

[181] "For whom he did foreknow, he also did predestine to be conformed to the image of the Son. . . . Moreover, whom he did predestine, them he also called: and whom he called, them he also justified: and whom he justified, them he also glorified."

[182] *On Heresies* 79 (PL 42, 4 = CCSL 46, 336). The English translation in: L. G. Müller, *The "De Haeresibus" of Saint Augustine: A Translation with an Introduction and Commentary*, Patristic Studies 90 (Washington, D.C., 1956), p. 115. Cf. Filastrius of Brescia, *The Book on Heresies* 125 (97) (CCSL 9, 288–289). For an analysis of Augustine's and Filastrius' references to the "heresy" in question see, in particular: R. Gounelle, *La descente du Christ aux Enfers*, pp. 67–87.

ion that Christ descended to hell in the flesh,[183] arguing that this teaching contradicts scriptural testimony.[184]

Augustine continues by setting forth the view that Christ led from hell all who were there as, indeed, among them were "some who are intimately known to us by their literary labours, whose eloquence and talent we admire—not only the poets and orators who in many parts of their writings have held up to contempt and ridicule these same false gods of the nations, and have even occasionally confessed the one true God . . . but also those who have uttered the same, not in poetry or rhetoric, but as philosophers."[185] Belief in the salvation of heathen poets, orators, and philosophers was quite popular in the Eastern patristic tradition, as is most vividly expressed by Clement of Alexandria. According to Augustine, however, many of the positive qualities of the ancient poets, orators, and philosophers originate not from "sober and authentic devotion, but pride, vanity and [the desire] of people's praise." Therefore they "did not bring any fruit." Thus the idea that pagan poets, orators, and philosophers could be saved, though not refuted by Augustine, still is not fully endorsed, since "human judgment" differs from "the justice of the Creator."[186]

Augustine neither rejects nor accepts unconditionally any opinion concerning the salvation of all those in hell. Though very careful in his judgment, it is clear that the possibility of salvation for those in hell is blocked in his perception by his own teaching on predestination,[187] as well as by his understanding of divine mercy and justice:

> For the words of Scripture that "the pangs of hell were loosed"[188] by the death of Christ do not establish this, seeing that this statement

---

[183]Concerning the teaching on the descent of Christ into Hades in the flesh, see: I. N. Karmirēs, "Hē Christologikē heterodidaskalia tou 16 aiōnos kai eis haidou kathodos tou Christou," *Nea Siōn* 30 (1935), pp. 11–26, 65–81, 154–165. See also: S. Der Nersessian. "An Armenian Version of the Homilies on the Harrowing of Hell," *Dumbarton Oaks Papers* 8 (1954), pp. 201–224.

[184]*Letter* 164, II, 3 (PL 33, 709).

[185]*Letter* 164, II, 3 (PL 33, 710).

[186]*Letter* 164, II, 3 (PL 33, 710).

[187]Cf. J. A. MacCulloch, *The Harrowing of Hell*, p. 123.

[188]Cf. Acts 2.24.

may be understood as referring to himself, and meaning that he so far loosed (that is, made ineffectual) the pangs of hell that he himself was not held by them, especially since it is added that it was "not possible for him to be held by them."[189] Or if any one [objecting to this interpretation] asks why he chose to descend into hell, where those pains were which could not possibly hold Him . . . the words that "the pains were loosed" may be understood as referring not to the case of all, but only some whom he judged worthy of that deliverance; so that neither he supposed to have descended thither in vain, without the purpose of bringing benefit to any of those who were there held in prison, nor is it a necessary inference that divine mercy and justice granted to some must be supposed to have been granted to all.[190]

While Augustine also considers the traditional teaching that Christ delivered from hell the forefather Adam, as well as Abel, Seth, Noah, and his family; Abraham, Isaac, Jacob, "and the other patriarchs and prophets"; he does not agree to it entirely. This is because he does not believe "Abraham's bosom" to be a part of hell. Those who were in the bosom of Abraham were not deprived of the gracious presence of Christ's divinity, and therefore Christ, on the very day of his death immediately before descending to hell, promises the wise thief that he will be with him in paradise.[191] "Most certainly, therefore, he was, before that time, both in paradise and the bosom of Abraham in his beatific wisdom (*beatificante sapientia*), and in hell in his condemning power (*judicante potentia*)," concludes Augustine.[192]

Also refuted by Augustine is the opinion that the righteous received that incorruption promised to people at the end of time, through Christ's death on the cross. If it were so, then St Peter would not have said about David that "his tomb is with us to this day"[193] unless David was still undisturbed in the tomb.[194]

---

[189]That is, the pangs of hell.
[190]*Letter* 164, II, 5 (PL 33, 710–711).
[191]Cf. Luke 23.43.
[192]*Letter* 164, III, 7–8 (PL 33, 710–711).
[193]Acts 2.29.
[194]*Letter* 164, III, 7–8 (PL 33, 711).

As for Christ's preaching in hell recorded in 1 Peter 3.18–21, Augustine rejects its traditional and commonly accepted understanding. First, he is not certain that it indicates those who have actually departed this life but rather those that are spiritually dead and nonbelievers in Christ. Second, Augustine offers the quite novel idea that after Christ's ascension from hell, any recollection of his sojourn there was eradicated. Therefore, the descent in Hades was a "one-time" event relevant only to those who were in hell at that time. Third, and finally, Augustine finds totally unacceptable any possibility that nonbelievers on earth could come to believe in Christ while in hell, calling this idea "absurd."[195]

Augustine is not inclined to view 1 Peter 3.18–21 as an indication of the Lord's descent into Hades. Rather, he reads the text allegorically: "the spirits" mentioned by Peter are clothed in the body but imprisoned in ignorance. Christ did not come down to earth in the flesh during the days of Noah, but he often came down to people in the Spirit, either to rebuke unbelievers or to justify believers. The days of Noah are representative of circumstances today; the flood acts as a precursor of baptism. Those who believe in our days are like whose who believed in the days of Noah: they are saved through baptism, just as Noah was saved through water. Similarly, unbelievers are like unbelievers in the days of Noah, and the flood is the prototype of their destruction.[196]

Although Augustine is the first Latin author to pay such close attention to the theme of Christ's descent into Hades, he neither clarifies to whom Christ preached in hell nor whom Christ delivered. He also expresses many doubts about particular interpretations of 1 Peter 3.18–21, but does not offer any convincing interpretation of his own. Nevertheless, later Western Church authors developed his ideas. St Thomas Aquinas, in particular, makes continuous references to Augustine in his chapter devoted to the descent of Christ into Hades.[197] However, during the Reformation, many theologians of the

---

[195] *Letter* 164, III, 10–13 (PL 33, 713–714).
[196] *Letter* 164, IV, 15–16 (PL 33:715).
[197] See below.

Protestant tradition criticized Augustine's teaching, especially his teaching that the recollection of Christ (after his ascent) did not survive in hell. Lutheran theologians, in fact, insisted on the reverse.[198]

Of the subsequent Latin authors, the teachings of St Gregory the Great (sixth century) on the descent, in certain aspects are closer to the traditional understanding than Augustine. Unlike the latter, and in accord with commonly accepted teaching, Gregory claims that the Old Testament righteous were detained in hell, from where they were delivered by Christ after his resurrection.[199] Following St Gregory of Nyssa, Gregory the Great speaks of the devil being caught "on a fishhook": "It is, then, as if the fishhook got caught in his throat as he was swallowing.... And he lost the mortal human beings whom he rightly held because he dared to crave the death of one who was immortal, over whom he had no claim."[200] Through an allegorical interpretation of the biblical story of Samson, Gregory speaks of the destruction of the "defences" of hell by the risen Christ:[201]

> Whom, dearly beloved, whom does Samson foreshadow by his deed but our Redeemer? What does the city of Gaza signify if not the lower world? What is indicated by the Philistines except the faithlessness of the Jews? When they saw that the Lord was dead and his body had been laid in the sepulchre, they assigned guards there. They were happy that they caught and held him, who shone out as the creator of life, behind the defence of the lower world. . . . Redeemer, rising before it was light, not only went out free from the lower world, but even destroyed its very defences (*claustra*).[202]

---

[198]See details in: F. Loofs, "Descent to Hades," in *Encyclopaedia of Religion and Ethics* (New York, 1912), vol. 4, p. 658.

[199]*XL homiliarum in Evangelia libri duo*, Homilia I, 19 (PL 76:1156bc). English translation in: Gregory the Great, *Forty Gospel Homilies*, translated from the Latin by Dom David Hurst, Cistercian Studies Series 123 (Kalamazoo, Michigan 1990), Homily 11, p. 81.

[200]*XL homiliarum in Evangelia libri duo*, Homilia II, 25 (PL 76:1195a). English translation in: Gregory the Great, *Forty Gospel Homilies*, translated from the Latin by Dom David Hurst, Homily 25, pp. 195–196.

[201]Cf. Judg 16.1–3.

[202]*XL homiliarum in Evangelia libri duo*, Homilia II, 21 (PL 76:1173bc). English

Gregory the Great also develops the traditional teaching on John the Baptist's descent into Hades and his preaching therein:

> John was at the river Jordan when he declared that Jesus was the Redeemer of the world; he had been cast into prison when he asked whether they were to look for another, or whether he had come. He did not ask because he doubted that Jesus was the Redeemer of the world, but to know if he who had come into the world in person would also go down in person to the courts of hell. By dying he was to precede into hell the one whose forerunner he was when he proclaimed him to the world. He said: "Are you he who is to come or shall we look for another?" as if saying, "Just as you deigned to be born on behalf of human beings, make manifest whether you will also deign to die on our behalf. Then I who was the forerunner of your birth may also become the forerunner of your death, and may proclaim you in hell as the one who is to come, as I have already proclaimed to the world that you have come."[203]

Responding to the question "Who was liberated from hell by the risen Christ?" Gregory follows Augustine: he definitely rejects the opinion that Christ saved all those who believed in him and labels such opinion "heresy."[204] Like Augustine, Gregory claims that only the "elect," or the "predestined," were freed. This leads him to the statement that Christ did not slay hell, but only "took a bite" from it. Here we find a significant difference between Gregory and the traditional early Christian understanding:

> By this solemnity the elect (*electes*) who, protected though they were in undisturbed rest, were yet being held within the bounds of the lower world, have been brought back to the pleasant places of para-

---

translation in: Gregory the Great, *Forty Gospel Homilies*, translated from the Latin by Dom David Hurst, Homily 21, pp. 162–163.

[203]*XL homiliarum in Evangelia libri duo*, Homilia I, 6, 1 (PL 76:1095d–1096a). English translation in: Gregory the Great, *Forty Gospel Homilies*, translated from the Latin by Dom David Hurst, Homily 5, pp. 28–29. Cf. similar interpretation in Gregory's *Homilies on Ezekiel* I, 1, 5 (PL 76:788d–789a).

[204]*Letter* VII, 15, in *S. Gregorii Magni Opera, Registrum epistularum*, libri I–VII, ed. D. Norberg, CCSL 140 (Louvain, 1982), p. 465.

dise. . . . By his resurrection the Lord fulfilled what he said before his passion, "when I am lifted up from the earth, I will draw all men to myself."[205] He who left none of his elect in the lower world did indeed draw all things to himself. He took from them all the predestinate. The Lord by his rising did not restore to pardon any unbelievers, or those whose wickedness had caused them to be given over to eternal punishment; he snatched away from the confines of the lower world those whom he recognized as his own as a result of their faith and deeds. Hence he says truly by the mouth of Hosea: "O death, I will be your death; O lower world, I will be your bite" (*morsus*).[206] . . . Because he completely slayed death in his elect, he became death for death; but because he took away a portion of the lower world, and left part of it (*partem abstulit, et partem reliquit*), he did not completely slay it but took a bite from it.[207]

As far as we can judge, Gregory the Great was the first Western father who categorically insisted that Christ, when he ascended from hell, "took away a portion of the lower world, and left part of it," an idea neither in Augustine nor in the Eastern fathers (with the exception of one pseudepigraphon). Both in the Greek and Latin traditions it was claimed that either Christ released *all* from hell or He released *some* (be it saints, righteous, patriarchs, prophets, "elect," Adam and Eve, and so on), but it was never made clear who, apart from the devil and demons, were left there. Gregory the Great brought the Augustinian teaching on the salvation of the elect and the predestined to its logical conclusion. All expressions in the liturgical texts, including the Latin ones, that imply that Christ destroyed hell,[208] must be understood as pure rhetoric: in reality Christ only harrowed hell but did not destroy it.

---

[205]John 12.32.

[206]Cf. Hos 13.14.

[207]*XL homiliarum in Evangelia libri duo*, Homilia II, 22, 6 (PL 76:1177bc). English translation in: Gregory the Great, *Forty Gospel Homilies*, translated from the Latin by Dom David Hurst, Homily 22, pp. 168–169.

[208]On the subject of the descent into Hades in Latin Christian hymnography see F. Cabrol, "Descente du Christ aux Enfers d'après la liturgie," *Dictionnaire d'archéologie chrétienne et la liturgie*, t. IV (Paris, 1921), pp. 688–691.

The degree to which this approach is foreign to traditional Eastern Christian understanding is clear from the correspondence between Gregory the Great and Kyriakos the Patriarch of Constantinople. They discussed the two clerics from Constantinople, George and Theodore, who claimed that "Jesus Christ, when He descended into hell, saved all who there acknowledged Him as God, and delivered them from the pains due to them" (*omnes qui illic confiterentur eum Deum salvasse atque a poenis debitis liberasse*). Contesting this view, Gregory writes:

> When He descended into hell, He delivered through His grace those only who both believed that He should come and observed His precepts in their lives. For it is evident that after the incarnation of the Lord no one can be saved, even of those who hold His faith, who have not the life of faith. . . . If, then, believers now are not saved without good works, while the unbelieving and reprobate without good action were saved by our Lord descending into hell, then the lot of those who never saw the incarnation of the Lord was better than that of these who have been born after the mystery of His incarnation. . . . Hold ye nothing but what the true faith teaches through the Catholic Church: namely, that the Lord in descending into hell rescued from infernal durance those only whom while living in the flesh He preserved through His grace in faith and good conduct (*in fide et bona operatione*).[209]

In the Roman Church after Gregory the Great, belief in the partial victory of Christ over hell became commonly accepted, being confirmed by the Council of Toledo in AD 625. In the mid-seventh century Pope Boniface attacked the Irish missionary Clement for teaching that Christ released all those detained in hell, whether believers or non-believers, whether worshippers of the true God or idolaters.[210] A Synod convened by Boniface at Rome condemned Clement and acknowledged, following the Toledo Council, that

[209]*Letter* VII, 4 in *S. Gregorii Magni Opera, Registrum epistularum*, libri I–VII, ed. D. Norberg, CCSL 140 (Louvain, 1982), pp. 447–452.
[210]Boniface, *Letter* LVII (PL 89:153).

Christ descended into hell not to release the damned but solely to redeem his righteous forefathers.[211]

The Latin doctrine on the descent of Christ into hell was systematized and brought to completion by the thirteenth-century theologian St Thomas Aquinas. In his *Summa theologiae* he divides hell into four "regions": first, purgatory (*purgatorium*), where sinners experience penal suffering; second, the hell of the patriarchs (*infernum patrum*), the abode of the Old Testament righteous before the coming of Christ; third, the hell of unbaptized children (*infernum puerorum*); and fourth, the hell of the damned (*infernum damnatorum*). In response to the question "Into which hell did Christ descend?" Thomas Aquinas admits two possibilities: Christ descended either into all parts of hell or only into the parts where the righteous were imprisoned, whom he was to deliver. In the first case, "for going down into the hell of the lost He wrought this effect, that by descending thither He put them to shame for their unbelief and wickedness: but to them who were detained in Purgatory He gave hope of attaining to glory: while upon the holy Fathers detained in hell solely on account of original sin (*pro solo peccato originali detinebantur in inferno*), He shed the light of glory everlasting." In the second case the soul of Christ "descended only to the place where the righteous were detained (*descendit solum ad locum inferni in quo justi detinebantur*)," but the action of his presence there was felt in some way in the other parts of hell as well.[212]

Thomas Aquinas teaches that Christ delivered the Old Testament righteous who had been imprisoned in hell because of original sin.[213] But sinners detained in "the hell of the lost" remained there, either because they had no faith or because their faith included no conformity with the virtue of the suffering Christ. They could not be

---

[211]J. A. MacCulloch, *The Harrowing of Hell*, pp. 259–260. Cf. the first canon of the Council of Toledo of AD 633 ("He descended into hell in order to release from it those saints who were detained there") in H. D. Bruns, *Canones Apostolorum et Conciliorum Veterum Selecti*, t. I (Berlin, 1839), p. 221.

[212]*Summa theologiae* IIIa, 52, 2 = St Thomas Aquinas, *Summa theologiae*, Latin text with English translation (London–New York, 1965), vol. 54, p. 158.

[213]*Summa theologiae* IIIa, 52, 5 (*Summa theologiae*, vol. 54, pp. 166–170).

cleansed from their sins, so Christ's descent brought them no deliverance from the pains of hell.[214] Likewise, children who had died in the state of original sin were also not delivered from hell, since only "by baptism children are delivered from original sin and from hell, but not by Christ's descent into Hades," since baptism can be received only in earthly life, not after death.[215] Finally, Christ did not deliver those who were in purgatory, for their suffering was caused by personal defects (*defectus personali*), whereas "exclusion from glory" was a common defect (*defectus generalis*) of all human nature after the fall. Christ's descent recovered the glory of God to those excluded from it by virtue of the common defect of nature, but did not deliver anyone from the pains of purgatory caused by one's personal defects.[216]

Aquinas' scholastic understanding of Christ's descent into Hades became the official teaching of the Roman Catholic Church for many centuries. It was severely criticised by Protestant theologians during the Reformation, and indeed many of today's Catholic theologians are also very skeptical about the teaching.[217] There is no need to discuss how far Thomas Aquinas' opinions on the descent fall from Eastern Christianity. No Eastern church father ever attempted to isolate those who may have been left in hell after Christ's descent; none ever spoke of unbaptized infants as subject to eternal punishment.[218] The division of hell into four regions and the teaching on purgatory are alien to Eastern patristics. Finally, this rigorous subjection of the most mysterious events of history to detailed analysis and rational interpretation is unacceptable for Eastern Christian theology. For the theologians, poets, and mystics of the Eastern Church, the descent of

---

[214] *Summa theologiae* IIIa, 52, 6 (*Summa theologiae*, vol. 54, pp. 170–172).

[215] *Summa theologiae* IIIa, 52, 7 (*Summa theologiae*, vol. 54, pp. 174–176).

[216] *Summa theologiae* IIIa, 52, 8 (*Summa theologiae*, vol. 54, pp. 176–178).

[217] See for instance: H. U. von Balthasar and A. Grillmeier, *Le mystère pascal* (Paris, 1972), p. 170 (where the Thomistic understanding of the descent to Hades is described as "bad theology").

[218] Speaking about those who die without baptism "from perfectly involuntary circumstances," such as unbaptized infants, Gregory Nazianzen says that they "will be neither glorified nor punished by the righteous Judge, as unsealed and yet not wicked, but persons who have suffered rather than done wrong" (*Discourse* 40, 23, 17–21 in SC 358, 248).

Christ into Hades remains, above all, a mystery—praised in hymns and subject to various but indefinite assumptions.

Notably, in the Middle Ages, the theme of the descent into Hades was developed not only in the scholastic-theological framework but also in the poetic-literary one. Traditions originating in the "Gospel of Nicodemus" and early Christian literature found reflection in the pages of Dante Alighieri's *Divine Comedy*, where the descent into Hades is mentioned on several occasions. Dante particularly references the destruction of hell's gates as well as the earthquake that accompanied Christ's descent.[219] Adam is said to have spent 4,302 years in hell,[220] and John the Baptist is said to have spent two years in limbo before Christ's descent.[221] Dante also describes the release of the Old Testament righteous:

> I was a novice in this state,
>> when I saw hither come a Mighty One,
>> with sign of victory incoronate.
> Hence he drew forth the shade of the First Parent,
>> and that of his son Abel, and of Noah,
>> of Moses the lawgiver, and the obedient
> Abraham, patriarch, and David, king,
>> Israel with his father and his children,
>> and Rachel, for whose sake he did so much,
> And others many, and he made them blessed;
>> and thou must know, that earlier than these
>> never were any human spirits saved.[222]

---

[219] *Divine Comedy, Inferno* 8, 125; 12, 36; 21, 112; 23, 136.

[220] *Divine Comedy, Inferno* 33, 61; *Paradiso* 26, 119.

[221] *Divine Comedy, Paradiso* 33, 31, et al.

[222] *Divine Comedy, Inferno* 4, 52–63 (translated by H. W. Longfellow). Here is the Italian text from Dante Alighieri, *La divina commedia* (Cittá del Vaticano, 1965), pp. 26–27:

> *Io era nuovo in questo stato,*
> *quando ci vidi venire un possente,*
> *con segno di vittoria coronato.*
> *Trasseci l'ombra del primo parente*
> *d'Abèl suo figlio e quella di Noè,*

*

However selective our survey of patristic sources may have been, some general conclusions can now be drawn from our comparison of the Eastern and Western interpretations of Christ's descent into Hades. It is clear that in the first four Christian centuries there was a significant degree of common understanding of this doctrine by theologians of the East and West. In particular, many Western authors shared the opinion of the Eastern fathers that all people, not only some, were saved by Christ when he descended into hell.[223]

From the fifth century onward, however, substantial differences become ever more noticeable. In the West the very idea of a conversion *post mortem* is rejected by several authors as heretical, and a juridical approach gradually begins to prevail. This approach gives increasingly more weight to notions of predestination (Christ delivering from hell those predestined for salvation from the beginning) and original sin (Christ's salvation as deliverance from the "universal" [original] sin, rather than from the "personal" [individual] sins). The range of those to whom the saving action of the descent into Hades extends becomes ever more restricted. First, those who might have believed in Christ when he descended into hell are excluded; then, sinners doomed to eternal torment, those in purgatory, and finally unbaptized infants are eliminated. Legalism of this kind is alien to the Orthodox East, which perceives the descent in the spirit expressed by the liturgical texts of Great Friday and Easter, that is, as an event significant not only for all people but also for the entire cosmos, for all created life.

---

di Moïsè legista e obediente;
Abraàm patriarca e Davíd re,
Israèl con lo padre e co' suoi nati
e con Rachele, per cui tanto fè';
e altri molti, e feceli beati;
e vo' che sappi che, dinanzi ad essi,
spiriti umani non eran salvati.
[223]See R. Gounelle, *La descente du Christ aux Enfers*, pp. 72–73.

Both Eastern and Western traditions support the view that Christ delivered the Old Testament righteous, beginning with Adam, but in the West this is perceived restrictively: Christ delivered *only* the Old Testament righteous, while leaving all the rest in hell to eternal torment. In the East, Adam is viewed as a symbol of the entire human race redeemed by Christ: the Old Testament righteous led by Adam *first* followed Christ and *then* followed those who responded to Christ's preaching in hell.

PART TWO

THE DESCENT INTO HADES
IN LITURGICAL TEXTS

Eastern Christian Liturgical Poetry of the Fourth through Sixth Centuries: From Ephrem the Syrian to Romanos the Melodist

T he works of the sixth-century Byzantine musician and hymn writer St Romanos the Melodist made a considerable impact on the formation of the annual liturgical cycle of sacred poetical texts bequeathed to the Orthodox Church. His major compositions in verse—the *kontakia*—became foundational for many of the hymns now sung during Orthodox services.

Most scholars consider Romanos to be the preeminent poet of the Byzantine period. His uniqueness lies in the fact that he was able to assimilate the achievements of the Syriac hymnographical tradition and transplant them into Byzantine terms. As a result, a highly unique and original poetic style emerged in which the elements of Greek poetry and of genres characteristic of the Syriac poetic tradition became interconnected. According to E. Wellesz, three poetic genres in the Syriac tradition exercised a marked influence on the emerging genre of the *kontakion* as introduced by Romanos the Melodist, namely, the *memra, madrasha,* and *soghitha.* The *memra,* a metrical sermon, presented a verse paraphrase of the Gospel text read at matins. The *madrasha* was a long didactic poem written in stanzas with an obligatory refrain, its strophes sometimes forming an acrostic. The *soghitha* was a poem made up of monologues and of dialogues between its main characters. Wellesz claims that it is from the *memra* that Romanos borrowed his skill of linking the poetical narrative with the Gospel. The *madrasha* shaped hymnody with many stanzas and a refrain, while the *soghitha* served as a repertory of dramatic devices used in the process of composition.[1]

Each of these three genres is first found in verses composed by the renowned Syrian hymnographer St Ephrem the Syrian. His hymns and metrical sermons in particular became a "binding link" between the Palestinian-Aramaic tradition and Byzantine didactic literature.[2] Romanos the Melodist was familiar with Ephrem's works and drew from them. He learned from Ephrem's poetical artistry as well as from his handling of particular literary plots and theological themes. Romanos was the recipient of a poetic tradition looking back to Ephrem. Some scholars presume that Romanos knew Ephrem's poems only in their Greek translation,[3] but he did, in fact, also know them in their Syriac original.[4]

These facts invite us to look closely at the works of both writers. In this chapter, however, our interest lies only in those poems that deal with or develop the theme of Christ's descent into Hades.

The Hymns of St Ephrem the Syrian

St Ephrem (AD 306–373) was born in the region of Nisibis and according to Syriac sources was ordained deacon by St Jacob of Nisibis. In AD 363, after the town of Nisibis had been handed over to the

---

[1]E. Wellesz, *A History of Byzantine Music and Hymnography*, 2nd ed. (Oxford, 1961), pp. 184–185.

[2]S. Averintsev, *Poetika rannevizantiiskoi literatury* (Moscow, 1997), pp. 188–189.

[3]Cf. observations made by J. Grosdidier de Matons on Kontakia 3 (SC 99, 129–165) and 50 (SC 283, 209–267), where he indicates points of contact between Romanos and "Greek" Ephrem.

[4]W. Petersen has proved that Romanos was familiar with the Syriac work of St Ephrem. He has not only established twelve main parallels between the kontakia of Romanos and hymns of Ephrem in Syriac but also found nine parallels between the kontakia of Romanos and the *Commentary on the Diatessaron* written by Ephrem. See: W. L. Petersen, "The Dependence of Romanos the Melodist upon the Syriac Ephrem: Its Importance for the Origins of Kontakia," *Vigilia Christiana* 39 (1985), pp. 171–187; W. L. Petersen, *The Diatessaron and Ephraem Syrus as Sources of Romanos the Melodist*, CSCO 475, Subsidia 74 (Louvain, 1985), pp. 169–194.

Persians, Ephrem, along with many other Christians, fled to find refuge in Edessa.[5] There he founded the "school of the Persians," a school for refugees, which later became a very important theological center for the entire Syriac-speaking Christian world. While the main subject of study in this school was the Holy Scriptures, a significant emphasis was also attached to church singing and recitation. With this in mind Ephrem composed his exegetical treatises as well as a host of poems for the school on theological, ethical, historical, and ecclesiastical themes.

Ephrem holds an important place among the fourth-century church fathers. He belonged to a tradition different than that of contemporary Greek fathers, who were chiefly engaged in precisely and comprehensively defining the tenets of the Christian faith and in setting doctrinal boundaries separating Orthodoxy from heresy. These tasks were definitively handled by the Ecumenical Councils, which opposed the heresies and set out Christian doctrine in special dogmatic statements known as *horoi*. Ephrem was also involved in this activity; he opposed heresies and formulated the dogmatic teaching of the church for his Syriac flock. His medium, however, was entirely different from that of the Greeks. He clothed theological truths not in the armor of precise dogmatic definitions but with the bright garments of poetic symbols and metaphors.[6] Differences in his theological method and approach presuppose a difference of means. Theology for Ephrem was not so much about definition or proof of certain philosophical issues; to theologize for Ephrem meant to glorify God rather than talk about or reflect upon God. He believed the truths of Christianity should not only be comprehended, reflected upon, defined, and established but also experienced by the faithful through prayer. This same avenue was followed by most of the writers of the liturgical texts in the tradition of the Orthodox Church.

In his prose works Ephrem attaches a particular importance to Christ's descent into Hades, which becomes even more apparent in

---

[5]Modern Urfa in southeast Turkey.
[6]See S. Brock, *The Luminous Eye: The Spiritual World Vision of St Ephrem the Syrian*, pp. 10–11.

his poetic writings. The most detailed account of the descent can be found in the "Nisibene Hymns" (*Carmina Nisibena*), written in the form of a *madrasha*. As such, the "Nisibene Hymns" are characterized by a regular syllabic rhythmical pattern, which makes them suitable for congregational singing. In each hymn, stanzas in a fixed meter end in a common refrain (*'onitha*). Hymns 35–42 are of particular interest to us as they are collected under the general title, "On Our Lord, Death, and Satan." These are treated as a thematically unified whole along with hymns 52–68, which follow under the common title, "On Satan and Death" and are also connected with our subject.

In these works many strophes, and therefore much importance, are given to monologues by the chief actors—Sheol, Satan, and Death—and to dialogues between them. (Similar dialogues are found in the "Gospel of Nicodemus" and in the "Questions of Bartholomew" et al.) Hymn 35 contains a monologue by Sheol. It refers to events in Old Testament history and to the deeds of Christ, who destroyed Sheol's power:

> Sheol said: "As he made water into wine
> so he makes the dead alive.
> And God caused the flood and
> cleansed the earth and destroyed its sin.
> Fire and sulphur he sent to it
> to whiten its stains.
> By means of fire he gave me the dwellers of Sodom,
> by means of a flood—the giants.
> He closed the mouth of the house of Sennacherib
> and opened the mouth of Sheol.
> All these and similar things I liked,
> but now instead of exercising justice
> he brought through his Son resurrection and grace."[7]

One of the most vivid presentations of the descent can be found in Hymn 36, which is also preserved in Arabic and Georgian transla-

---

[7] *Carmina Nisibena* 35, 6–7 (*Der heiligen Ephraem der Syrers Carmina Nisibena*, Bd. II, p. 3)

tions.[8] It contains an extensive monologue by Death, who boasts that no one has escaped his power, be they prophets or priests, kings or warriors, rich or poor, wise or foolish, old or young. There were only two escapees: Enoch and Elijah. In searching for them Death goes "to the place where Jonah came down," but even there they cannot be found. Death's monologue is suddenly shattered by a vast panorama of the resurrection. Descending into Sheol, Christ revives the dead, tearing the tombs open and leading the dead out of the nether regions. In due course there is a description of the struggle between Christ and Death. The latter rushes to close the gates of Sheol in the face of the Divine Visitor. Death is struck by the fact that, unlike all others who strive to escape from Sheol, Christ wishes to enter it. "The medicine[9] of life has entered Sheol and restored its dead back to life," says Death. Addressing Christ, Death acknowledges his own defeat and asks him to take Adam, ascend to heaven, and leave the regions of Sheol. The hymn ends on a note of the final glorification of Christ's victory over Death. Following is the complete text of the hymn:

> Our Lord subjected his might, and they seized him
> so that through his living death he might give life to Adam.
> He gave his hands to be pierced by nails
> to make up for the hand which plucked the fruit; he was
>   struck
> on his cheek in the judgment room
> to make up for the mouth that ate in Eden; and while
>   Adam's foot was free
> his feet were pierced; our Lord was stripped that we might
>   be clothed;
> with gall and vinegar he sweetened
> the poison of the serpent which had bitten man.

---

[8]The Arabic and Georgian homilies, "On Death and Satan," present a paraphrase of this hymn. G. Garitte, "Homélie d'Éphrem sur la Mort et le Diable, Version géorgienne et version arabe," *Le Muséon* 77 (Louvain, 1969), pp. 123–163.

[9]The same word is employed in the *Demonstration* 22, 5 with the meaning of the "venom" that has poisoned Sheol from within. Cf. also the *Odes of Solomon* 42.12 in J. Charlesworth's edition.

Blessed is he who has conquered me[10]
and brought life to the dead to his own glory!

Death: "If you are God, show your might,
and if you are man, make trial of our might!
Or if it is Adam you are wanting, be off:
he is imprisoned here because of his debts; neither cherubim
    nor seraphim are able
to secure his release: they have no mortal amongst themselves
to give himself up for him. Who can open the mouth of
    Sheol,
dive down and bring him up from thence,
seeing that Sheol has swallowed him up and holds him tight
    for ever?"

Blessed is he who has conquered me
and brought life to the dead to his own glory!

"It was I who conquered all the sages;[11]
I have them heaped up in the corners of Sheol.
Come and enter, son of Joseph, and look at the horrors;
the limbs of the giants, Sampson's huge corpse,
the skeleton of cruel Goliath; there is Og, the son of the
    giants, too,
who made a bed of iron, where he reclined:
I cast him off it and threw him down,
I leveled that cedar at Sheol's gate."

Blessed is he who has conquered me
and brought life to the dead to his own glory!

"I alone have conquered many,
and now the Only-begotten (*ihidaya*)[12] seeks to conquer me!

---

[10]The refrain is written on behalf of Death.

[11]As "Death" is masculine in Syriac, it explains the symbols of Death as runner, reaper, victor, etc.

[12]The Syriac word *ihidaya* also used to be a designation for hermits (in the sense of the "solitary ones") and Christ himself (the "Only-begotten"). See H. Alfeyev, *The Spiritual World of Isaac the Syrian* (Kalamazoo, Michigan, 2000), pp. 61–62.

I have led off prophets, priests, and heroes,
I have conquered kings with their array, giants with their
    hunts,
the just with their fine deeds—rivers full of corpses
I cast into Sheol, who remains thirsty no matter how many I
    pour in!
Whether a man is near or far,
the final end brings him to Sheol's gate."

Blessed is he who has conquered me
and brought life to the dead to his own glory!

"I have spurned silver in the case of the rich
and their presents have failed to bribe me;
owners of slaves have never enticed me
to take a slave in place of his owner, or a poor man in place
    of a rich,
or an elder in place of a child. Sages may be able to win over
wild animals, but their winning words do not enter my ears.
All may call me 'hater of requests,'
but I simply perform what I am bidden."

Blessed is he who has conquered me
and brought life to the dead to his own glory!

"Who is this? Whose son?
And of what family is this man who has conquered me?
The book with the genealogies is here with me—
I have begun and taken the trouble to read all the names
    from Adam onward,
and none of the dead escapes me; tribe by tribe they are all
    written down
on my limbs. It is for your sake, Jesus,
that I have undertaken this reckoning,
in order to show you that no one escapes my hands."

Blessed is he who has conquered me
and brought life to the dead to his own glory!

"There are two men—I must not deceive—
whose names are missing for me in Sheol:
Enoch and Elijah did not come to me;
I looked for them in the whole of creation, I even descended
to the place where Jonah went, and groped around, but they
were not there; and when I thought
they might have entered paradise and escaped,
there was the fearful cherub guarding it.
Jacob saw a ladder:
perhaps it was by this that they went up to heaven."

Blessed is he who has conquered me
and brought life to the dead to his own glory!

"Who has measured out the sea sand
and only missed two grains?
As for this harvest, with which illnesses like harvesters
are daily busied, I alone carry
the sheaves and bind them up. Sheaf-binders in their haste
leave sheaves, and grape pickers forget whole clusters,
but only two small bunches have escaped me
in the great harvest that I have been gathering in by myself."

Blessed is he who has conquered me
and brought life to the dead to his own glory!

"It is I," says Death, "who have made
all kinds of catches on sea and land:
the eagles in the sky come to me,
so do the dragons of the deep, creeping things, birds and
    beasts,
old, young and babes; all these should persuade you,
Son of Mary, that my dominion reigns over all.
How can your cross conquer me,
seeing that it was through the wood that I was victorious
    and
conquered at the beginning?"

Blessed is he who has conquered me
and brought life to the dead to his own glory!

"I should like to say much more—
for I do not have any lack of words!—
but there is no need for words, for deeds
cry out close by; I do not, like you, promise
hidden things to the simple, saying that there will be a
    resurrection;
when, I ask, when? If you are so very strong,
then give a pledge on the spot
so that your distant promise may be believed."

Blessed is he who has conquered me
and brought life to the dead to his own glory!

Death finished his taunting speech
and our Lord's voice rang out thunderously in Sheol,
tearing open each grave one by one.
Terrible pangs seized hold of Death in Sheol; where light
had never been seen, rays shone out from the angels who
    had
entered to bring out
the dead to meet the Dead One who has given life to all.
The dead went forth, and shame covered the living
who had hoped they had conquered him who gives life to all.

Blessed is he who has conquered me
and brought life to the dead to his own glory!

"Would I were back in Moses' time,"
says Death, "he made me a feast day:
for that lamb in Egypt gave me
the first fruits from every house; heaps upon heaps of
    firstborn
were piled up for me at Sheol's gate. But this festal Lamb
has plundered Sheol, taken his tithe of the dead and led
    them off from me.

That lamb filled the graves for me,
this one empties the graves that had been full."

Blessed is he who has conquered me
and brought life to the dead to his own glory!

"Jesus' death is a torment to me,
I wish I had chosen to let him live: it would have been
    better
for me than his death.
Here is a dead man whose death I find hateful;
at everyone else's death I rejoice, but at his death I am
    anxious,
and I expect he will return to life: during his lifetime he
    revived
and brought back to life
three dead people. Now through his death
the dead who have come to life again trample me at Sheol's
    gates
when I go to hold them in."

Blessed is he who has conquered me
and brought life to the dead to his own glory!

"I will run and close the gates of Sheol
before that Dead One whose death has plundered me.
He who hears of it will wonder at my humiliation,
because I have been defeated by a dead man outside: all the
    dead want to go outside,
and he is pressing to enter. The medicine[13] of life has
    entered Sheol
and brought its dead back to life. Who is it who has
    introduced for me and hidden
the living fire in which the cold and dark
wombs of Sheol melt?"

---

[13]In the Syriac tradition it is a symbol of Christ.

Blessed is he who has conquered me
and brought life to the dead to his own glory!

Death saw angels in Sheol,
immortal beings instead of mortal,
and he said: "Trouble has entered our abode.
On two accounts am I tormented: the dead have left Sheol,
and the angels, who do not die, have entered it—one has
entered and sat at the head
of his grave, another, his companion, at his feet.
I will ask and request him
to take his pledge (*rahbona*)[14] and go off to his kingdom."

Blessed is he who has conquered me
and brought life to the dead to his own glory!

"Do not reckon against me, good Jesus,
the words I have spoken, or my pride before you.
Who, on seeing your cross, could doubt
that you are truly man? Who, when he sees your power,
will fail to believe that you are also God? By these two
indications
I have learned to confess you both Man and God.
Since the dead cannot repent in Sheol,
rise up among the living, Lord, and proclaim repentance."

Blessed is he who has conquered me
and brought life to the dead to his own glory!

"Jesus king, receive my request,
and with my request, take your hostage,
carry off, as your great hostage, Adam
in whom all the dead are hidden—
just as, when I received him, in him all the living were
concealed.

---

[14]The word "pledge," or "hostage" (*rahbona*), corresponding to the Greek *arrabon*, is a circumlocution for the saved Adam. This image also appears in the homily "On the Soul and Body and the Passion of Our Lord" ascribed to St Athanasius of Alexandria (see chapter two).

As first hostage I give you Adam's body,
ascend now and reign over all,
and when I hear your trumpet call,
with my own hands will I bring forth the dead at your
    coming."

Blessed is he who has conquered me
and brought life to the dead to his own glory!

Our living King has arisen and is exalted,
like a victor, from Sheol.
Woe is doubled for the party of the left,
dismay for evil spirits and demons, suffering for Satan and
    Death,
lamentation for Sin and Sheol, but rejoicing for the party of
    the right
has come today! On his great day, then,
let us give great praise to him
who died and came to life again, so that he might give life
    and
resurrection to all!

Blessed is he who has conquered me
and brought life to the dead to his own glory!

This hymn presents a clear theological statement: Death tries in vain to impede Christ's entrance into Sheol. Having descended into it, he resurrects everyone there and leads them out. Sheol is left bare and destitute; there are no longer any dead inside. Only the evil spirits (demons), Satan, Death, and Sin remain waiting in Sheol for the second coming of Christ. On this day Death himself must hand over his victims to Christ. Ephrem does not segregate the prophets and the righteous from the rest of the dead but calls our attention to the fact that everyone is saved and resurrected in Christ.[15]

---

[15]While other hymns by Ephrem refer to the removal of the righteous from Hades (*De Azymis* 3, 7), none specifies whether the poet speaks only of the Old Testament righteous people.

Hymn 37 has the theme of the resurrection of the dead connected with reference to Ezekiel's prophecy:

> Death shed tears over Sheol
> seeing that her treasures were despoiled,
> and he said: "Who has stolen your riches?" . . .
>
> "I saw that Ezekiel in the valley,
> who resurrected the dead as he was bidden.
> And I saw the bones in disarray brought into motion.
> There was a commotion of the bones in Sheol,
> for a bone sought its companion
> and would reunite with its pair. And no one asked there
> as well as no one was asked:
> 'Are those bones indeed going to be brought back to life?'
> For without questioning the voice of Jesus, the Ruler of
>   Creation,
> has resurrected them."
> "Sheol was afflicted as she saw them.[16]
> She cried for Lazarus, as he abandoned [her].
> Inside and outside there was weeping;
> for his sisters wept for him as he
> came down to me to the grave,
> and I wept for him because he left it.
> Upon his death there was a great mourning among the
>   living,
> and in Sheol there was a great mourning as he rose."
>
> "Now I also have learned the taste of grief of
> those who bemoan their loved ones.
> If dead are so pleasing to Sheol,
> Still more, how much they should have been loved by their
>   fathers! . . ."
>
> "That suffering (*hasha*) which I bring to humans, which
> afflicts them because of their loved ones,

---

[16]The entire hymn is a monologue by Death.

eventually, has befallen me.
For when the dead will leave Sheol
everyone will undergo resurrection.
Only I alone will undergo torture.
And truly, who will be able to endure this
which still lies ahead of me? For I will see Sheol in solitude
    (*balhudeh*),
for that voice which destroyed the tombs,
has emptied it. And he took out the dead that there
    remained."

"When one reads prophets
and learns about fair wars,
one who meditates upon the life of Christ,
learns charity and compassionate mercy.
And if he thinks about Jesus as a stranger (*nukhraya*), [17]
he offends me.
No other key would match
the gates of Sheol, except for the key of the Creator
who has opened them.
He will open them [again] at his second coming."

"Who can knit the bones together, if not the power
which has created them? The parts of the body who can
join if not the hand of the Maker?
What will restore the bodies but the finger of the Creator?
The one who created them and turned into [dust] and
    destroyed,
only he is able to renew and resurrect.
No other God can enter
and restore the creatures which do not belong to him." [18]

"If there be any other divine power existing,
I would be very glad if it could visit me.

---

[17] Or strange, foreign. This term is also used in relation to false gods as opposed
to the true God.
[18] Literally, "who are not His."

It would go down into the entrails of Sheol and
learn that there is only one God.
Mortals who erred and preached
about many gods, are now bound in Sheol for me,
and their gods were never saddened because of them.
I know only one God
and only his prophets and apostles I acknowledge."[19]

In Hymn 38 Ephrem describes how Sheol took Christ for a mere mortal because the latter had concealed his divinity with his body.[20] Ephrem draws a clear distinction between Sheol and Gehenna, saying that Judas would have preferred death in Sheol to life in Gehenna.[21] Thus "Sheol" designates a place where all the dead repose, while Gehenna means a place where sinners suffer retribution for their transgressions.[22]

Ephrem puts all of these ideas into the mouths of the personifications of Death, Sheol, and Satan. In this hymn, humor, a distinctive feature, also serves as a literary device. Characters appear to ridicule themselves by acknowledging their own weaknesses and falsehoods while at the same time they present arguments that attempt to prove the contrary. Matters may be depicted distortedly because the despicable characters dwell on them. Therefore it is up to the reader to unravel this unassuming riddle and to define the original, intended message of the text. For instance, in Hymn 41 Satan delivers a long speech on how, despite his old age, he still does not neglect small children but takes care of them. This care consists of his attempt to accustom youngsters to evil from a tender age.[23] Similar techniques will later be transmitted from Ephrem to Romanos the Melodist, and from the latter to Byzantine hymnographers and authors of liturgical texts. The following example is the entire text of Hymn 41:

---

[19]*Nisibene Hymns* 37, 1–11 (*Carmina Nisibena*, Bd. II, pp. 15–18).

[20]*Nisibene Hymns* 38, 6 (*Carmina Nisibena*, Bd. II, pp. 20–21).

[21]*Nisibene Hymns* 38, 11 (*Carmina Nisibena*, Bd. II, p. 22).

[22]See *The Letter to Publius* 22–25, in which St Ephrem develops the idea that Gehenna is a place where sinners are tortured for being separated from God. Critical edition of the text in *Le Muséon* 89 (Louvain, 1976), pp. 261–305.

[23]*Nisibene Hymns* 41, 4 (*Carmina Nisibena*, Bd. II, p. 33).

Said the Evil One:[24] "I am afraid of
that Jesus. He will destroy my ways.
I am a thousand years old and have never been idle:
Nothing in creation which I saw
did I neglect or miss, and now comes
he, who teaches profligate chastity.
I weep now, for he has destroyed everything I had built.
For it took me much effort and labor
to entangle the whole of creation in wiles."

*Blessed is he who came and destroyed the
guiles of the Evil One.*

"I used to set off with the fastest [runners]
and would outrun them. I would do battle,
and confusion of crowds would be my weapon.
I would rejoice in people's agitation
for it gave me a fast opportunity to harden
the onslaught of the crowd.
By means of a crowd I built
a great mountain—a tower reaching up to heaven.
Had they declared war on the heights [of heaven]
how much simpler would it have been for them to overcome
that one on earth!"

*Blessed is he who came and destroyed the
guiles of the Evil One.*

"Along with time and its benefits
I struggled prudently.
The people heard that God is one,
but made for themselves a multitude of gods.
Because, having seen the Son of God,
they rushed toward the One God,
so that under the pretext of confessing God to deny him.
On the pretext of being zealous they ran away from him.

---

[24]I.e., Satan.

Thus, every time they would be found perverse,
for they are godless."

Blessed is he who came and destroyed the
guiles of the Evil One.

"I am a great many years old,
but I never despised a child.
I have taken particular care of infants,
so that from the very beginning
they would acquire bad habits,
so that their defects would grow with them.
But there are foolish fathers who
do not harm the seed I have
sown in their sons.
And there are such who like good farmers,
uproot vices out of the minds of their children."

Blessed is he who came and destroyed the
guiles of the Evil One.

"Instead of chains I bound people by sloth,
and they sat down in idleness.
I deprived their senses of everything good:
their eyes—from reading,
their lips—from psalm singing[25]
their minds—from learning.
How excellent they are at barren stories,
how expert at empty talk and stories,
but if the word of salvation[26] falls on their ears,
they will push it aside,
or stand up and leave."

Blessed is he who came and destroyed the
guiles of the Evil One.

---

[25]Literally: "from alleluias" (*hullale*). In the Syriac tradition the Psalter was divided into *hullale*-alleluias.

[26]Or "the word of life." The Syriac word *hayye* means both "life" and "salvation."

"How many satans are inside a man,
but it is me everyone curses!
For the anger of man
is like a demon, who every day harasses him;
other demons are like wayfarers,
they leave when they are compelled to.
However, when anger is concerned,
all righteous put it under oath,
and cannot eradicate it.
Instead of hating a destructive envy,
everyone hates a weak and miserable demon!"

Blessed is he who came and destroyed the
guiles of the Evil One.

"The magician and a snake charmer was put to shame,
he who binds snakes every day;
a viper inside of him rebels,
for he cannot subdue the lust within him.
Concealed sin is like an asp;
when someone blows on it, he gets burned.
Even if he catches the viper through his craft,
falsehood has invisibly struck him:
he puts the snake to sleep by his incantations,
but also arouses great wrath against himself by his very
        incantations."

Blessed is he who came and destroyed the
guiles of the Evil One.

"I have prepared my sting and sat waiting.
Who is able to subject anyone to his own opinion?
. . . . . .[27]
Who else is so patient with everyone?
And little by little I led him astray,

---

[27]A line is missing in the original text.

so that he fell into listlessness."[28]

"The one [who] shrinks from wrongdoing,
habits subject him: little by little I trained him,
until he fell under my yoke;
and grew accustomed to it, so that he did not wish to
abandon it."

Blessed is he who came and destroyed the
guiles of the Evil One.

"I have noticed and seen
that patience is able to overcome everything.
In the time when I triumphed over Adam, he was alone.
So I left him, till he begat descendants
and meanwhile looked for another job to do,
so that idleness did not overtake.
I began to count sea sand,
so that through this my spirit became more patient
and to train my memory, so that it did not let me down,
when sons of men will become a multitude.
Before they became numerous
I tested them in many ways."

Blessed is he who came and destroyed the
guiles of the Evil One.

Servants of the Evil One argued with him
and refuted his words by objections:
"Here Elisha revived a dead one
and won over death in the high chamber,
and brought to life
the son of the widow;
now he is bound in Sheol."
However, the intellect of the Evil One is far greater:
he beat them with their own words:

---

[28]In Syriac this word occurs in late monastic literature and is analogous to the Greek *akēdia*.

"How can Elisha be overpowered
if in Sheol his remains still
bring dead to life?"

*Blessed is he who came and destroyed the
guiles of the Evil One.*

If Elisha who is so weak
has such a great power in Sheol
that he could revive the dead,
then how many dead ones would be resurrected
by the death of strong Jesus?
Thus, following that you may learn,
how considerably Jesus surpasses us, my friends!
For, behold, his cunning has deceived you,
and you have not been able to discern his greatness,
for you simply compared him with prophets.

*Blessed is he who came and destroyed the
guiles of the Evil One.*

"Therefore your consolation is in vain"—
said the Evil One to his comrades.
"For how could Death take hold of the one
who resurrected Lazarus?
And even if Death would be victorious over him,
this is because he would subject himself to it.
And if he subjects himself to Death voluntarily,
you should be still more terrified,
for he would not die for nothing.
Great tumult he has caused us,
for having died, he would enter in to revive Adam."

*Blessed is he who came and destroyed the
guiles of the Evil One.*

Death looked out of its cavern
and was astounded for he saw Our Lord crucified
and said: "Waker of the dead, where are you?

Will you become my nourishment
instead of sweet Lazarus,
whose taste is still on my lips?
Jairus' daughter will come to look at your cross;
the son of the widow will look up at you.
The tree has ensnared Adam for me;
blessed is this cross which has
ensnared the son of David for me."

Blessed is he who came and destroyed the
guiles of the Evil One.

Death opened its gullet and said:
"Have you never heard, O Son of Mary,
about Moses who was great and surpassed everybody?
About how he became a god[29] and performed divine
    actions,
put firstborns to death and saved firstborns,[30]
warded off death from the living ones?
However, I ascended to the mountain with this Moses;
[God] handed him over to me
let his might be praised!
No matter how great was the son of Adam
lo, dust returns to dust,
for he came from earth."

Blessed is he who came and destroyed the
guiles of the Evil One.

Satan came with his servants
to look at Our Lord in Sheol
and to rejoice with Death, his ally.
But he saw Death sad and mourning for the dead,
who at the voice of the Firstborn,
returned to life and went forth from Sheol.

---

[29]See Exod 4.16; 7.1.
[30]I.e., put to death the firstborn of the Egyptians and saved the firstborn of Israel.

The Evil One began to console Death,
his relative: "You have not lost as much as you have
    acquired.
Unless Jesus is within you,
in your hands you will hold all who have lived and are
    living."

Blessed is he who came and destroyed the
guiles of the Evil One.

"Open to us [the door], so that we can see
and laugh at him. We will respond and ask: "Where is your
    might?"
It is three days already, so let us tell him:
"O, three days old, you have resurrected
four days old Lazarus. So bring yourself back to life."
Death has opened the doors of Sheol,
and the light of the face of the Lord gushed out from there,
and like the Sodomites they were destroyed
groping and looking for the door of Sheol, but it has
    disappeared.[31]

Blessed is he who came and destroyed the
guiles of the Evil One.

Hymns 52–68 present a collection of dramatic dialogues in verse between Satan and Death, interspersed with the poet's remarks. Satan and Death, who have "never prevailed and will never prevail," argue with each other about which side the victory is on.[32] In the course of this argument Satan and Death do no more than prove their helplessness in the face of God; they talk about Christ's death on the cross as the source of their own torment and defeat. Each stanza is accompanied by a refrain that bears the central message: "Praise to you, O Son of the Shepherd of all, who has saved his flock from the hidden wolves, the Evil One and Death, whom he has swallowed

---

[31]Literally, "which has disappeared."
[32]*Nisibene Hymns* 63, 1 (*Carmina Nisibena*, Bd. II, p. 99).

up,"[33] "Praise to you, who has prevailed over the Evil One and through your resurrection has triumphed over Death."[34] In a condensed form the refrains contain the principal theological idea, which the reader would otherwise have to derive from the dialogues between Satan and Death. This particular way of presenting the material serves a didactic purpose and enables the reader to grasp the core idea of the poem in greater depth. The dialogue between Death and Satan in Hymn 52 demonstrates this.

> I heard Death and Satan loudly disputing
> which was the stronger of the two amongst men.
>
> Death has shown his power in that he conquers all men,
> Satan has shown his guile in that he makes all men sin.
>
> *Death*: "Only those who want to, O Evil One, listen to you,
> but to me they come, whether they will or not."
>
> *Satan*: "You just employ brute force, O Death,
> whereas I use traps and cunning snares."
>
> *Death*: "Listen, Evil One, a cunning man can break your
>   yoke,
> but there is none who can escape from mine."
>
> *Satan*: "You, O Death, exercise your strength on the sick,
> but I am the stronger with those who are well . . ."
>
> *Satan*: "Sheol is hated for there is no chance of remorse
>   there:
> it is a pit which swallows up and suppresses every impulse."
>
> *Death*: "Sheol is a whirlpool (*samarta*), and everyone who
>   falls in it is resurrected,
> but sin is hated because it cuts off a man's hope."
>
> *Satan*: "Although it grieves me, I allow for repentance;
> you cut off a sinner's hopes if he dies in his sins."

---

[33] *Nisibene Hymns* 52, refrain (*Carmina Nisibena*, Bd. II, p. 73).
[34] *Nisibene Hymns* 58, refrain (*Carmina Nisibena*, Bd. II, p. 87).

Death: "With you his hope was cut off long ago;
if you had never made him sin, he would have made a good
    end."

Chorus: "Blessed is he who set the accursed slaves against
    each other
so that we can laugh at them just as they laughed at us."

Our laughing at them now, my brethren, is a pledge
    (*rahbona*)[35]
that we shall again be enabled to laugh, at the resurrection.[36]

After Ephrem, dialogue poems of a similar kind will become popular in Syrian liturgical hymnography. The entire corpus of anonymous dialogue poems, dated approximately to the fifth century and preserved in Syriac, feature not only characters such as Satan and Death, but also contain separate exchanges between biblical characters, for example, Abel and Cain, Abraham and Sarah, the prophet Elijah and the widow of Sarepta, Mary and Joseph, Mary and the Angel, Mary and the Magi, John the Baptist and Christ, and the Cherub and the Thief.[37] In due course Byzantine hymnographers, including St Romanos the Melodist,[38] St Theophanes Graptos,[39] and others will become heirs to this particular technique.

Syriac liturgical manuscripts have preserved numerous *madrasha* attributed to Ephrem, but they almost certainly belong to authors of the fifth, sixth, and subsequent centuries. A collection of funeral hymns (*Necrosima*), in which considerable attention is paid to the theme of Christ's victory over Hades and death, also belongs to this category.[40] Identification of the original authorship of these hym-

---

[35]See note 14 above.

[36]*Nisibene Hymns* 52, 1–27 (*Carmina Nisibena*, Bd. II, pp. 73–75).

[37]S. Brock, *A Brief Outline of Syriac Literarture* (Kottayam, 1997), pp. 32–33.

[38]There are numerous dialogues in his *kontakia*.

[39]In particular, his Canon on the Annunciation of the Holy Mother of God, still in use in the Orthodox Church, which is written in the form of a dialogue between Mary and the Archangel.

[40]Syriac text in *Sancti Ephraem Syri Opera Omnia in Sex Tomos Distributa*, ed. Stephanus Evodius Assemanus, Archiepiscopus Apamensis, vol. III (Rome, 1744).

nodic cycles has proved to be difficult.[41] The texts of these *madrasha* were published by J. Assemani from Syriac liturgical books, which customarily attribute them to Ephrem. Certain hymns in the cycle cite authentic works almost word for word,[42] while others are a far cry from the opus of Ephrem, differing radically in style and content. It is obvious that we are dealing with a compilation by some late imitator of Ephrem.

One hymn belonging to this cycle, "A Solemn Ode on the Death of the Righteous," depicts the annihilation and final destruction of Death:

> "And I saw Death, which since long ago is dead and became nought.
> And I said to it: 'Where is your sting, you omnivorous one? Behold, even your memory has disappeared among the mortals!' "
> Death silently replied to the one who was questioning him: "Stay in peace, O mortals: my reign came to its end.
> The sin of Adam engendered death in the sons of men, and now the nature of the mortals is justified, and Death is put to death."
> Thus, said Death, silently, without uttering a word, though typically he neither talks nor is silent.
> Through the condemnation of sinners he received his name; but as soon as the nature of mortals became justified, he was brought to an end.[43]

Another poem, "Christ's Victory over Death," presents the story of Christ's descent into Hades, victory over Satan, and the devastation of Sheol:

---

[41]F. Burkitt, who tried to identify the manuscript sources used by Assemani in the edition of his *Necrosima*, was unable to come to any definite conclusion about the authorship of these works. See F. C. Burkitt, *Saint Ephraim's Quotations from the Gospels* (Cambridge, 1901), p. 9.

[42]*Necrosima* 58 ("Dispute between Satan and Death") in particular has a literal quotation in the initial strophes taken from the *Nisibene Hymns* 52, 53, and 68.

[43]*Sancti Ephraem Syri Opera Omnia in Sex Tomos Distributa*, ed. Stephanus Evodius Assemanus, Archiepiscopus Apamensis, vol. III, p. 249.

This whole region is the region of the dead; terrifying
darkness is the keeper of its treasures; its lord, Death,
roars as a lion every day. . . .

Who can imagine the terrors of this region? who will
describe by what horrors it is surrounded? Everyone
who enters it, shudders. . . .

Death rejoices and makes merry, Sheol jubilates but keeps
silent.

With gladness she opens its gates and gulps down ages and
generations.

And as this fierce tyrant is accustomed to swallowing up the
beautiful ones, so he has swallowed up and stolen the
most Beautiful and the Most Holy One.

He ushered him in into his halls and concealed the Giant.

But the Strong One arose in glory, bound Death in his own
dwelling, enchained and deposed the Tormentor, who
boasted of his power over humanity.

Finally he plundered the insatiable Sheol who gulped down
and tormented even the bodies of the righteous; he
cried out and the demons trembled, and darkness
shrank from his voice.

He put to terror the hordes and retinue of Death; that
moans in his fetters; loudly howls Sheol in her
domains. . . .

Death has been put to shame, the head of this rebel, who
willed to become God, has drooped. The voice of Christ
resounds in the realm of perdition, and the rebel,
besieged, has surrendered.

Christ has cried out to Adam in the darkness, into which he
had been plunged, and said: "Where are you beautiful
Adam, once seduced by the counsel of a wife?

Rise up now, O splendid one, rise up, you majestic and
corrupt image! The head of the dragon has been
crushed, Death and Satan are put to death." . . .

Adam rose up, bowed down to the Lord who had come in
search of him, and said: "Together with my own

children I bow down to you, my Lord, who has come to restore us, the fallen ones."[44]

Salvation's all-embracing character, as given by Christ, is emphasized in another ode with the same title, "Christ's Victory over Death":

> Blessed is Christ! He gave to us the dead, hope for life, and consoled our race. Although now we are subject to decay, we will be renewed.
>
> Listen, you mortals, to the mystery of the resurrection which is hidden now, but in the Last Days will be revealed in the Holy Church.
>
> Jesus a traveler [in the realm] of Death for three days, liberated his captives, robbed his camp, and renewed our race.
>
> Previously Death had prided himself and boasted, saying: "Priests and Kings are enchained in my dwellings."
>
> But the glorious Warrior suddenly broke into the realm of Death; as a thief his voice stole therein and put an end to his glory.
>
> The dead in Sheol perceived the fragrance of life and began preaching to each other that their hopes come to fulfillment.
>
> Death reigned over mortals from the beginning, until the one Sovereign shone over and destroyed his pride.
>
> His voice, like peals of mighty thunder, reached the dead and heralded to them that they were liberated from bondage."[45]

There are numerous other texts attributed to Ephrem—some genuine, others spurious, extant in both Syriac and Greek[46]—which

---

[44] *Necrosima* 29, p. 281.

[45] *Necrosima* 48, p. 301.

[46] There is an entire corpus of the Greek writings attributed to St Ephrem; almost all of them are spurious, with one exception: a homily "On Jonah and the Repentance of Nineveh," preserved in Syriac as well as in Greek, Latin, Armenian,

develop the theme of Christ's descent into Sheol. The aforementioned fragments, however, provide an impression of how the great Syriac hymnographer and his closest adherents would handle this subject. The central motif of the whole corpus of texts devoted to the descent is Christ's victory over Death and Hades. To convey this idea, an entire system of images was developed. They find expression in "The Gospel of Nicodemus" and other early Christian documents that mention the *Höllensturm*. The main protagonist is Christ himself: he breaks the gates and bars of Hades, steps into the darkness of the abyss, overpowers Satan and his ministers, and breaks their resistance. He illumines Sheol with his light, destroying Death and opening the way back to paradise for the dead.

The Kontakia of St Romanos the Melodist

St Romanos was born toward the end of the fifth century in the city of Emesa,[47] located in the west of Syria. It is presumed that he was born into a Jewish family and that Syriac was his native language.[48] Romanos served as a deacon in Berytus (modern Beirut) and then moved to Constantinople during the reign of Emperor Anastasios, ending up at the Church of the Theotokos in the Kyrou quarter.[49] In a short time he gained fame for his elaborate metrical sermons written in Greek and known as *kontakia*[50]—a genre accredited to him.

---

and Ethiopian versions. See *Des Heiligen Ephraem des Syrers Sermones* II, hrsg. von. E. Beck, CSCO 311, Scriptores Syri 124 (Louvain, 1970); Greek, Georgian, and Latin texts are edited in *Le Muséon* 80 (1967), pp. 47–119. Research into the Greek text of this homily has shown that translations of the genuine works of St Ephrem in Greek into verse form were being made already in the third quarter of the 4th century. See C. Emereau, *Saint Ephrem le Syrien, son oeuvre littéraire grecque* (Paris, 1919), p. 66. As for the spurious writings, they were composed in Byzantium beginning from the 5th century.

[47]Now Homs in Turkey.

[48]*Sancti Romani Melodi Cantica genuina*, ed. P. Maas and C. A. Trypanis (Oxford, 1963), pp. XV–XVI.

[49]See Basil's *Menologion* (PG 117:81).

[50]Literally, the Greek word *kontakion* means a stick onto which a scroll was rolled. On the genre of the *kontakion*, see P. Maas, "Das Kontakion," *Byzantinische*

Kontakia usually consist of an introduction (*prooimion*) and several stanzas (*oikoi*[51]), each followed by a refrain (*ephymnion*). In its developed form the *kontakion* was a lyric homily in which the faithful were instructed based on a strong narrative or storyline, dramatic dialogues between the main characters, and commentary. Romanos died no later than AD 565 but no earlier than AD 555 (a *terminus post quem* established by his 51st *kontakion*).[52] According to legend he composed more than a thousand hymns.

During the sixth and seventh centuries the *kontakia* of Romanos were in wide circulation. However, at the turn of the eighth century they were gradually supplanted by new genres of liturgical poetry, particularly the *kanon*, a non-dramatic and non-narrative hymn of praise based on the biblical odes. Liturgical practice has retained only the introductory stanzas (*prooimia*) and one *oikos* of the older *kontakia*. Once the complete hymns had been removed from liturgical practice the designation *kontakion* came to be used in this narrow sense in the liturgical books. The only extant *kontakion* that retains its complete form in the liturgical books is the famous "Akathistos to the Holy Virgin," which many scholars attribute to Romanos.[53]

Although the large corpus of Romanos' hymnodic legacy is no longer included in today's repertory of hymns in Orthodox services, his influence on the formation of subsequent liturgical texts can be hardly overestimated. Beautifully crafted *kontakia* dedicated to various events celebrated in the church calendar set a standard for many Byzantine hymnographers of subsequent generations. Among those writing under Romanos' influence were St Andrew of Crete (seventh century), St John Damascene (eighth century), St Theophanes Graptos (ninth century), and St Symeon Metaphrastes (tenth century).

Zeitschrift 19 (1910); E. Wellesz, *A History of Byzantine Music and Hymnography*, pp. 179–197.

[51]The Greek word *oikos* means "house."

[52]W. L. Petersen, "The Diatessaron and Ephraem Syrus as Sources of Romanos the Melodist," p. 3.

[53]E. Wellesz, *The Akathistos Hymn* (Copenhagen, 1957); Idem., *A Hystory of Byzantine Music and Hymnography*, 2nd ed, pp. 191–197; S. Averintsev, *Poetika*, pp. 243–249.

Romanos uses a wide variety of sources. Among them, apart from the writings of St Ephrem, are the works of St Cyril of Jerusalem, St Basil of Seleucia, St Dorotheus of Gaza, St John Chrysostom, and many others. He also refers to and quotes the writings of Syriac poets.[54] Moreover, Romanos was familiar with the "Diatessaron," a harmonization of the four Gospels compiled in the second century and widely disseminated in Syriac.[55] He may have also used the apocryphal "Gospel of Nicodemus," the influence of which is particularly conspicuous in his 38th *kontakion*, as well as in particular stanzas of Kontakia 40–45, dedicated to the resurrection of Christ.

The fact that Romanos used a comparatively wide range of sources that include apocryphal writings cannot be explained simply by the statement that he was not a theologian (an assertion of J. Grosdidier de Matons).[56] The point, rather, is that the church, by his lifetime, had not yet rejected all of the apocryphal gospels as part of the canon of Scripture. Many, including "The Gospel of Nikodemus," became an indispensable part of the ecclesiastical tradition. Although Romanos never wrote a theological treatise, he was a theologian exactly in the same sense that Ephrem the Syrian was. For Ephrem to be a theologian did not merely mean to "philosophize about God"[57] but rather to praise and glorify God. Both Ephrem and Romanos fit in perfectly with the classic definition of "theologian" as formulated by Evagrius: "If you are a theologian, you will pray in truth; if you pray in truth, you are a theologian."[58]

One of the most typical characteristics of a Romanos *kontakion* is the presence of a plotline, which could be developed by several characters in dialogue with the author or with one another. In these verse

---

[54]J. Grosdidier de Matons, *Romanos le Mélode* (Paris, 1977), pp. 254–255.

[55]We know this chiefly from *The Commentary on the Diatessaron* written by St Ephrem. On the "Diatessaron" as a common source for Ephrem and Romanos see W. L. Petersen, *The Diatessaron and Ephraem Syrus as Sources of Romanos the Melodist*; on the influence of Ephrem to Romanos see S. Brock, "From Ephrem to Romanos," *Studia Patristica* 20, ed. E. A. Livingstone (Louvain, 1989), pp. 139–151.

[56]Introduction, SC 99, 51.

[57]See St Gregory Nazianzen, *Oration* 27, 3 (On Theology I).

[58]Evagrius, *On Prayer* 61.

exchanges Romanos does not reproduce sacred events in a historical manner. Rather, he offers an iconographic outline of the events: putting words that carry the inner theological message of the event into the mouths of his characters. In his *kontakia* Romanos' characters know the outcome in advance. Even evil characters give the impression that they are fully aware of their wrongdoing, which they express in colorful verse.

Refrains play an important structural role in Romanos' *kontakia*. Quite often they are not directly connected with the plotline but appear to be artificially added to individual *oikoi*. At times the general tone of the refrain reverses the mood and message of the *kontakion* to which it belongs. For instance, a mournful *kontakion* may contain a joyful refrain or vice versa. In this way the antinomic and paradoxical character of the *kontakion*'s subject matter is emphasized. Thus one meaningful dimension of this philosophical-theological antinomy is localized in the main text and the other in the refrain.[59]

The aforementioned poetic style of Romanos originates from the Semitic tradition to which Ephrem the Syrian also belonged. The influence of the "Nisibene Hymns" on Romanos' *kontakia* is most conspicuous as, for example, in the dialogue between Sheol (or Hades) and Satan in Kontakion 38:[60]

> Three crosses Pilate fixed on Golgotha,
> two for the thieves and one for the Giver of Life,
> whom Hell saw and said to those below,
> "My ministers and powers,
> who has fixed a nail in my heart?
> A wooden lance has suddenly pierced me and I am being
>   torn apart.
> My insides are in pain, my belly in agony,
> my senses make my spirit tremble,
> and I am compelled to disgorge

---

[59]S. Averintsev, *Poetika*, p. 230.

[60]This is one of the so-called *staurosima kontakia*, dedicated to the Passion and Cross of Christ. Translation in St Romanos, *On the Life of Christ. Kontakia*, trans. Archimandrite Ephrem Lash (New York, 1996), pp. 155–163.

Adam and Adam's race. Given me by a tree,
a tree is bringing them back
again to paradise."

When he heard this the cunning serpent
ran crawling and cried, "What is it, Hell?
Why do you groan for no reason? Why produce these
    wailings?
This tree, at which you tremble,
I carpentered up there for Mary's Child.
I intimated it to the Jews for our advantage,
for it is a cross, to which I have nailed Christ,
wishing by a tree to do away with the second Adam.
So do not upset yourself. It will not plunder you.
Keep hold of those you have. Of those whom we rule,
not one escapes
again to paradise."

"Away with you, come to your senses, Beliar," cried Hell.
"Run, open your eyes, and see
the root of the tree inside my soul.
It has gone down to my depths,
to draw up Adam like iron.
Elisha of old painted its image in prophecy
when he drew the axe head from the river.[61]
With a light object the prophet dragged a heavy,
warning you and teaching you
that, by a tree, Adam is to be brought up
from wretchedness
again to paradise."

"Who gave you such an idea then, Hell?
From where now this cowardly fear, where once there was
    no fear,
of a worthless tree, dry and barren. . . . "

---

[61] 4 Kgdms 6.5–7.

"You have suddenly lost your senses, you of old the cunning
    serpent. . . .
Behold that tree, which you call dry and barren,
bears fruit; a thief tasted it
and has become heir to the good things of Eden. . . . "

"Wretched Hell, cease this cowardly talk. . . .
Were you afraid of a cross and of the Crucified?
Not one of your words has shaken me. . . ."

Suddenly Hell began to call out to the devil—
The eyeless to the sightless, the blind to the blind—
"Look . . . the tree which you boast of has shaken the
    universe,
has convulsed the earth, hidden the sky,
rent the rocks together with the veil,
and raised up those in the graves. . . ."

"Has the Nazarene's tree been strong enough to scare you?"
said the devil to Hell the destroyer,—
"Have you been slain by a cross, you who slay all?"[62]

    The classical, quantitative metrical patterns based on alternating
of "long" and "short" vowels were rejected by Romanos in favor of
tonic or accentual measures. This style is based on alternating lines of
identical syllable count, with accents falling on corresponding syllables. An example of tonic versification may be seen in the opening
lines of Kontakion 40, on Christ's descent into Hades:

> *Ei kai en tafō katēlthes athanate,*
> *alla tou Hadou katheiles tēn dynamin*
> *kai anestēs hōs nikētēs, Khriste ho theos,*
> *gynaiksi myroforois to khaire fthegksamenos*
> *kai tois sois apostolois eirēnēn dōroumenos*
> *ho tois pesousi parekhōn anastasin.*

---

[62] *Kontakion* 38, 3–8 (SC 128, 288–296).

> Though you descended into the tomb, O Immortal,
> yet you destroyed the power of hell,
> and you arose as victor, O Christ God,
> calling to the myrrh-bearing women, "Rejoice!"
> and giving peace to your apostles, O you
> *who grants resurrection to the fallen.*[63]

Reading this passage one observes isosyllabic forms in the first and second strophes. The syllabic patterns in lines four and five are also equivalent. This text gives a good example of *homoioteleuton*—when the consonant ending of the final syllables is the same in consecutive lines—a precursor of modern rhyme. As a literary device *homoioteleuton* adds an uplifting solemnity to the poem. While *homoioteleuton* is one of the important stylistic devices used by Romanos, its presence or absence in a stanza is not determined by any metrical scheme. It may be altogether absent or it may occur with final syllables in adjacent lines. It may also be found within a stanza or in successive stanzas, or even in the middle of a stanza. The opening of Kontakion 42 presents one of a multitude of vivid examples:

> *Katepothē ho thanatos eis nikos*
> *tē ek nekrōn egersei sou, Khriste ho theos.* . . .
> *Tēn zōēn tē tafēi, tō thanatō theon*
> *kai tō Haidēi ton Haidēn skyleusanta*
> *paredōke pote tōn anomōn laos,*
> *hōs thnēton tous thnētous athanatēsanta,*
> *hōs de nekron tous nekrous anastēsanta rhēmati.*
> *Fylakas ethento mnēmati tou panta ferontos neumati.*

> Death is swallowed up in victory[64]
> by your resurrection, O Christ God. . . .
> Life to the tomb, God to death
> and the One who despoiled Hades to Hades,
> once was handed over by the host of lawless people,
> as a mortal who made mortals immortal,

---

[63] *Kontakion* 40, Introduction (SC 128, 380).
[64] 1 Cor 15.54; Isa 25.8.

and as a dead who raised up the dead by his Word:
The guards were placed at the tomb of the One who
summons all at his nod.[65]

These lines abound in *homoioteleuta*, scattered throughout the text. *"Rhēmati"* and *"neumati"* are the final sounds of adjacent lines, and *"theos"* and *"laos"* are also consonant endings that are two lines apart. *"Thnēton tous thnētous"* and *"nekron tous nekrous"* (a double *homoioteleuton*) are placed in the middle of neighboring lines. Moreover, *"athanatēsanta—anastēsanta,"* and *"rhēmati—neumati"* are so artfully constructed. It seems as if one *homoioteleuton* takes hold of, or clings to, the other, forming a chain.

Sometimes *homoioteleuta* do not differ at all from modern rhyme:

Ainos soi, hymnos soi, hagie tafe,
mikre kai megiste, ptōkhe kai plousie,
zōēs tameion, eirēnēs dokheion,
kharas sēmeion, Khristou mnēmeion.

Praise to you, a hymn to you, Holy Tomb,
small, yet very great, poor, yet rich,
treasury of life, vessel of peace,
sign of joy, grave of Christ.[66]

Kontakia 40 and 41, from which these examples are taken, belong to the *Anastasima* group, dedicated to the resurrection of Christ. Kontakia 42 to 45 are also dedicated to the resurrection, and the theme of the descent is also extensively developed in them. The resurrection of Christ has been the subject of liturgical worship since the earliest Christian decades; indeed, the liturgical calendar initially developed around celebrations connected with this very feast. Sermons, encomia, and hymns dedicated to the resurrection were already composed in the second century. The liturgical poem of St Melito of Sardis, *"Peri Pascha,"* provides evidence for the existence of other similar compositions in this vein.

---

[65]*Kontakion* 41, Introduction (SC 128, 430–432).
[66]*Kontakion* 40, 17 (SC 128, 408).

Turning again to Kontakia 42 to 45, we note in number 42 that Hades himself articulates the descent. The hymn refers to the harrowing and destruction of Hades and Christ's release of all therein:

> Your path into Hades, O my Savior,
> no one has fathomed clearly, except for Hades himself,
> for by what he had seen and endured
> he could perceive your power. . . .
> So, tell me first, Hades, eternal enemy of my race,
> how could you hold in the tomb the one who loved my
>   race?
> Who did you take him for? . . .

> "Do you desire to learn from me, O man,
> how my murderer descended against me?
> I have been annihilated, and I do not have the strength
> to tell you, for I am still dumbfounded. . . .
> And the hands which I had previously bound, he places
> around my throat,
> and all the people I had swallowed
> I disgorge as they cry:
> *'The Lord is risen!'*"

> "Why do I mourn for the dead of whom I am despoiled?
> I mourn for myself and the way I am mocked. . . .
> For gluttonous and omnivorous they call me, those who
>   have escaped me.
> And with such words they irritate me, saying:
> 'Why do you open up your large gullet?
> Why do you thrust in your mouth any old thing in any old
>   way?'
> O greedy and insatiable one
> why do you rush for food, causing distress to your stomach?
> For, lo, having emptied you,
> *the Lord is risen!*

> ". . . No one had ever imagined or accomplished against me
>   what he did

I ruled over the kings and was in control of prophets
and of those who cry out:
'*The Lord is risen!*'"

"And now, once a master, I became captive,
once a ruler, I turned into a slave . . .
I am entirely naked for he has taken from me all my
    possessions;
he commanded, and suddenly all surrounded him
as bees a honeycomb.
And then having bound me tightly, he told them to mock
    me,
and to strike my head and to bend my back,[67]
and crush my unyielding heart, exclaiming:
'*The Lord is risen!*'"

"It was night when I endured these things,
but by dawn I saw a different sight,
as the fiery assemblies rushed in to greet him,
while fears from without and battles within held me,[68]
I dared not to look one way or the other, since all threatened
    me,
And so, hiding my face between my knees,
I cried out, tearfully:
'You, who have crushed my gates and
shattered my bars, move on, since I cry out:
"*The Lord is risen!*"'"

He, smiling at these words, said to those behind him:
"Follow me"
to those in front he said: "Precede me, since it is
for this that you have come."
Suddenly, silence and fear prevailed over the whole creation.
For the Lord of Creation came forth from the tomb,

---

[67]A play on words. In Greek, the idiom "to bend somebody's back" means to put
somebody in distress.

[68]2 Cor 7.5.

and in front of him were all the prophets, repeating what
    they had prophesied,
and making known to all that "This is the One,
who voluntarily came down to earth,
and of his will departs from it."
The Lord is risen!

". . . These things Hades said to me as he answered me;
and he did not persuade me by words;
But he was revealed by facts, demonstrating
how naked and destitute he was."
The Lord is risen!

You are without beginning and without end,
Creator and Lord of Truth,
You have caused Death to die, and made man immortal,
in the last hour, when you come to resurrect me,
have mercy on me, my Savior. . . .
And do not then condemn me . . . so that I may say:
"Not for my punishment but for my redemption
the Lord is risen!"[69]

The genesis of the main ideas in this text can be easily pinpointed.
Its source, "The Gospel of Nicodemus," was already used by Ephrem
in developing his "Nisibene Hymns." Common to both Ephrem and
Romanos is the notion that Hades seizes everyone "without discern-
ment,"[70] "any old thing in any old way." Neither Ephrem nor
Romanos restricts those led out of Hades to the Old Testament
prophets and righteous. In their view Christ liberated all from Hades
despite the fact that Romanos places the prophets in front of Christ
in this procession while the others follow behind. Who remains in
Hades after Christ's departure from the nether world? According to
Ephrem these are the evil spirits, demons, Satan, and Death.[71]
Romanos is not so specific, though it would appear that he proceeds

---

[69] *Kontakion* 42, 1–6; 8–10; 12; 23 (SC 128, 460–482).

[70] *De Domino nostro* (as quoted above).

[71] *Carmina Nisibena* (as quoted above).

from the same assumption. Both authors assert that Sheol is left naked and destitute, having been despoiled by Christ. Christ was mistaken for a mere mortal but turned out to be God and destroyed Sheol from within.

In Kontakion 43 (where there is a segment thematically akin to Kontakia 38 and 42 and with individual lines almost identical to some in Kontakion 45)[72] the same themes are developed in the form of a dialogue between the serpent (the devil) and Death. As to its content, the dialogue is reminiscent of similar exchanges in Ephrem's *Nisibene Hymns*. Specifically, Ephrem elaborates on a conversation between the "two defeated," who came to realize that they did not perceive the Incarnate God behind the facade of a human who eventually destroyed their realm:

> When you illumined the whole world by your resurrection
> and arose in your own power,
> you who brought life to all by your divinity.
> Then the beginner of evil, the Serpent, lamented to Death,
>   crying:
> "Now we are defeated, for seizing one, we are deprived of
>   many
> I took him to be merely a man (*anthrōpon psilon*)[73]
> and, wretched, knew I not that he concealed his eternal
>   nature,
> to vanquish me by the same he had been subjected to by
>   me. . . ."[74]

> "It is because of you that I submit to all these things,
> for you have become the cause of our defeat,"
> said Death to the wily Serpent:
> "Because of you I have lost my kingdom.

---

[72]See the remarks by J. Grosdidier de Matons (SC 128, 488), who does not see sufficient grounds for doubting the authenticity of this work.

[73]It is interesting to note that an opponent of Theodore of Mopsuestia, Paul of Samosata (Bishop of Antioch 260–268), also taught that Christ was a *psilos anthrōpos*. Here this passage might have polemical undertones.

[74]I.e., death.

From the very beginning I told you: 'Do not bring Christ to
    me,'
for I knew about the power resting in him
because of the daughter of Jairus, whom he has
snatched from me by his voice alone,
and because of Lazarus, who had been set free from my
    bonds. . . . "
"But it is to me that the Son of Mary has done more violent
    things,"
said the Enemy to Hades. . . .
"For I thought that if I bring him to death,
I would hold prisoners those whom I formerly flogged;
and, wretched, I did not know that he would end my power,
he who has destroyed the weapons of Belial,
the victory of Hades and the sting of Death. . . ."

Hades answered the wily one: "Let us both weep bitterly,
since in his descent he has attacked my stomach,
so that I vomit forth those whom I formerly devoured.
But now lament with me for we have been stripped of our
    glory.
For Adam has been set free from my former chains,
and the prophet cries out: 'Where is your victory, O Hades?'
Eve, too, rejoices for she was saved by
him, who has destroyed the weapons of Belial,
the victory of Hades and the sting of Death. . . ."

Continuing his words, Hades cried out in fear:
"Death, come here, let us see, how the light is shining in
    darkness,
and has illumined all our kingdom below,[75]
and it has raised up the descendants of Adam from the
    graves. . . . "
Saying this, then the evil Hades runs

---

[75]Cf. Isa 9.2 and *Acta Pilati* 22, Latin version (ed. A Tischendorf), p. 378 ("tam
tanti luminis claritatem, dum Christum repente in suis sedibus viderunt").

and tries to seize him from his suffering flesh.
For he seemed mere man, but he is God and Word
he who has destroyed the weapons of Belial,
the victory of Hades and the sting of Death.[76]

The final ten strophes of Kontakion 43, which highly resemble the corresponding strophes in Kontakia 38 and 45, were possibly added to the main body of the text at a later date. The following passage dwells on how Christ, having descended into Hades, bound the hands of Hades, who acknowledges his defeat:

Then Jesus Christ rose as if from a sleep,
he violently bound the hands of Hades,
crying to those in Hades, "Rise up, and mock Hades, crying
    out to him,
And saying 'Where is your victory?'
As for him, I shall hand him over to chains in Tartarus. . . ."

To the rest Hades responded, crying out,
Like a master, immediately commanding to his attendants,
    saying to them:
"Now seeing me suffer unjustly
run now, as you have power, and shut the bronze gates
for the Son of Mary wishes to pass sentence upon me,
he who has destroyed the weapons of Belial,
the victory of Hades, and the sting of Death."

Having said this, Hades the deceiver,
immediately answered the Savior and cried to him:
"All men were subject to me, I was master of the race of
    Adam,
tell me now, who are you, O man?
How have you arrived here?
For it is clear that you are a man,
and I see you have a human body,
and everyone from the race of men is my possession.

---

[76]*Kontakion* 43, 25–27 (SC 128, 530–534).

How then do you subject me to violence,
having come for the sake of all?
But you are the Resurrection and the Life of the dead,
he who has destroyed the weapons of Belial,
the victory of Hades, and the sting of Death."[77]

In Kontakion 44 the same theme is developed in a dialogue between Adam and Hades. Adam, waiting for the coming of the Savior, informs Hades of his imminent delivery from captivity. Hades replies that all mortals are in his power and none can resist him. Adam responds that he has recruited himself into the host of Christ, who will triumph over Hades and take him to supernal heights. Eventually Christ himself descends into Hades "to deceive Death" (here one may recall Gregory of Nyssa's teaching on the "divine deception"). Following is the complete narrative in the *kontakion*:

"By your passion, our Savior, we are set free from passions"
Adam cried out to you, and Hades was astounded
because of *your resurrection.*

As the earth gladly accepts the rain from heaven,
so Adam, who was held captive in Hades, awaited
the Savior of the world and Giver of Life,
and said to Hades: "Why are you conceited?
Wait, wait a short time, and you will soon see
your power destroyed and mine exalted;
now you hold in bondage me and my race,
after a while you will see that I am freed from you,
for Christ will come for me, and you will tremble;
and he will bring to an end your tyranny
through *the resurrection.*"

"No one has ever possessed such abundance of power of this
       sort;
for I am master of all," said Hades to Adam.
"For what other person will control me and rise superior to me?

[77] *Kontakion* 43, 17–24 (SC 128, 521–530)

Who will take my kingdom from me?
Abraham and Isaac and Jacob and Joseph
and all the prophets I hold in my power,
and you I possessed first as the firstborn among them all.
How, then, can you say that someone will come and trample
  on me?
Would this person, then, be superior to all these others,
so that he will deliver you, as you say,
through *the resurrection?*"

Adam heard Hades boasting in this way,
and at once, the first created of mortals said to him:
"Hear my words, and do not in vain exalt yourself,
for I whom you possess you cannot dominate;
I was thrown out from the joy of paradise because of you, O
Treacherous One, and I was sent down to you a short time
  ago;
you are my guard; but you do not have the power to destroy
  me,
for I have a King who will destroy your domain,
to him, the Helper of humankind, I have volunteered to be
  a recruit in his host,
so that he may raise me to supernal heights
through *the resurrection.*"

"No one is going to defend you and tear up your sentence,
The One whom you call your Helper, I rule over as King.
I shall seize him as I do all men,
for there is no one anywhere greater than I am.
Do not delude yourself, Adam! Why do you exhaust
  yourself in vain?
I hold you in the tomb, and I rule over your race.
The One whom you think you have as protector
you will now see crucified and swallowed up by me.
How, then, can you say that he will free you from me?
I have been given orders to hold your race in my power
because of *the resurrection.*"

"Just as he will be made a second Adam, and be my Savior
        because of me,
he would not for my sake beg off from wounds.
He will undergo my punishment for me,
since like me he wears flesh.
They will pierce the side of him whom the Cherubim do
        not behold,
and water will gush forth and quench my burning heat.
You think that you will hold him as man;
you will devour him as a mortal; but you will disgorge him
        as God
after three days; for you will not be able to endure
the torment which he will inflict upon you
through *the resurrection*."

Let us learn, brothers, what the Lord does!
For when he had tasted the vinegar and gall on the cross,
he said: "This is the end of my sufferings,"
and bowing his head, he gave up his spirit.
The sun and moon and stars of heaven
were not able to endure this gross insult and hid their
        brilliance.
Little hills and mountains took thought of flight,
and even the veil of the temple was torn in twain.
But the first-created man cried out from the abyss,
"O my God, deliver me from Hades
through *the resurrection*."

But Christ, the Life itself, came to deceive Death;
Hades received Christ like each of the earth-born.
He devoured the heavenly bread like bait,
he was wounded by the hook of divinity.
And Hades, lamenting, cried out:
"I am pierced in the stomach; I do not digest the One
        whom I devoured;
what I have devoured became a strange food to me!
No one of those whom I have eaten before has troubled me.

Perhaps he is the One whom Adam had announced to me
saying, 'When he comes, he will chastise you
through *the resurrection.*'"

"Now you will recall my words, which I said to you a long
     time ago,
'My King is stronger than you.'
But you considered these words a fantasy.
Experience will teach you his force.
For not only myself but also my descendants
and all men will you lose; you will be deprived of all.
The Christ whom you saw hanging on the tree,
he himself will enchain you, and joyfully I shall reply:
'Where, O Hades, is your victory, and where is your power?'
God has destroyed your strength
through *the resurrection!*"

"Just as, on the third day, the whale disgorged Jonas.
Now I disgorge Christ and all of those who are Christ's;
because of the race of Adam I am being chastised."
Uttering these laments, Hades cried out with groans.
"I did not believe Adam when he told me these things in
     advance;
but I boasted and loudly proclaimed: 'No one will prevail
     over me.'
For formerly I was king of all;
But now I have lost all men, and taunting me, they say:
'Where, O Death is your victory, or where is your power?'
God has destroyed your strength
through *the resurrection!*"

"In his coming, Christ has humbled your proud strength;
in assuming my whole natural form, he has put you to
     flight.
I am now bought by his precious blood.
He who knows no corruption has freed me from corruption.
Wherever you may turn, you see on all sides

tombs which are emptied, and you, yourself naked and ugly.
Where are your bolts and bars, strong one?
My Jesus has come down and shattered all your possessions.
Where, O Death is your victory, or where is your power?
God has destroyed your strength
through *the resurrection!*"

"He has lifted me to the heavens; you he has put to flight;
for the rest of time I share the throne, I am no longer
subject to you.
He assumed my body that he might make it new;
he will make it immortal and cause it to share his throne.
I shall reign with him, for I have been resurrected with him.
You no longer possess me, but I rule over you.
My pledge of surety is now on high,
but you are trampled on below by those who cry,
'Where, O Death, is your victory, or where is your power?'
God has destroyed your strength
through *the resurrection!*"[78]

Of all Sunday *kontakia,* the most profound in theological content
is Kontakion 45, "On the Ten Drachmas," rightly belonging among
the acknowledged masterpieces of world literature.[79] It begins with a
proclamation of Christ's triumph over Hades and Death:

Those who buried themselves with Christ by baptism into
death
and risen with him, sing praises and cry out, saying:
"Where is your victory, O Death? Hades, where is your
sting?
For the Lord is risen, the *Life and Resurrection.*"[80]

This *kontakion* contains a commentary on the parable of the lost

---

[78]*Kontakion* 44, 7 (SC 128, 558)
[79]*Oxford Dictionary of the Christian Church,* ed. F. L. Cross, 3rd edition by E. A.
Livingstone (Oxford, 1997), p. 1411.
[80]*Kontakion* 45, Introduction (SC 128, 576).

drachma (Luke 15.8). The nine drachmas symbolize the nine angelic orders and the lost drachma denotes humanity. This interpretation, as J. Grosdidier de Matons[81] points out, is also to be found in the homily "On the Gospel of Luke on the Drachma and on [the words], 'A Certain Man Had Two Sons,'" ascribed to St John Chrysostom.[82] Romanos may have borrowed this motif from this homily, but it is also possible that both Romanos and a pseudo-Chrysostom derived their ideas from a common source.

Developing this theme, Romanos goes on to say that in order to find "the creation which has gone astray" the Son of God came down to earth, became incarnate, "ascended to the cross, as a lamp in a lampstand,[83] and from there saw ancient Adam, sitting in darkness and gloom." After his death Christ descends into Hades. His divinity remains united with his humanity; his light illumines and fills up the nether world. Hades tries to keep the body of Christ in its hold but Christ, "as though arising from sleep, enchains Hades violently and puts him down." Addressing himself to those in Hades, Christ says:

> "Rise up, all, and trample down Hades!
> Adam, come to me with Eve now. Do not be afraid,
> liable for past debts, I have paid them all, I,
> *the Life and Resurrection.*"
> "You mortals, strike the face of Hades,
> mock him, and trample on his neck;
> come to them, exclaiming: 'Hades and Death are swallowed
>   up!'
> For your sake I have come, for I am the Life and
>   Resurrection of all,
> now, joyfully sing psalms and songs:
> Where is your victory, O dishonored Hades,
> Where is your sting, O Death?
> You lie exhausted, O Death, you are dead!

---

[81]SC 128, 572–573.
[82]PG 61:781–784.
[83]Matt 5.15; Luke 8.16; 9.33.

And you, O Hades, are skillfully bound down,
once masters, you became slaves, seeing that he has arrived
the Life and Resurrection!"[84]

Again, as in the other *kontakia,* Hades tries to resist Christ and, as a master, commands his attendants: "Run, close the bronze gates and guard them, put up the iron bars on the gates and permit none of those resurrected by him to come forth from the tomb" (this theme is reminiscent of "The Gospel of Nicodemus"). A dispute erupts between Hades and Christ. The former, astonished by the fact that Christ, being a man, performs the deeds of God, decides to put him to the test. "Every descendant of Adam is my property," he says. "Why, then, do you do violence unto me? . . . Every human being is subject to me. . . . How then have you become more than human and a redeemer of men?" Christ replies that as God he is not subject to judgment, but as a human being (literally, "Adam") he is ready to plead his case with Hades and win. Hades has power only over those who are subject to sin, but Christ is faultless.[85] Therefore Hades should justify him and give him back those on whose behalf he came:

"I shall conquer you and overthrow you
from the power which you possess. . . .
I am the Creator of all things, I am the life which really
    exists
and you, O Hades, did not exist in the very beginning,
nor O Death had you any substance,
you both are the fruit of passion, of the dreadful sin. . . ."

"But everyone born of Adam, born in sin, was liable to me.
He was born of corruption, and of union with husband, and
    intercourse,
but I am free from all this, from sin and from intercourse,
for even if I became man out of my will,
a virginal womb brought me forth blameless,

---

[84] *Kontakion* 45, 6–7 (SC 128, 584).
[85] *Kontakion* 45, 8–11 (SC 128, 586–590).

and gave my blood to the one who engendered me for the
sake of all men,
the Life and Resurrection."

"Examine me and see for yourself
that you will not find any unjust word or deed. . . .
If you find in me any remnant of sin,
then bring an indictment against me, O Unjust One,
and if you will find nothing, then give back immediately
the record you keep . . . and make yourself ready
to give back those whom you seized in advance,
those whom I have raised up, I,
the Life and Resurrection."[86]

In this poem Romanos rephrases a traditional teaching of the
Eastern church fathers, namely that Hades and Death have no independent substance for they were not created by God. According to
Anastasios of Sinai (seventh century), Hades and Death have no
hypostasis, being, or essence.[87] Another anonymous seventh-century
writer says that what is "unhypostatic is all that does not originate
from God. It exists because of the absence of better things, and
includes darkness, illness, sin, and death."[88] For St Isaac the Syrian
(seventh century), Death and Hades were engendered by sin, and as
such are subject to annihilation. "Sin, Gehenna, and Death do not
exist at all with God, for they are effects, not substances. . . . There
was a time when sin did not exist, and there will be a time when it
will not exist. Gehenna is the fruit of sin. At some point in time it had
a beginning, but its end is not known."[89]

Kontakion 45 contains yet another important thought, namely,
that Christ's victory was relevant not only for the generations of men
in Hades but also for subsequent generations:

---

[86] *Kontakion* 45, 11–14 (SC 128, 590–592).

[87] *Hodegos* 2 (PG 89:61b).

[88] See *Doctrina Patrum de Incarnatione Verbi*, hrsg. F. Diekamp (Münster, 1909),
p. 253.

[89] Mar Isaacus Ninevita, *De perfectione religiosa*, quam edidit Paulus Bedjan
(Leipzig, 1909), p. 189.

"Not only will you give back
those whom you have taken and whom I have resurrected
and now take with me, as I leave here,
but also those who in the future will be sent to you will
arise . . ."[90]

Romanos continues, "Hades, hearing these words, shuddered. The doorkeepers threw down their keys and ran off. Seeing that Christ had crushed and destroyed Hades' bars, the bodies of the dead became animated as 'suddenly, all of the tombs were opened of themselves and all the dead were released therefrom and rejoiced.'"[91] Christ redeemed all those in hell at the moment of his descent, and the victory was valid also for future generations—the general resurrection awaits all: "Christ opened every tomb and set free all the dead,"[92] and because of this, he is the Savior and Redeemer of all humanity.

Having summed up the works of Romanos the Melodist, we may now point out the particular function of Christ's descent into Hades. The following motifs are fully developed and widely represented in his writings: first, Christ's descent into Hades was voluntary; second, Christ was a victor in Hades, liberating and redeeming the dead; third, Christ descended into Hades as God, but Hades mistook him for a mere mortal, having swallowed the "bait" of his humanity (motif of divine deception); fourth, Christ despoiled and trampled down Hades and triumphed over Satan and Death (motif of victory); fifth, Christ removed from Hades all who were held therein; and sixth, Christ's victory over Hades applies to all subsequent generations.

---

[90] *Kontakion* 45, 15 (SC 128, 594).
[91] *Kontakion* 45, 17 (SC 128, 596).
[92] *Kontakion* 45, 19 (SC 128, 598).

CHAPTER FOUR

Liturgical Texts of the Orthodox Church

T he teaching on Christ's descent into Hades was an integral part of the Christian liturgical tradition from the early centuries. The descent was referred to both explicitly and implicitly in ancient baptismal rites, in the eucharistic prayers, in the prayers and hymns of the paschal cycle, in the monastic offices of the ninth and twelfth hours, as well as in Sunday and festal hymns of the ancient church.[1] This theme continues to play a central role in the Church today. Christ's descent into Hades is mentioned more than fifty times in the services of Good Friday and Great Saturday, more than two hundred times during the Pentecost period, and more than one hundred and fifty times in the Sunday and festal hymns throughout the church year.[2]

The corpus of texts that compose the liturgical books of the Orthodox Church was formed during the seventh through ninth centuries, although some texts belong to earlier or later periods. Some bear the names of great Byzantine hymnographers: Sts Romanos the Melodist (sixth century), Sophronius of Jerusalem (seventh century), Andrew of Crete (seventh and eighth centuries), John of Damascus (eighth century), Kosmas of Maiouma (eighth century), Theodore the Studite (eighth and ninth centuries), Joseph the Studite (eighth and ninth centuries), Theophanes Graptos (ninth century), and

---

[1]For a detailed treatment of the theme of the descent in the liturgical practices, see: R. Gounelle, *La descente du Christ aux Enfers*, pp. 149–249.

[2]Cf. N. Vasiliadis, *Tainstvo smerti* (Holy Trinity-St Sergius Lavra, 1998), pp. 166–167.

Joseph the Hymnographer (eleventh century).[3] As with many other hymnographers whose works entered the service books but whose names remain unknown to us, these authors were not just "professional" poets and hymnographers but also outstanding theologians who succeeded at expressing the riches of the Orthodox Church's dogmatic teaching in poetic forms.

A good number of liturgical texts bearing the names of the abovementioned authors are actually not their works. Modern scholarship has almost no critical editions of liturgical texts at its disposal, making it extremely difficult to confirm the authorships. Many studies examining this problem explain this situation only in a general manner.[4] In numerous cases not only do we not know the names of the authors, but we have very little idea of the time of their writing, making it impossible to examine them from within their historical context.

All this, while making research on liturgical texts difficult, does not constitute a barrier to their exploration from the theological point of view. Being the product of many authors, liturgical books, like the Bible, compose a coherent, theological unit. Liturgical texts contain harmonious, well-developed theological systems and serve as indisputable doctrinal authorities for Orthodox Christians.

---

[3]Cf. Archimandrite Kallistos Ware, "The Meaning of the Great Fast," in *The Lenten Triodion* (London, 1977). pp. 40–43.

[4]In Russian liturgical scholarship there are many studies on the origins of the liturgical cycle, various liturgical books and hymns. Among these studies are: M. Skaballanovich, *Tolkoviy Typikon*, vols. I–II (Kiev, 1913); I. Mansvetov, *Tserkovniy ustav* (Moscow, 1885); A. Dmitrievsky, *Opisanie slavyanskikh rukopisey v bibliotekakh pravoslavnogo Vostoka*, vols. I–III (Kiev–St Petersburg, 1895–1917); Idem, *Bogosluzheniye strastnoy i paskhalnoy sedmits vo sv. Ierusalime IX–X v.* (Kazan, 1894); I. Karabinov, *Postnaya Triod'* (St Petersburg, 1910); N. Uspensky, "Chin vsenoshchnogo bdeniya na pravoslavnom Vostoke i v Russkoy Tserkvi," *Bogoslovskiye Trudy* 18 (Moscow, 1978), pp. 5–117. Valuable observations on the authorship and time of writing of various liturgical texts can be found in these and other works of these authors. Among modern western studies we should mention: J. Mateos, *Un horologion inédit de S.Sabas: Mélanges E. Tisserant* III, Studi e testi 233 (Vatican, 1964), pp. 47–76; Idem, *Le typicon de la Grande Eglise* (Ms. Saint-Croix No. 40, Xe siècle), t. 1–2, OrChrAn 165–166 (Rome, 1962–1963); M. Arranz, *Le Typicon du Monastère du Saint Sauveur à Messine*, OrChrAn 185 (Rome, 1969); R. Taft, *The Liturgy of the Hours in East and West* (Collegeville, Minn., 1986).

THE OCTOECHOS

The *octoechos* ("Book of the Eight Tones"), or *paraklitike*, contains liturgical texts for every day of the week beginning with Sunday.[5] This book is divided into eight parts according to the eight "tones" used in the services. Each tone has its own variations of liturgical texts, and the *octoechos* is read or sung in church in its entirety over the course of eight weeks. The Orthodox Church traditionally regards St John of Damascus as the compiler of the *octoechos*, although in reality he is the author of only some of its hymns, among which are several Sunday canons. Some other authors of the *octoechos* are St Romanos the Melodist,[6] St Theodore the Studite,[7] Metropolitan Metrophanes of Smyrna, Metropolitan Theophanes of Nicea, and St Theophanes Graptos, all of whom lived in the ninth century. Certain hymns are ascribed to the Emperors Leo VI the Wise (AD 886–912) and Constantine Porphyrogenetes (AD 913–959).

This study will examine texts from vespers (the *stichera* sung at "Lord, I have cried," those at the *litiya*, *aposticha*, and *troparia*), matins (sessional hymns, *hypakoe*, canons, *kontakia*, *oikoi*, and the verses at the lauds), compline (canons), and the liturgy (verses on the Beatitudes).[8] Among the hymnographic genres found in the *octoechos* the most ancient are the *troparion*, some of which go back to the fourth century; the *kontakion* and *oikos*, from the fifth through eighth centuries;

---

[5]According to a custom dating from the early years of Christianity, the counting of the days of the week begins with Sunday, and the days themselves, in accordance with the Old Testament division of time inherited by the Christian church, are counted beginning with the evening. Thus the first service of the week is vespers on Saturday, which actually belongs to Sunday.

[6]Some *kontakia* and *oikoi* in the *octoechos* are actually fragments of *kontakia* written by St Romanos the Melodist.

[7]The Sunday "antiphons of the degrees" are also attributed to him.

[8]In quoting texts from the *octoechos*, we shall abbreviate the day of the week and the number of the tone (e.g., "Tu.1," indicates "Tuesday, first tone"), the name of the service (Mat. = Matins; Ves. = Vespers; Gt. Ves. = Great Vespers; Lit. = Liturgy), and the name of the species of hymn (Can. = Canon; StichLC = Stichera at "Lord, I have cried"; StichLit. = Stichera at the litiya; StichAp. = Stichera at the aposticha; Lau. = Stichera at lauds, Beat. = Verses at the Beatitudes, etc.). We also indicate the number of the ode of the canons (e.g., "O.5" = fifth ode).

and the canons and *stichera*, which are of later origin, written in the seventh through ninth centuries.[9]

The theme of Christ's descent into Hades and his victory over hell and death is thoroughly developed in the Sunday services of the *octoechos*. Other services of importance are those used on Tuesdays, when St John the Forerunner is commemorated; Wednesdays and Fridays, when Christ's sufferings and death on the cross are remembered; and Saturdays, when the church commemorates the departed.

The *octoechos* often refers to how Christ's preaching in hell was preceded by St John the Baptist's, who also taught there:

> To the dead, blessed Forerunner, you preached the coming of our life.[10]

> The dead were brought the good news that the Light from Light had shone on earth by your Light . . .[11]

> To those in hell you foretold by the Divine Spirit the Life that was near at hand, by your entreaties, O Prophet, give life to my deadened soul . . .[12]

> You brought to the dead the good tidings of the coming of the One who was put to death for us . . .[13]

This theme, a part of Orthodox tradition from the first centuries of Christianity, is also developed in the service of the beheading of John found in the "Festal Menaion," a liturgical book containing various festal services.[14] According to the church's teaching, John the

---

[9]For more details cf.: E. Wellesz, *A History of Byzantine Music and Hymnography*, as well as: Archimandrite Kallistos Ware, "The Meaning of the Great Fast," pp. 13–68.

[10]Tu.1. Mat. Can. O.1. I.e., he preached about Christ, who was to come to those in hell (EL). Here and below, translations from liturgical sources belong to Archimandrite Ephrem Lash (EL), or to the Holy Trinity Monastery, Jordanville (J), or to Deacon Basil Bush (BB). In some instances Fr Ephrem's or the Holy Trinity Monastery's translations have been edited by Deacon Basil Bush (EL-BB or J-BB).

[11]Tu.1. Mat. Can. O.5 (EL-BB).

[12]Tu.3. Mat. Can. O.1 (EL-BB).

[13]Tu.5. Mat. Can. O.4 (EL).

[14]"For he preceded the Life in hell, to preach to those sitting in darkness and

Baptist is the last of the prophets and the first of the apostles. He stands "between the Law and Grace,"[15] on the border between the Old and New Testaments, foretelling the advent of the Savior. John also became an "honorable martyr of the Lord,"[16] leading the host of Christian martyrs. The beheading of John, which occurred not long before the death and resurrection of Christ, was a result of the divine plan for the salvation of mankind: John died so that he could "ready the way of the Lord and make his paths straight,"[17] not only on earth but also in Hades.

It could be argued that the very theme of Christ's descent into Hades is one of the main ideas of the *octoechos*, inseparably linked to the events of Christ's death and resurrection. Christ's victory over hell, death, and the devil; his vanquishing the devil's power; and his deliverance of people from death and Hades are subjects that run through the *octoechos* like a leitmotif. Below are some of the most significant of these texts:

> When you announced the glad tidings of peace by your Cross and proclaimed deliverance for captives, my Saviour, then, O Christ, you put to shame him who held them all in thrall and showed him naked and destitute by your Divine Rising.[18]

> O Christ, you destroyed the misery and wretchedness within the gates and strongholds of hell.[19]

---

the shadow of death the Orient from on high, Christ our God" (StichLC); "The honorable head is cut off, and he preaches the resurrection from the dead to those in hell" (StichLit.); "He who outran your birth and divine passion came through a sword to the lowest parts of the earth as Prophet and messenger of your entrance there" (Can. O.8); "You who preached Christ's coming to those in hell . . ." (Can. O.8); "You were sent to the souls in hell to preach him who was about to come and save all the faithful who passed away after Adam" (Can. O.9); "Christ's herald is sent even to those in Hades" (Lau.) (all BB).

[15]Tu.7. Mat. Can. O.3 (BB).

[16]Service of the Beheading. Can. O.9 (BB).

[17]Mark 1.3. Cf. kontakion of the service of the Beheading: "The glorious beheading of the Forerunner became a divine dispensation, that he might proclaim to those in hell the coming of the Saviour" (EL).

[18]Sun.1. Mat. Can. O.5 (EL-BB).

[19]Sun.1. Mat. Can. O.8 (EL).

Our horrible death has been slain by your resurrection from the dead, for you appeared to those in hell, O Christ, and granted them life.[20]

When you were nailed to the Cross, the might of the enemy was put to death . . . hell was taken captive by your might, you raised the dead from the graves and opened Paradise to the thief.[21]

The gates of death opened to you, O Lord, in fear; Hades' gate-keepers shuddered when they saw you, for you have destroyed the gates of brass and crushed to powder the iron bars . . .[22]

When you descended unto death, O Life Immortal, you slew Hades by the lightning of your divinity.[23]

Most blessed are you, O Virgin Theotokos, for through him who became incarnate of you is Hades taken captive, Adam recalled, the curse annulled, Eve set free, death slain, and we are given life . . .[24]

Hell was emptied and made helpless by the death of one man.[25]

By your Cross, Christ Saviour, death's might has been abolished and the devil's deception destroyed . . .[26]

The Redeemer has emptied the tombs and taken hell captive . . .[27]

In your mercy you entered the tomb for our sakes, O Master, and emptied the tombs as God.[28]

. . . by descending into Hades, O Powerful one, you tore apart the bonds of death as God . . .[29]

---

[20]Sun.1. Mat. Can. O.9 (BB).

[21]Sun.1. Mat. Lau. (BB).

[22]Sat.2. Ves. StichLC (EL-BB).

[23]Sat.2. Ves. Troparion (BB).

[24]Sun.2. Mat. Sessional Hymn (J-BB). In the contemporary Greek *octoechos* the words "Adam is recalled, the curse is annulled, Eve is set free" are absent. The Slavonic *octoechos* follows a more ancient reading.

[25]Sun.2. Mat. Can. O.6 (BB).

[26]Sat.3. Gt. Ves. StichLC (EL-BB).

[27]Sun.3. Mat. Lau. (BB).

[28]Sat.3. Mat. Can. O.4 (BB).

[29]Sat.4. Gt. Ves. StichLC (EL).

... the alien was bound, death terribly despoiled, and all those in hell cried aloud at your Life-bearing Rising: Christ, the giver of life, has risen and abides to the ages.[30]

who rose from the dead and emptied hell, wealthy before with many people . . .[31]

You laid waste the mighty strongholds of the enemy and plundered his wealth with your all-powerful hand, raising me with you from the vaults of hell, O Christ . . .[32]

... by your death you have destroyed the devil who tyrannized over our nature, by your Rising you have filled all things with joy . . .[33]

By your life-bearing death you slew the death bringer, Christ God . . .[34]

You rose from the tomb on the third day, despoiled hell and enlightened the world; with one mind we the faithful magnify you.[35]

Lord, having smashed the eternal bars and burst the bonds asunder, you rose from the tomb . . .[36]

... In hell you trampled on death . . .[37]

You despoiled hell and emerged unscathed . . .[38]

Jonah foretells your tomb . . . for you descended as a corpse into the tomb and destroyed the gates of hell . . .[39]

---

[30]Sun.4. Mat. Sessional Hymn (EL).
[31]Sun.4. Mat. Can. O.7 (EL).
[32]Sun.4. Mat. Can. O.9 (EL-BB).
[33]Sun.4. Mat. Lau. (EL).
[34]Sat. 4. Mat. Can. O.1 (EL).
[35]Sun.5. Mat. Can. O.9 (EL).
[36]Sun.5. Mat. Lau. (EL-BB).
[37]Sun.6. Gt. Ves. StichLC (BB).
[38]Sun.6. Gt. Ves. Troparion (EL).
[39]Sun.6. Mat. Sessional Hymn (EL).

The tyranny of hell has ended, and its reign has finally been abolished. For the God of all was raised on the Cross and defeated its might . . .[40]

Let creation rejoice and blossom like a lily, for Christ, as God, is risen from the dead. Let us cry out: "Death, where is your sting now? Hell, where is your victory? He who in his mercy exalted our horn has defeated you."[41]

Come, let us rejoice in the Lord, who has smashed the might of death and enlightened the human race . . .[42]

For our sakes you endured the Cross and burial, O Saviour, but as God you slew death by death . . .[43]

Hades drew near you, and having no strength to crush your body with its teeth, it broke its jaws . . .[44]

What return shall we make to the Lord for all that he has given back to us? For us God came among men; for our corrupted nature the Word became flesh and dwelt among us;[45] the Benefactor to the ungrateful; the Liberator to the prisoners; the Sun of justice to those who sat in darkness; the passionless One to the Cross; the Light to Hades; Life to death; Resurrection for the fallen . . .[46]

. . . By your divinity you bound the strong one and scattered his spoil.[47]

Who now is not amazed, O Master, as they see death destroyed through suffering, corruption taking flight through the Cross, and hell emptied of its wealth through death? [48]

---

[40]Sun.6. Mat. Can. O.8 (BB).
[41]Sun.6. Mat. Can. O.9 (BB). "Exalted our horn," i.e., granted us victory.
[42]Sat.7. Gt. Ves. StichLC (EL).
[43]Sat.7. Gt. Ves. StichLC (BB).
[44]Sun.7. Mat. Can. O.1 (EL-BB).
[45]John 1.14.
[46]Sun.7. Mat. Lau. (EL-BB).
[47]Sun.8. Mat. Can. O.3 (EL).
[48]Sun.8. Mat. Can. O.4 (EL-BB).

Murky darkness has been abolished, for from hell Christ, the Sun of justice, has dawned, enlightening all the ends of the earth.[49]

The Redeemer tasted death, the ancient sentence, that he might abolish the reign of corruption, and when he had descended to those in hell, Christ rose and saved, as he is powerful, those who sing the praise of his Resurrection.[50]

When you entered the gates of hell, Lord, and destroyed them, the prisoner cried out: who is this, for he is not condemned to the lowest parts of the earth, but has torn down death's prison-house like a tent? I received him as a mortal, and I tremble at him as God . . .[51]

In these excerpts from the *octoechos*, metaphors similar to those found in the "Gospel of Nicodemus" are used to describe Christ's victory over hell and death. Christ destroys the "chains," "bars," "seals," "gates," and "stronghold" of hell; breaks the "shackles" with which the dead were bound; and plunders the "treasure chests" of the devil. All of these images, also found in Orthodox iconography, reflect the understanding of hell as a prison that was impossible to escape from until Christ's victory over Hades and his abolition of the devil's power.

The *octoechos*' teaching can be systematized by the following questions: Who benefited from Christ's saving accomplishments? To whom was his preaching in hell addressed? Whom did he resurrect from the dead? Whom did he free from the power of hell, and whom did he lead to paradise? The church fathers answered these questions differently. St Gregory Nazianzen did not answer the question: "Will Christ save all or just the faithful?"[52] St Amphilochius of Iconium believed that *all* those who were in hell followed Christ after his descent and preaching.[53] Theologians of the Alexandrian tradition were inclined to believe that God "redeemed and led *all of us* out of

---

[49]Sun.8. Mat. Can. O.9 (EL-BB).
[50]Sun.8. Mat. Can. O.6 (EL-BB).
[51]Sun.8. Mat. Lau. (EL-BB).
[52]Homily 45, 24.
[53]Homily 6, *Against Heretics.*

hell, or rather, *the entire human race* from death."[54] Clement even numbered pagans among the saved.[55] St Romanos the Melodist and St Ephrem the Syrian maintained that after Christ's descent into Hades "*all tombs* were opened, and *all* the dead came out of them and rejoiced."[56] St Hippolytus of Rome, on the contrary, wrote that Christ preached only to the "*souls of the saints*,"[57] and St Cyril of Jerusalem believed that through Christ "*all the righteous swallowed by death* were redeemed."[58] According to St John Damascene, Christ preached to all of the dead, but for some his preaching led to salvation while for others it only exposed their unbelief."[59]

As in the writings of the Eastern fathers, we find several different answers in the hymns of the *octoechos*. One has Christ leading out (resurrecting, saving) all who awaited his coming (all the pious, righteous, and holy) from hell. This version is found in the *octoechos* quite infrequently (in about five out of one hundred cases):[60]

Having slain hell by your invincible power . . . You liberated *the souls of the pious* from it and its sentence . . .[61]

For the sake of mortals, O Christ, Giver of life, willingly you underwent the Passion; as Powerful you descended into hell, snatching as from the hand of a mighty one *the souls of those who were waiting there for your coming* and, instead of Hades, you granted them to dwell in Paradise . . .[62]

The sun was ashamed at your crucifixion and hid its rays, while the rocks broke apart and hell below was taken by fear. But the souls of the *righteous* rejoiced, O Word, awaiting their final liberation.[63]

---

[54]Paschal Epistle 10, 10.
[55]*Stromateis* 6, 6.
[56]*Kontakion* 45, 17.
[57]*On Christ and the Antichrist* 26.
[58]*Catechetical Homily* 14, 19.
[59]*Exact Exposition of the Orthodox Faith* 3, 28.
[60]Henceforth only approximate figures will be given in order provide a general idea of the frequency of viewpoints in the liturgical texts.
[61]Sat.1. Mat. Can. O.4 (BB).
[62]Sat. 2. Gt. Ves. StichAp. (EL-BB).
[63]Wed.2. Mat. Can. O.8 (BB).

When it received him who is strong by his divinity, pitiful hell . . . spewed out the souls of the *righteous*.[64]

Having destroyed, O Lover of mankind, the temple of your body, you divided the tomb and hell, condemning both of them so that, against their will, the latter had to disgorge the souls of the *Saints*, while the former, O Immortal One, gave up their bodies.[65]

Another response found even more rarely in the *octoechos*, possibly in two or three out of one hundred cases, is that Christ granted salvation to all the "faithful." This does not specify whether it refers to those who believed in God during their lives or to those who came to believe in him as a result of Christ's preaching in hell:

All that is beneath the earth, Hades and death, trembled today before one of the Trinity; the earth quaked, the gate-keepers of hell quailed when they saw you. . . . Let us shout with joy and cry out to Adam and to Adam's race, "The tree has led him once again (into Paradise); come out, *you faithful*, to the Resurrection!"[66]

Today Christ has risen from the tomb, granting *all the faithful* incorruption.[67]

In some cases (also quite rare), the hymnody speaks of the death of Christ for the "unrighteous," of the liberation of "those who sinned voluntarily," and of the resurrection of the "fallen":

You voluntarily endured crucifixion in order to redeem and save those who sinned voluntarily, O Merciful one . . .[68]

For the sake of mortals you die, O Life; for the sake of the unrighteous you, O righteous Jesus, endure a shameful death . . .[69]

---

[64]Sun.3. Mat. Can. O.7 (BB).
[65]Sun.4. Mat. Can. O.5 (BB).
[66]Sun.7. Mat. Oikos (EL-BB).
[67]Sun.8. Lit. Beat. (EL).
[68]Fri.3. Mat. Can. O.4 (BB).
[69]Wed.7. Mat. Can. O.4 (BB).

You destroyed the gates of brass and shattered the bars of hell, and
as almighty God raised the fallen human race.[70]

Each of the texts referred to above speaks of Christ saving one or
another group of the dead, be they the "faithful," "pious," or "those
who sinned" and "the fallen." However, in the *octoechos* the universal
character of Christ's death and resurrection is stressed much more
frequently. Thus we find in it the idea that Christ, while descending
into Hades, enlightened the "peoples":

> We offer you our evening worship, O Light that knows no evening,
> who . . . descended as far as hell, abolished the darkness there and
> showed the nations (*ethnē*) the light of the Resurrection.[71]

In a Christian context, the Greek word used here (*ethnē*) very often
means "pagans." It could be reminiscent of Clement of Alexandria's
belief that Christ's preaching in hell was salutary for the pagans, but
we are inclined to understand *ethnē* in a more general way as a reference to all peoples, the entire human race.

Quite often the *octoechos* speaks of Christ raising "Adam the forefather" and leading him out of hell. Adam is understood not as a con-
crete personality but rather as a symbol of fallen humanity. As such,
his liberation from the chains of hell signifies the renewal of all:

> Being King of heaven and earth, O Incomprehensible One, you were
> crucified willingly through your love for mankind; when Hades met
> you he was embittered, and the souls of the righteous receiving you
> rejoiced, while Adam, seeing you his Creator in the nethermost
> parts, arose . . .[72]

> You rose from the grave in glory as God and raised the world up with
> you; mankind praises you as God, and death disappeared; Adam
> dances, Master, and now Eve, freed from her chains, rejoices . . .[73]

---

[70]Sat.6. Gt. Ves. StichAp. (BB).
[71]Sat.5. Gt. Ves. StichLC (EL).
[72]Sat.1. Gt. Ves. StichAp. (EL-BB).
[73]Sun.1. Mat. Kontakion (EL-BB).

You arose today, O Merciful One, and led us out from the gates of death. Adam dances today and Eve rejoices. The prophets too, along with the Patriarchs, praise without ceasing the divine might of your authority.[74]

Girded with power you ascended the Cross and came to grips with the tyrant, and as God hurled him from on high; but Adam you raised up with your invincible might.[75]

Let us all who are born of earth sing the praise of Christ the giver of life, who rose from the tomb on the third day and by his power today destroyed the gates of death, slew Hades, crushed the sting of death, and set Adam free with Eve . . .[76]

. . . for by his rising from the dead, the world has been saved from error; the choir of Angels rejoices, the error of demons flees, fallen Adam arises, the devil has been overthrown.[77]

You despoiled death and smashed the gates of hell; while Adam, the prisoner, was released and cried out to you: your right hand has saved me, O Lord! [78]

You descended into hell, my Saviour, destroyed its gates as all-powerful, raised the dead with yourself as Creator, annihilated the sting of death, and delivered Adam from the curse . . .[79]

Having been deceived, Adam fell into the depths of hell; but being God and Merciful by nature, you went looking for him, carried him on your shoulders and resurrected him with you.[80]

On the third day you rose from the tomb, O Christ, as it is written, and raised our Forefather with you . . .[81]

---

[74]Sun.3. Mat. Kontakion (EL-BB).
[75]Sun.4. Mat. Can. O.6 (EL-BB).
[76]Sun.4. Mat. Oikos (EL-BB).
[77]Sat.5. Gt. Ves. StichLC (EL).
[78]Sun.5. Mat. Can. O.6 (EL).
[79]Sun.5. Mat. Kontakion (EL-BB).
[80]Sun.6. Mat. Can. O.6 (BB).
[81]Sun.6. Mat. Lau. (EL-BB).

You descended into hell as you willed, O Christ; you despoiled death as God and Master, and rose on the third day, raising with yourself Adam from the bonds of hell and from corruption . . .[82]

You were laid in a tomb, O Lord, as one who slept, and rose on the third day as one powerful in strength, raising Adam with yourself from the corruption of death . . .[83]

Fearful you appeared, O Lord, as you lay in the tomb; but rising on the third day in power you raised with yourself Adam . . .[84]

. . . You raised with you Adam by your almighty hand . . .[85]

You raised Adam, and Eve rejoices in your resurrection . . .[86]

The hymnographers quite often identify themselves, and with them the entire church or even all mankind, with those who benefit from Christ's saving work. In their verses Christ's saving of the dead and the exodus from Hades were not "one-time" events that occurred in the past without significance for the present. These are events that transcend time, whose fruits were reaped not only by those who were imprisoned in hell before Christ's descent but also by future generations. This universal, transcendental significance of Christ's descent and victory over hell and death is stressed in the *octoechos*:

Today salvation has come into the world; let us sing to him who arose from the tomb and is the author of our life. For having destroyed death by death, he has granted us victory and great mercy.[87]

You have led us out of hell, Lord, by slaying the all-devouring monster, destroying his power by your might . . .[88]

Let the heavens be glad and let earthly things rejoice; for the Lord has wrought might with his arm. He has trampled down death by

---

[82]Sat.7. Gt. Ves. StichLC (EL-BB).
[83]Sat.7. Gt. Ves. StichLC (EL-BB).
[84]Sat.7. Gt. Ves. StichAp. (El-BB).
[85]Sat.8. Gt. Ves. StichAp. (BB).
[86]Sun.8. Mat. Kontakion (BB).
[87]Sun.1–3–5–7. Mat. Troparion after the doxology (J-BB).
[88]Sun.1. Mat. Can. O.6 (EL-BB).

death and become the firstborn of the dead. From the belly of Hades has he delivered us and granted the world great mercy.[89]

Hell opened its gullet and swallowed me down, and the fool puffed up his soul; but Christ came down and brought out my life, for he is the lover of mankind.[90]

. . . You dwelt in a tomb, that you might free us from hell . . .[91]

Come you peoples, let us hymn the Saviour's rising on the third day, through which we were redeemed from the unbreakable bonds of hell and all received incorruption and life . . .[92]

Angels and men hymn your Rising on the third day, O Saviour, through which the ends of the world were filled with light, and we were all redeemed from the slavery of the foe . . .[93]

Lord, the King of the ages and Maker of all things, who for us accepted crucifixion and burial in the flesh, that you might free us all from hell, you are our God and we know no other but you.[94]

By your voluntary and life-giving death, O Christ, you destroyed the gates of hell as God, opened to us Paradise, and, having risen from the dead, you redeemed our lives from corruption.[95]

Glory to your Rising, our Saviour, for you, as the Almighty One, have saved us from the hell of corruption and death . . .[96]

In taking on the corruption of death, you kept your body free from corruption; and your life-giving and divine soul, Master, was not left in hell. But you arose as from sleep and raised us with you.[97]

---

[89]Sat.3. Gt. Ves. Troparion (J-BB).
[90]Sun.4. Can. O.6 (EL-BB).
[91]Sun.4. Mat. Lau. (EL).
[92]Sat.4. Gt. Ves. StichLC (EL).
[93]Sat.4. Gt. Ves. StichLC (EL-BB).
[94]Sun.5. Mat. Lau. (EL).
[95]Sun.6. Mat. Hypakoe (EL-BB).
[96]Sun.6. Mat. Can. O.3 (BB).
[97]Sun.6. Mat. Can. O.9 (BB).

Come, let us worship the one who rose from the dead and enlightened all things; for he has freed us from the tyranny of hell through his Rising on the third day, granting us life and his great mercy.[98]

O Christ, by descending into hell you despoiled death, and by rising on the third day you raised us with you . . .[99]

Let us glorify Christ who rose from the dead: for having taken on a body and a soul, he parted them from one another by the passion; for his soul descended into Hades, whom he despoiled, while the holy body of the Redeemer of our souls did not know corruption in the tomb.[100]

We glorify your Resurrection from the dead, O Christ, in psalms and hymns. Through it you have freed us from the tyranny of Hades, and as God granted us eternal life and your great mercy.[101]

Glory to your Rising on the third day, through which you have granted us eternal life and forgiveness of sins . . .[102]

The One who raised me, the fallen, out of the lowest hell . . . all you works of the Lord, bless the Lord . . .[103]

I worship, I glorify, and I praise your Resurrection from the tomb, O Christ, through which you have freed us from the unbreakable bonds of hell and as God granted the world eternal life . . .[104]

When speaking of those whom Christ resurrected and of those whom he led out of hell, the liturgical texts of the *octoechos* most frequently (in approximately forty out of one hundred cases) refers in a general way to the "dead," "those who passed away," those "born of earth," the "human race," "the race of Adam," the "world," or the "uni-

---

[98]Sat.7. Gt. Ves. StichAp. (EL-BB).
[99]Sat.7. Gt. Ves. StichAp. (EL-BB).
[100]Sat.8. Gt. Ves. StichAp. (EL).
[101]Sat.8. Gt. Ves. StichAp. (EL).
[102]Sat.8. Gt. Ves. StichAp. (EL).
[103]Sun.8. Mat. Can. O.8 (EL).
[104]Sun.8. Mat. Can. O.9 (BB).

verse" (the Greek *oikoumene* can mean both "the inhabited world" and "the people of the world"):

> You were willingly nailed to the Cross, O Merciful one, and laid in a tomb as a mortal, O Giver of life. By your death, O Powerful one, you crushed its might; for hell's gatekeepers trembled before you; you raised with you *the dead from every age* . . . [105]

> *You rose from the tomb, all-powerful Saviour, and seeing the marvel hell was struck with fear, and* the dead arose . . . [106]

> *Those who slept in darkness*, O Christ, seeing you the Light in the lowest depths of hell, rose up. [107]

> Going down *to those in hell*, Christ proclaimed the good tidings, saying: "Be of good courage, now I have conquered! I am the Resurrection; I will bring you up, abolishing the gates of death." [108]

> *Death* gave up the dead it had swallowed, while hell's reign, which brought corruption, was destroyed when you rose from the tomb, O Lord. [109]

> . . . He raised *the prisoners* from the tombs . . . today as the Giver of life he drew *people* out of hell and raises them together to heaven. He lays low the uprisings of the foe and smashes the gates of hell . . . [110]

> Having revived, as God, *the dead in hell* by your three-day burial, you raised them with you; and as God you became for all of us a source of incorruption . . . [111]

---

[105] Sun.1. Mat. Sessional Hymn (EL-BB).

[106] Sun.2. Mat. Kontakion (EL).

[107] Sun.2. Lit. Beat. (EL).

[108] Sat.3. Gt. Ves. StichLC (EL). Cf. Melito of Sardis, *On Pascha* 100–103. "The Lord . . . rose from the dead and called with these words: '. . . I am he who destroyed death, vanquished the enemy, trampled down hell and bound the strong one . . . I am your resurrection . . . I shall raise you to the heavenly heights.'"

[109] Sun.3. Mat. Can. O.4 (EL-BB).

[110] Sun.3. Mat. Oikos (EL-BB).

[111] Sun.3. Lit. Beat. (BB).

Having fallen alseep as a man, as God did you raise through your invicible power *those sleeping in the tombs* . . .[112]

You destroyed the gates of hell, O Lord, and by your death you destroyed the reign of death; you freed *humanity* from corruption, granting the world life and incorruption, and your great mercy.[113]

. . . your descent into hell is fearful for the devil and his angels; for having trampled on death you rose on the third day, granting *mankind* incorruption . . .[114]

. . . by descending into Hades you freed *those enchained* from every age, granting incorruption to *the human race* . . .[115]

Truly Christ is risen, granting those in hell life and resurrection.[116]

. . . you opened the gates of hell for *the souls from every age* . . .[117]

My Saviour and Deliverer, from the tomb as God you raised *those born of earth* from their bonds and destroyed the gates of hell, and as Master arose on the third day.[118]

Dead you were reckoned with transgressors; *for the dead* you became a source of immortal life . . .[119]

He who grants resurrection to the human race was led as a sheep to the slaughter; all the princes of hell trembled before him and the gates of pain were lifted up; for Christ the King of glory had come in, saying to *those in bondage*: Come forth! and to *those in darkness*: Reveal yourselves![120]

---

[112] Sat. 3. Lit. Beat. (BB).

[113] Sat.4. Gt. Ves. StichLC (EL-BB).

[114] Sat.4. Gt. Ves. StichLC (EL).

[115] Sat.4. Gt. Ves. StichAp. (EL).

[116] Sun.4. Mat. Sessional Hymn (EL-BB).

[117] Sun.4. Mat. Can. O.3 (EL-BB).

[118] Sun.4. Mat. Kontakion (EL-BB).

[119] Sat.4. Mat. Can. O.8 (BB).

[120] Sat.5. Gt. Ves. StichLC (EL-BB).

Strange is your crucifixion and your descent into Hades, O Lover of mankind; for having despoiled it and gloriously raised with yourself as God those who were *prisoners*, you opened Paradise and bade it welcome them . . .[121]

. . . with himself he raised *the dead* from the graves, as God having despoiled the might of death and the devil's strength, and he made light dawn for *those in hell*.[122]

When the Saviour went down as mortal to the prisoners, *the dead from every age* arose with Him . . .[123]

You rose from the dead and raised with you *those in hell*; blessed are you, the God of our Fathers.[124]

By your death, O Christ, you destroyed the power of death and raised up *those who were dead from every age* . . .[125]

Victorious over hell, O Christ, you ascended the Cross that you might raise up with yourself *those who sat in the darkness of death* . . .[126]

Your Cross and burial, O Giver of life, we the faithful hymn and venerate; for you, Immortal one, bound hell as all-powerful God, and raised *the dead* with you, and destroyed the gates of death, and as God brought down the power of hell . . .[127]

. . . When you descended into hell, you raised with you *the whole man*, lying in dust . . .[128]

By your burial for three days you despoiled death, and by your life-bearing Rising you raised corrupted *humanity*, O Christ God, as you love humankind. Glory to you![129]

---

[121]Sat.5. Gt. Ves. StichAp. (EL-BB).
[122]Sun.5. Mat. Sessional Hymn (EL).
[123]Sun.5. Mat. Can. O.4 (EL).
[124]Sun.5. Mat. Can. O.7 (EL).
[125] Sun.5. Lit. Beat. (EL).
[126] Sat. 6. Gt. Ves. StichLC (EL).
[127]Sun.6. Mat. Oikos (BB).
[128]Sun.6. Mat. Can. O.8 (BB).
[129]Sun.7. Mat. Sessional Hymn (EL).

By dwelling in a tomb and rising on the third day Christ granted *mortals* the expectation of incorruption . . .[130]

You rose from the tomb on the third day and made life dawn for *the world*, as Giver of life and God; establish my mind to do your will . . .[131]

With hymns we glorify you that destroyed all the power of the tyrant by the incomprehensible strength of your Godhead and raised *the dead* by your Resurrection.[132]

When you rose from the dead by your power, O Saviour, you raised up with you *the human race*, granting us life and incorruption . . .[133]

When you rose from the dead by your power, O Saviour, you raised up with you *the human race*, granting us life and incorruption . . .[134]

The One who abolished the power of death rose from the tomb in glory and saved the *human race*; praise him, you Priests, supremely exalt him, you peoples, to all the ages.[135]

By your mighty power, O Lord, you have smashed the gates of Hades and destroyed the might of death; and raised with yourself *the dead* who slept from eternity in darkness, by your divine and glorious Resurrection . . .[136]

. . . He has raised *the dead* with himself from the unbreakable bonds of Hades . . .[137]

The light of the Resurrection has shone out for *those who sat in darkness and the shadow of death* . . .[138]

---

[130]Sun.7. Mat. Can. O.1 (EL).

[131]Sun.7. Mat. Can. O.3 (EL).

[132]Sun.7. Mat. Can. O.5 (EL).

[133]Sun.7. Mat. Can. O.6 (EL-BB).

[134]Sun.7. Mat. Can. O.6 (EL-BB).

[135]Sun.7. Mat. Can. O.8 (EL-BB).

[136]Sun.7. Mat. Lau. (EL-BB).

[137]Sun.7. Mat. Lau. (EL-BB).

[138] Sun.8. Mat. Can. O.3 (EL).

You foresee all things in your wisdom, O Lord, and established the nethermost parts with your mind; by your descent you did not deprive of the resurrection, Word of God, *those who were created in your image.*[139]

Having risen from the tomb, you raised *the dead*...[140]

When you had taken captive the kingdom of hell and raised *the dead*...[141]

At your divine descent the regions beneath the earth were filled with light, and the darkness, which before pursued, was driven out. Therefore *the prisoners from every age* arose...[142]

Finally, the texts of the *octoechos* very frequently (perhaps in thirty-five out of one hundred cases) speak of how Christ led *all* people out of hell:

Christ has despoiled hell, as alone mighty and powerful, and has raised up with himself *all* those in corruption...[143]

Let us praise as almighty God the One who rose on the third day, smashed the gates of hell, and roused the age-long dead from the grave.... Therefore ... hell groans, death laments, *the world* exults and all rejoice together: For you, O Christ, have granted Resurrection to *all*.[144]

When you, O Supremely Exalted, had willingly for our sakes become as one with no help and a slain corpse among the dead, you freed us *all* and raised us up with you with your mighty hand...[145]

You are the light of those in darkness, you are the resurrection of *all* and the life of mortals, and you have raised up *all* with yourself,

---

[139]Sun.8. Mat. Can. O.3 (BB). I.e., all humans.
[140] Sun.8. Mat. Kontakion (BB).
[141] Sun.8. Mat. Oikos (BB).
[142]Sun.8. Mat. Can. O.7 (EL).
[143]Sun.1. Mat. Sessional Hymn (EL-BB).
[144]Sun.1. Mat. Oikos (EL-BB).
[145]Sun.1. Mat. Can. O.7 (EL-BB).

despoiling the might of death, O Saviour, and smashing the gates of hell, O Word. And when the dead saw the miracle they were amazed, and all creation rejoices in your Resurrection . . .[146]

Let us all with faith worship God, who by his own death destroyed with might the power of death; for he raised with him the age-long dead, and to *all* he grants life and Resurrection.[147]

Rising from the tomb, you broke the bonds of Hades and destroyed the sentence of death, O Lord, delivering *all* from the snares of the enemy.[148]

The first-created man transgressed of old the first commandment, taking death from the Garden; but the Immortal One, who was raised on the Cross and tasted death, granted immortality to *all* people . . .[149]

Having been nailed to the Cross . . . You have poured forth salvation, O Christ, to *all people*.[150]

By your Resurrection, O Lord, *all things* have been filled with light and Paradise has been opened again, while *all* creation as it sings your praise, constantly offers you its hymn.[151]

In a mortal body, O Life, you were acquainted with death . . . and having destroyed the corrupter, Supremely Exalted One, you raised *all* with you . . .[152]

Your soul made divine, O Saviour, plundered the treasuries of hell and raised with it the souls from every age; while your life-bearing body became a source of incorruption for *all*.[153]

---

[146]Sun.2. Mat. Oikos (EL-BB).
[147]Sun.2. Mat. Lau. (EL-BB).
[148]Sun.2–4–6–8. Mat. Troparion after the doxology (J-BB).
[149]Wed.2. Mat. Can. O.1 (BB).
[150]Wed.2. Mat. Can. O.5 (BB).
[151]Sun.3. Gt. Ves. StichLC (EL-BB).
[152]Sun.3. Mat. Can. O.4 (BB).
[153]Sun.4. Mat. Can. O.4 (EL).

You came down to my aid as far as hell, and having made a road to the resurrection for *all*, you went up once more . . .[154]

. . . the gate-keepers of hell trembled when you were placed as a mortal in the sepulchre; for you destroyed the strength of death and gave incorruption to *all* the dead . . .[155]

. . . numbered among the dead you bound the tyrant there, so delivering *all* from the bonds of hell by your Resurrection . . .[156]

You despoiled hell, my Saviour, by your burial, and you filled *all things* with joy by your Resurrection.[157]

At your descent, O Christ, hell became a laughing stock and disgorged *all* those who of old had been slain by the devil's deception . . .[158]

Destroyed by death, the miserable one [death] lies without breath; for it, the strong one, could not endure the encounter with the divine life and is slain, and resurrection is granted to *all*.[159]

Having by his life-bestowing hand raised up *all the dead* out of the dark abysses, Christ God, the Giver of life, has granted resurrection to *all*; for he is the Saviour of *all*, the Resurrection, the Life and God of *all*.[160]

Though you descended into the grave as a mortal, O Life-giver, you destroyed the power of hell, O Christ, raising with you the dead that it had swallowed; and you, as God, granted resurrection to *all* who magnify you with faith and love.[161]

---

[154]Sun.4. Mat. Can. O.8 (EL-BB).
[155]Sun.4. Mat. Lau. (EL-BB).
[156]Sun.4. Lit. Beat. (EL).
[157]Sun.5. Mat. Can. O.5 (EL-BB).
[158]Sun.5. Mat. Can. O.8 (EL-BB).
[159]Sun.6. Mat. Can. O.3 (BB).
[160]Sun.6. Mat. Kontakion (J-BB).
[161]Sun.6. Mat. Can. O.9 (BB).

You smashed the gates and bars of hell, O Giver of life, and you raised *all* the dead, O Saviour, as they cried, "Glory to your Rising."[162]

You were laid in the tomb as a mortal, O Christ, the Life of all; you broke the bars of hell and by your resurrection on the third day as the Powerful one, you enlightened *all* . . .[163]

By rising from the grave, you raised with you *all* the dead in hell . . .[164]

Rising from the tomb as from sleep, O compassionate Lord, you saved *all* from corruption . . .[165]

If we add to the above texts those that speak of Christ's descent and victory as a complete "emptying" of hell, it becomes clear that the authors of the liturgical books saw Christ's descent as significant for *all people* without exception. Sometimes various categories of the dead are mentioned, such as "the pious" or "righteous," but nowhere do the hymns speak of selectivity—the existence of certain groups that were unaffected by Christ's descent. Nowhere in the *octoechos* is it stated that Christ preached to the righteous but left sinners without his saving words or that he led the holy fathers out of hell but left all the rest. It is never indicated that someone was excluded from God's providence for the salvation of people, accomplished in the death and resurrection of the Son of God.

Had Christ shed mercy only on the Old Testament righteous who awaited his coming, what miracle is this? Had he freed from Hades only the righteous, leaving behind the sinners, why would the "assembly of Angels" have been amazed? One of the Orthodox evening prayers, attributed to St John Damascene, reads: "for to save a righteous man is no great thing, and to have mercy on the pure is nothing wonderful, for they are worthy of your mercy."[166] Had Christ saved

---

[162]Sun.6. Lit. Beat. (EL).

[163] Sun.7. Lit. Beat. (BB).

[164]Sun.8. Mat. Can. O.4 (EL).

[165]Sun.8. Mat. Can. O.7 (BB).

[166]Cf. *Kanonnik* (Moscow, 1986), in Slavonic, p. 283.

only those to whom salvation belonged by right, it would not have been so much an act of mercy as the fulfillment of duty or a restoration of justice. "Should you save me for my works, this would not be grace or a gift, but rather a duty," reads one of the morning prayers.[167]

This is precisely the reason that the liturgical texts return again and again to the theme of Christ's descent into Hades, and why church hymnographers express their wonder and astonishment at this event. The descent into Hades does not fit in with our usual, human ideas of justice, retribution, fulfillment of duty, the rewarding of the righteous, and the punishment of the guilty. Something extraordinary happened that made the angels shudder and be seized with wonder: Christ descended into Hades, destroyed its "strongholds" and "bars," unlocked the gates of hell, and "opened up the path of resurrection to all people." He opened up the way to paradise for everyone without exception.

Liturgical poetry gives no clear answer to the question: did all in Hades respond to Christ's preaching, follow him, and receive salvation? One could conclude that the possibility of believing or not believing in Christ rested with those in hell who already believed or who came to believe in him and then followed him into paradise. But did all come to believe in him? If so, then not a single mortal remained in hell, and hell would have been emptied. On the other hand, if Christ preached to everyone but some did not respond to him, or if he opened the doors for all but not all followed him, then those who so willed it would have stayed in hell.

Here there is value in St Maximus the Confessor's teaching on how God, having taken on human nature and healed it once and for all, did so entirely without anyone's participation and independent of external participation. Nevertheless, every person still must free himself from sin by personal struggle.[168] Thus Christ's descent was significant for all those of mankind whose wills did not resist the divine will and followed Christ into paradise. In other words, Christ preached to all "those under the earth" and freed from chains all who

---

[167]Eighth Prayer, to Our Lord Jesus Christ. Cf. *Kannonik*, p. 298.
[168]G. Florovsky, *Vizantiyskie Otsy V–VIII vekov* (Paris, 1933), p. 220.

were bound from the ages, which was saving only for those who came to believe in him. The key to solving the question of who was led out of hell by Christ is in the teaching of free will. God does not save anyone against one's will. Although he grants the possibility of salvation, he also respects freedom and grants the right to refuse paradise.

The possibility of salvation is granted not just once, however. Those described in chapter eight of the Book of Genesis were created by God so that with his help they might walk the path to salvation while on earth. They did not make use of the chance that God gave them but instead chose another path and perished in the waters of the flood. However, in taking their earthly lives from them, God did not deprive them of salvation. He gave them still one more chance to turn to him by sending them his Only-Begotten Son, who suffered and died for them on the cross, descended into hell, and preached to them the same good news they ignored while living on earth.

The theological teaching yielded from the *octoechos* can be expressed in the following manner: The salvation of humanity, a fruit of synergy between God and man, had already been accomplished by Christ through his incarnation, suffering, death, descent into Hades, and resurrection. He vanquished hell, bound the devil, and opened up the way to paradise for all who desire to believe in him and respond to his call, even those who rejected it during their earthly lives. To enjoy the fruits of Christ's victory one must believe in him, trust him, and follow him, freely and consciously rejecting the devil. Each person must vanquish hell and the devil within and overcome the inner power that opposes the will of God.

THE LENTEN TRIODION

The Lenten Triodion is the service book that contains liturgical texts for the period from the week of the Publican and Pharisee to Great Saturday. Like the *octoechos*, the Lenten Triodion was formed over the course of many centuries. Its earliest texts can be dated to the sixth century, while the latest were written in the fifteenth or perhaps the sixteenth centuries. The most ancient hymns are perhaps the short

"Troparia of prophecy" read before the Old Testament reading during the Sixth Hour. The Akathist to the Most Holy Theotokos dates to the sixth or seventh centuries, while the Great Canon of St Andrew of Crete was written in the first half of the eighth century. Among other authors of the sixth through eighth centuries are the Palestinian hymnographers St Sophronius (Patriarch of Jerusalem), St John Damascene, and St Kosmas of Maiouma. In the ninth century the center of hymnographic activity was transferred from Palestine to Constantinople. There the brothers Theodore and Joseph the Studite, St Theophanous Graptos, and Joseph the Hymnographer produced their celebrated works. Emperor Leo VI the Wise (ninth to tenth centuries) and the court poetess Kassia (ninth century) also are authors of liturgical texts that entered the Lenten Triodion. Among later writers are St Symeon Logothetos (tenth century); John, Metropolitan of Euchaita (ninth century); and the Patriarchs of Constantinople, St Philotheos Kokkinos (1354–1354; 1364–1376) and Gennadios Scholarios (1454–1456).[169]

The theme of Christ's descent into Hades appears repeatedly in the liturgical texts of Great Lent, especially in the service of the Sunday of the Veneration of the Cross. On this day the church glorifies the cross of Christ, a shameful instrument of death that became the symbol of salvation for the human race. According to the hymnographers, Christ's victory over hell and death was decided when the cross was raised on earth. Even at that moment hell felt that its days were numbered and was convinced of it when Christ died, descending into its darkness in order to resurrect the dead:

> A day of festival! At Christ's Rising, death has disappeared without trace and the light of life has dawned. Adam has arisen and dances for joy . . .[170]

---

[169]Cf. Archimandrite Kallistos Ware, "The Meaning of the Great Fast," pp. 40–43. The service to St Gregory Palamas on the Second Sunday of Great Lent was written by Philotheos Kokkinos, while the canon to St Gregory was composed by Gennadios. For details on the origin and development of the Lenten Triodion cf.: I. Karabinov, *Postnaya Triod'*.

[170]Sunday of the Veneration of the Cross. Mat. Can. O.1 (EL-BB).

Come, let us sing a new song as we celebrate the overthrow of hell, for Christ has risen from the tomb; capturing death, and saving the whole universe.[171]

No sooner had the Tree of your Cross been set up, Christ our Lord, than the foundations of death were shaken. Hell swallowed you eagerly, but it let you go with trembling. You have shown us your salvation, O Holy One, and we glorify you, Son of God . . .[172]

Having crushed death, O Christ, you rose as a great King, calling us back from the storehouses of hell to the enjoyment of the Kingdom of Heaven, to the land of immortality.[173]

Three crosses Pilate fixed on Golgotha, two for the thieves and one for the Giver of life, whom Hades saw and said to those below, "My ministers and powers, who has fixed a nail in my heart? A wooden lance has suddenly pierced me and I am being torn apart. My insides are in pain, my belly in agony. My senses make my spirit tremble, and I am compelled to disgorge Adam and Adam's race, given me by a tree, for this tree is bringing them back again to Paradise."[174]

You rose on the third day from the tomb as one who slept, O Lord, and by your divine power struck down the gatekeepers of hell; you raised up all our forebears from of old . . .[175]

You went down into the tomb, O God the Giver of Life, and you broke all the bolts and bars, raising up the dead who cry aloud: Glory to your Resurrection! O Christ, the Saviour all-powerful.[176]

Your tomb, O Christ, has brought me life: for you, the Lord of life, came and cried to those who were dwelling in the grave, "All who

---

[171]Sunday of the Veneration of the Cross. Mat. Can. O.3 (EL).

[172]Sunday of the Veneration of the Cross. Mat. Can. O.3 (EL).

[173]Sunday of the Veneration of the Cross. Mat. Can. O.6 (EL).

[174]Sunday of the Veneration of the Cross. Mat. Oikos of St Romanos the Melodist (EL) (cf. the Greek text, which differs somewhat from the one in the Lenten Triodion, in SC 128, 286).

[175]Sunday of the Veneration of the Cross. Mat. Can. O.7 (EL-BB).

[176]Sunday of the Veneration of the Cross. Mat. Can. O.9 (EL).

are in bonds, be loosed: for I have come, the Ransom of the world."[177]

Allusions to Christ's descent are also found in services on week-days following the Sunday of the Veneration of the Cross, as well as in all Friday and Saturday services throughout Great Lent. These hymns are similar to the *octoechos* hymns dedicated to the cross.

The weekend of Lazarus Saturday and Palm Sunday lead the Orthodox faithful into Holy Week, which immediately precedes Pascha—the feast of Christ's holy resurrection. The overall spirit of the services during that weekend is festal, since their main theme is the resurrection of Christ, but the theme of Christ's sufferings and death are also present in the services. The paradox of both feasts, which comprise a single liturgical unit, is that they testify to two things: the power and might of God, who took upon himself the sins of the world and the weakness of man, who was unable to respond to this sacrifice and unready to accept Christ. Christ, "confirming the common resurrection,"[178] resurrects Lazarus, but the response of high priests and Pharisees is the conspiracy to kill him. Christ enters Jerusalem and the crowds welcome him with palm leaves in their hands, crying "Hosanna to the Son of David," but some of that same crowd would also cry "Crucify, crucify him" in just a few days. In the services of Holy Week, the theme of this inconsistency—between God's love and man's weakness revealed in the last days of Christ's earthly life—is continued. From God: meekness, forgiveness, prayer for enemies, and self-sacrifice unto death; from man: unbelief, doubt, treachery, and cruelty. These are the cardinal themes of the Holy Week services.

The resurrection of Lazarus, dead for four days in the grave, is seen in the liturgical texts as a foreshadowing of that victory over hell and death made possible through Christ's death on the cross. Obey-ing the authoritative word of the incarnate God, hell hands over with amazement and fear a dead man who had been held in its power. For the first time the strength of hell over the human race is shaken:

---

[177]Sunday of the Veneration of the Cross. Mat. Can. O.9 (EL).
[178]Troparion of the Saturday of Lazarus and Palm Sunday (J).

Your voice, O Saviour, destroyed all the power of death, and the foundations of hell were shaken by your divine might.[179]

The depths are afraid at your presence, O Lord, the Source of all. All the waters serve you; the bars of hell tremble before you, O Christ, and its locks are destroyed by your might when Lazarus rises from the grave at your command . . .[180]

O voice, uttering the divine words! O divine power of your might, Saviour, with which you destroyed the voracious gates of Hades . . .[181]

Love, O Lord, led you into Bethany to Lazarus; and as God you raised him, already undergoing corruption, and saved him from the bonds of hell.[182]

O Saviour and Treasury of Life, you aroused the mortal one as if from sleep, and having ripped open the depths of hell by your word, resurrected him . . .[183]

As a man you searched for the tomb, but as Creator you resurrected the mortal by your authoritative command, before which Hades shuddered . . .[184]

By your word, O Word of God, Lazarus now springs up and runs to life, while the people, Master, honour you with leaves, for you will finally destroy hell by your death.[185]

Christ already destroys you through Lazarus, O Death; and Hades, where is your victory?[186]

Before your death, O Christ, you raised Lazarus from hell, dead for four days, thereby shaking the power of death and foreshadowing

---

[179]Saturday of Lazarus. Mat. Can. O.4 (BB).
[180]Saturday of Lazarus. Mat. Can. O.4 (BB).
[181]Saturday of Lazarus. Mat. Can. O.5 (BB).
[182]Saturday of Lazarus. Mat. Can. O.6 (BB).
[183]Saturday of Lazarus. Mat. Can. O.7 (BB).
[184]Saturday of Lazarus. Mat. Can. O.8 (BB).
[185]Saturday of Lazarus. Mat. Exapostilarion 1 (BB).
[186]Saturday of Lazarus. Mat. Exapostilarion 2 (BB).

through the raising of one beloved man the salvation of all people from corruption.[187]

In Bethany you raised Lazarus, dead for four days. As soon as you stood before the tomb your voice gave life to the dead one, and hell gave him up groaning. How great is the miracle; Most Merciful Lord, glory to you![188]

One particularity of the cycle of pre-paschal liturgical texts is their "iconographic character."[189] Events from the last days of Christ's life are depicted from the perspective of the "mystery of salvation" rather than from a historical perspective. In icons, events that took place at different times are often depicted as parts of a single composition. The holy images do not depict a chain of temporal events but expound the soteriological content. They do not so much describe each of them separately as give meaning to the whole. The same temporal overlapping occurs in the liturgical understanding of the events of sacred history. For example, the service of Palm Sunday speaks of how the crowd greeted Christ as a vanquisher of death with palm branches even though the victory over death and hell took place later:

Since you, Immortal One, bound hell, slew death, and raised the world, with palms the infants praised you, O Christ, as victor, crying out to you today, "Hosanna to the Son of David. For no more," they say, "will infants be slaughtered because of Mary's babe, but for all, infants and elders, you alone are crucified." . . . Therefore we rejoice and say, "Blessed are you who comes to call back Adam."[190]

Already noticeable is the familiar theme of Christ's suffering for the "unrighteous" in the service of Palm Sunday:

---

[187]Palm Sunday. Mat. Lau. (BB).

[188]Palm Sunday. Mat. Lau. (BB).

[189]Incidentally, this observation holds true for most other liturgical texts. Cf. also our note on the iconographic character of St Romanos the Melodist's kontakia.

[190]Palm Sunday. Mat. Oikos by St Romanos the Melodist (EL-BB); cf. Greek text in SC 128, 30–32.

How can death not be horrified, my Saviour? How can hell not be frightened at meeting you, who willingly went to the Passion, and seeing you, the Righteous One, suffering for the unrighteous?[191]

The theme of humanity's salvation by Christ is developed with special thoroughness and power in the services of Great Saturday. These services are highly original in that the death of Christ is experienced not as the end of the gospel drama but as the beginning of a new life, not as a defeat or a source of sorrow but as a victory and a source of joy. The services of Great Saturday are not yet infused with paschal rejoicing, but neither are they filled with sorrow as the attention of the faithful is drawn to Christ's sufferings. His death opens the way to the resurrection, and his tomb becomes "life-giving": a source of life for all humanity.

As Fr John Meyendorff notes, the theological foundations of the Great Saturday services are to be found in the "theopaschism" of St Cyril of Alexandria. The incarnate God, not just the man Jesus Christ, died on the cross, was entombed, and descended into hell. The theological opponents of Cyril (among them Nestorius) refused to talk of the "death of God." Cyril considered the salvation to be accomplished by virtue of the fact that "One of the Trinity" suffered. Only God can save. In order to save man, he voluntarily "lowered himself not only to mankind itself, but to the very depths of human fallenness, to the very last degree of disintegration—unto death itself." For death is inextricably tied with sin: it enslaves a person to sin and engulfs one in one's own self-interest, forcing one to fight for one's own survival, often sacrificing the lives of others. Not being involved in sin, the incarnate God took on death, a result of sin, breaking the vicious cycle of sin and death. "In a world in which the battle for survival at the price of others has become a law, he showed death for others as the highest revelation of love. When this highest manifestation of love was accomplished by God himself, a truly new life entered into the world."[192]

---

[191]Palm Sunday. Compline. Can. O.8 (BB).
[192]J. Meyendorff, "Vremya Velikoy Subboty," *Journal of the Moscow Patriarchate* 4 (1992), pp. 33–34.

In the hymns of vespers on Good Friday, with which the services of Great Saturday begin, the paradoxical and saving character of the "death of God" for all of mankind is stressed:

A dread and marvelous mystery is seen to come to pass today. The Invisible is grasped, the One who loosed Adam from the curse is bound . . . he who judges the living and the dead is condemned to a Tree; the destroyer of hell is shut up in a tomb. You bear all things with compassion, and save all from the curse, O long-suffering Lord, glory to you![193]

Christ's victory over hell and death crosses over from vespers on Good Friday to matins of Great Saturday:

When in the new tomb you, the Redeemer of all, had been laid for the sake of all, hell became a laughing stock (*paggelastos*) and, seeing you, quaked with fear; the bars were smashed, the gates were shattered, the graves were opened, the dead arose . . .[194]

When in the tomb you were enclosed in the flesh by your own will, O Christ, who by the nature of your Godhead are uncircumscribed and unbounded, you unlocked the storehouses of hell and emptied all its palaces . . .[195]

When you went down to death, O immortal Life, you slew hell with the lightning flash of your Godhead; but when from the depths below the earth you raised the dead, all the Powers beyond the heavens cried out: Giver of life, Christ our God, glory to you![196]

The central moment of Great Saturday matins is the singing of the long Psalm 118, which is divided into three parts. This psalm has been used by Christians at funerals since ancient times. In this service, short praises by an unknown poet (no later than the fourteenth century) are appended to each verse of the psalm.[197] In the praises

---

[193]Great Friday. Ves. StichLC. Theotokion (EL-BB).
[194]Great Friday. Ves. StichAp. (EL).
[195]Good Friday. Ves. StichAp. (EL-BB).
[196]Great Saturday. Mat. Troparion at "The Lord is God" (EL-BB).
[197]These praises appear for the first time in manuscripts dated to the 14–15th

there are several central ideas that alternate with each other. They speak of how the Son of God suffered and died, fulfilling the will of the Father who sent him for the salvation of the world. At the same time his death is referred to as "voluntary."[198] They also speak especially of the Mother of God, who stood by the cross of Christ and wept for her Son. Some of the praises are addressed to the Mother of God and Joseph of Arimathea, while others, written on behalf of the Mother of God, are addressed to Jesus. The author accuses Judas of treachery and the Jews of deicide, since they did not accept their Messiah but gave him over to a shameful death.

The main subject of the praises, however, is Christ's redemption and salvation of mankind. Searching for fallen Adam but not finding him on Earth, the incarnate God entered the depths of hell to redeem him. This image is reminiscent of the parable of the lost sheep and the drachma. As in many hymns of the *octoechos*, the universal character of Christ's redemption—not for one category of people but for all of mankind and every human being—is stressed. They also speak of Christ's resurrecting the dead, described as an "emptying" of hell by the risen Lord:

> Life, how can you perish, or how can you dwell in a tomb? Yet the reign of death you now bring to naught, and from Hades' realm you raise the dead.
>
> You who established the ends of the earth, today you are placed in a small tomb, O Jesus, King of all, who raises the dead from the tombs.
>
> O my Jesus Christ, King of all, what were you looking to do when you came to Hades? Was it to free mankind?
>
> The Master of all is seen dead, and he who emptied the tombs of the dead is placed in a new tomb.

---

centuries. Cf. Archimandrite Kallistos Ware, "The Meaning of the Great Fast," p. 42. Fr John Meyendorff ("Vremya Velikoy Subboty," p. 35) dates them to the 14–16th centuries, but this dating must be considered inaccurate.

[198]Such an understanding is based on the traditional Eastern Christian doctrine on the will of the Son of God as expressed by St Maximus the Confessor, among others. Accordingly, his will, although not identical to the will of the Father, is nevertheless in complete unity with it.

O Life, you were placed in a tomb, and you destroyed death by your death, O Christ, and became a source of life for the world.

How does Hades endure, O Saviour, your coming, and does not suffer miserably, blinded by the lightning flash of your glory?

When you were placed in the tomb, O Christ the Creator, the foundations of hell shook, and the graves of the dead opened.

After you died, you rose from corruption, my Saviour and Life; and you came to the dead and broke the bars of hell.

Like a burning lampstand, here the flesh of our God, as beneath a bushel measure, now lies concealed under the earth and puts the gloom of hell to flight.

You descended to earth so that you might save Adam; not finding him on earth, O Master, you descended as far as Hades in search of him.

Like a wheat grain buried in the bosom of earth, you have yielded harvest in great abundance, O Lord, raising up all Adam's progeny.

Life itself, Christ the Saviour, having tasted of death, freed all mortal kind from death, liberated us, and the gift of life he now bestows on all.

Having appeared as the new Adam in the flesh, O Saviour, by your death you led back into life Adam, who of old was slain by envy.

Willingly as mortal, you went down beneath the earth; from the earth's depths you led back up to Heaven's height all of those, O Jesus, who lay fallen there.

Though a corpse we see you, yet alive as our God you gave life again to mortals who once were slain, putting to death the one who brought me to my death.

O the joy, O the boundless delight, with which you filled those who lay bound in hell, when you made light blaze throughout its murky depths.

Though you are buried in a tomb, O Lord, and descend into hell, yet, O Saviour, you have emptied the sepulchres and stripped naked mighty Hades, O my Christ.

Willingly, O Saviour, you went down beneath the earth, granted life again to mortals whom death had slain and led them up in the glory of the Father.

You obeyed your Father and descended, O Word, to the depth of dreadful hell, and raised up again the race of mortal kind.

By your will we see you, O Word, as a corpse in the tomb; but you live, as you foretold, and by your Resurrection you raise mortal kind, my Saviour.

Buried, O my Christ, you shattered the palaces of hell, put death to death by your death, O Lord, and from corruption you set free those born of earth.

When you descended beneath the earth, Light-bearer of justice, you aroused the dead as if they but slept, as you put to flight the murk and gloom of hell.

Adam trembled as God walked in Paradise, but he rejoices now as God enters hell. As of old he fell, so now he rises up.

Hades, O Saviour, shuddered seeing you, the Life-giver, plundering its riches and raising those dead from the ages.

O Life-giving Word, even stretched out on the Cross and nailed there, you, as Lord of Life, did not kill the Jews, granting resurrection even to their dead.

Adam lay asleep, and while sleeping, from his side brought forth death. You, O Word of God, who are sleeping here, now are pouring forth from your side life for the world.

For a while you slept, and brought life to the dead. Rising up, O Good One, you then raised up the multitudes of the dead from every age.

O Merciful One, while remaining in your Father's bosom, you willingly became man and descended into hell, O Christ.

Dreadful Hades shuddered when he saw you, immortal Sun of glory, and gave up his prisoners in haste.

Terrible indeed and great is the sight that is now seen, O Saviour; He, the cause of life, endures death, wishing to grant life to all.

O Giver of Life and Saviour, glory to your might, which destroyed hell.

Arise, Merciful One, and raise us from the depths of hell.[199]

---

[199] All verses above translated by EL-BB.

Immediately following the praises, the Sunday *troparia* from the *octoechos* are sung. One speaks of the descent into Hades: "The assembly of Angels was amazed, seeing how you were numbered among the dead, O Saviour, and that you had destroyed the stronghold of death, raised up with yourself Adam and freed all from Hades."[200] The other *troparia* deal with the resurrection of Christ. Their use at matins on Great Saturday initiates a gradual transformation from the funeral atmosphere to "paschal" joy. In essence, the celebration of Christ's resurrection begins not on Pascha night but on Great Saturday. Sunday hymns are sung at matins, in the Liturgy a Gospel reading of the resurrection is read,[201] and the clergy change from dark vestments into light-colored ones.[202]

One more key text in the lenten services, older than the praises, is the canon, which is attributed to three authors: the Irmoi by Kassia (ninth century); the last four odes by Kosmas of Maiouma (eighth century); and the first four by Mark, bishop of Idrunto (ninth to tenth centuries).[203] The canon's *troparia*, addressed to the buried and risen Son of God, vividly express the ideas of hell's death, thanks to Christ's descent, and of the end of hell's power over people:

O Lord, my God, I will sing a song for your departure, a funeral hymn for you who by your burial opened up for me the entrance to life, and by your death put death and hell to death.[204]

That you might fill all things with your glory, you went down into the lowest parts of the earth; for my substance, which is in Adam, was not hidden from you; and by being buried you renewed me who had been corrupted, O Lover of humankind.[205]

---

[200]Translated by BB.

[201]Matt 28.1–20.

[202]In contemporary practice the changing of vestments takes place after the reading of the Epistle. According to the ancient Jerusalem *typicon*, the clergy donned light-colored vestments before the beginning of the vespers of Great Saturday. This was because the baptism of catechumens took place during the Old Testament readings. Cf. I. Mansvetov, *Tserkovniy ustav* (Moscow, 1885), p. 215.

[203]For more information on Mark of Idrunto cf.: I. Mansvetov. *Tserkovniy ustav*, pp. 216–217.

[204]Great Saturday. Mat. Can. O.1 (EL-BB).

[205]Great Saturday. Mat. Can. O.1 (EL-BB).

Multiplying visions, you revealed symbols of your burial; while now, as God and man, you have also made clear your secrets, O Master, to those in hell . . .[206]

Hell, when it met you, O Word, was embittered, seeing a mortal made divine, marked by wounds and all powerful, and it shrank back in terror at the sight.[207]

Through death you transform mortality, through burial corruption; for in a manner befitting God you make incorruptible the nature you took on and make it immortal. For your flesh did not know corruption, O Master, nor was your soul, like a stranger, abandoned in hell.[208]

Hell reigns, but not for ever, over the race of mortals; for you, O Mighty One, when placed in a tomb, shattered with your Life-giving hand the bars of death, and proclaimed to those who slept there from every age no false redemption, O Saviour, who have become the first-born of the dead.[209]

Hell has been wounded, having received in its heart the One whose side was pierced by a lance,[210] and consumed by divine fire groans aloud at the salvation of us who sing, "O God, our Redeemer, blessed are you!"[211]

The immaculate temple has been destroyed, but he raises up the fallen tabernacle; for the second Adam, who dwells in the highest, has come down to the first as far as the storehouses of hell . . .[212]

"Earth covers me by my own will, but the gatekeepers of hell shudder as they see me clothed in the blood-stained robe of vengeance,

---

[206]Great Saturday. Mat. Can. O.3 (EL).
[207]Great Saturday. Mat. Can. O.4 (EL). Literally "it lost its voice beholding the terrible sight."
[208]Great Saturday. Mat. Can. O.5 (EL-BB).
[209]Great Saturday. Mat. Can. O.6 (EL-BB).
[210]Another variant of the translation: "hell was wounded in the heart, receiving him who was wounded by a spear."
[211]Great Saturday. Mat. Can. O.7 (EL-BB).
[212]Great Saturday. Mat. Can. O.8 (EL-BB).

O Mother; for having trampled on my enemies by the Cross, I shall arise again and magnify you."[213]

"Let creation rejoice, let all born of earth be glad; for hell, the enemy, has been despoiled; let women come to meet me with myrrh; for I am rescuing Adam and Eve with all their race, and on the third day I shall rise again."[214]

How should we understand the words, indicated above in italics, which declare that the reign of hell is not eternal? Can we see in them an echo of the *theologoumenon* on the finiteness of hell's torments, expressed in the fourth century by Gregory of Nyssa, or does it say that hell, unlike God, is not eternal since it appeared as something "introduced from the outside," foreign to God and therefore subject to annihilation? Again we stand before questions to which there are no single, easy answers. The services of Great Saturday raise the curtain of a mystery that cannot be solved. The answer to this mystery will be revealed only in the kingdom to come, in which we will see God as he is[215] and in which God will be "all in all."[216]

What can be said is that the power of hell over mankind has been terminated by the death and resurrection of Christ. If the torments of hell are eternal, they are so only for those who eternally resist the will of God. But hell's attempt to *eternally* wrest from God a certain autonomous kingdom, to place locks and bars over its gates and imprison souls inside, suffered defeat. Hell will continue to reign over mankind as long as there is even one person who responds "no" to God. It will reign, but *not eternally*, for its power was shattered once and for all by Christ, who by his death sentenced it to death. It will reign, but *not eternally*, for its very existence henceforth depends on the will of man, and no longer on its own will or that of the devil.

The matins of Great Saturday end with *stichera* that speak of the Lord's "keeping of the Sabbath" in the grave. The *stichera* draw parallels between the burial of Christ, who by his death completed the

---

[213]Great Saturday. Mat. Can. O.9 (EL-BB).
[214]Great Saturday. Mat. Can. O.9 (EL-BB).
[215]I John 3.2.
[216]I Cor 15.28.

"dispensation of the salvation" of mankind, and the Sabbath rest, with which the creation of the world ended:

> Today a tomb holds him who holds all creation in his palm. A stone covers him who covered the heavens with glory. Life sleeps, hell trembles and Adam is being released from his bonds. Glory to your dispensation,[217] O God, through which you, having completed the eternal Sabbath rest, have granted us your all-holy resurrection from the dead![218]

> What is this sight that is seen? What is this present rest? The King of the ages, having accomplished his dispensation through suffering, takes his Sabbath rest in a tomb, granting us a new Sabbath rest . . .[219]

> Come, let us see our Life lying in a tomb, that he may give life to all those who lie in the tombs.[220]

> Joseph asked for the body of Jesus, and laid it in his new grave; for it was right that he should come forth from a tomb as from a bridal chamber. O Lord, who destroyed the might of death and opened the gates of Paradise for humankind, glory to you![221]

> Great Moses mystically prefigured this present day when he said, "And God blessed the seventh day."[222] For this is the blessed Sabbath, this the day of rest on which the only-begotten Son of God rested from all his works . . .

The Liturgy on Great Saturday begins with vespers, which is already considered part of the Feast of Pascha.[223] This service

---

[217]The Greek word *oikonomia*, which can be translated as "dispensation" or "economy," signifies in this context the divine plan for salvation of the humankind.

[218]Great Saturday. Mat. Lau. (EL-BB).

[219]Great Saturday. Mat. Lau. (EL-BB).

[220]Great Saturday. Mat. Lau. (EL).

[221]Great Saturday. Mat. Lau. (EL-BB).

[222]Gen 2.3.

[223]According to the *typicon*, both Vespers and Liturgy of Great Saturday should be served in the evening, although in contemporary practice both are served in the morning.

includes the reading of fifteen Old Testament excerpts that were seen in the early church as reminiscent of Christ's death and resurrection. They are preceded by *stichera* that praise Christ's victory over hell. In these *stichera*, just as in early Christian writings (particularly in "The Gospel of Nicodemus," the hymns of St Ephrem the Syrian, and the *kontakia* of St Romanos the Melodist), hell is personified:

> Today hell groans and cries, "It were better for me had I not accepted the one born of Mary, for he has come upon me and destroyed my might. He has smashed the gates of brass. Souls which before I held, he, being God, has raised."[224]

> Today hell groans and cries, "My authority has been destroyed. I received a mortal as one of the dead, but have no strength at all to hold Him, but with him I shall lose those over whom I reigned. I held the dead from every age, but see, he raises them all."[225]

> Today hell groans and cries: "my power has been devoured. The Shepherd is crucified and has resurrected Adam; I have lost those over whom I ruled, and whomever I was able to swallow, I have disgorged. The crucified one emptied the tombs, and the rule of death is made powerless."[226]

The idea of hell being emptied, its losing of *all* its prisoners after Christ's descent, is compellingly expressed. The "Pascha of the Crucifixion," or the liturgical remembrance of Christ's death and burial, ends on this victorious note. After the Old Testament readings, the service definitely acquires the character of the "Pascha of the Resurrection." The path along which the Lenten Triodion had led the faithful for ten weeks finally comes to an end. It begins with the repentance of the lenten services, continues with the remembrance of Christ's sufferings, death, and burial, and through this remembrance leads the faithful to the joy of Christ's resurrection.

---

[224]Great Saturday. Ves. StichLC (EL-BB).
[225]Great Saturday. Ves. StichLC (EL-BB).
[226]Great Saturday. Ves. StichLC (BB).

THE PENTECOSTARION

The *pentecostarion* contains the services of the paschal period beginning with paschal nocturnes that are served just before the paschal matins and ending with the service of the first Sunday after Pentecost. There is much less original material in the *pentecostarion* than in the *octoechos* and the Lenten Triodion, and a significant part of the texts have simply been taken from the *octoechos*. The main theme of the *pentecostarion* is Christ's resurrection, and many of its texts also mention his victory over hell.

The main idea of celebrating Christ's resurrection as a transition from death to life is contained in the paschal canon of St John of Damascus, sung at Easter matins:

> It is the Day of Resurrection, let us be radiant, O people! Pascha, the Lord's Pascha: for Christ God has brought us from death to life and from earth to heaven, as we sing the hymn of victory.[227]

> Let the heavens be glad as is meet, let the earth rejoice, and let the whole world, both visible and invisible, keep festival. For Christ is risen, the eternal gladness.[228]

> Now all things are filled with light; heaven, earth, and the nethermost parts. Let all creation, therefore, celebrate the rising of Christ, in which it is strengthened.[229]

> Seeing your infinite compassion, those who were bound in Hades hastened to the light, O Christ, with gladsome feet, praising the eternal Pascha.[230]

> O my Saviour, the living and unslain sacrifice; as God you voluntarily offered yourself to the Father and, having risen from the tomb, resurrected with yourself Adam, the forefather of all.[231]

---

[227]Easter matins. Can. O.1 (J-BB).
[228]Easter matins. Can. O.1 (J-BB).
[229]Easter matins. Can. O.3 (J-BB).
[230]Easter matins. Can. O.5 (J-BB).
[231]Easter matins. Can. O.6 (J-BB).

Even though you descended into the grave, O Immortal One, you destroyed the power of hell and rose as victor, O Christ God . . .[232]

We celebrate the death of death, the destruction of Hades, the beginning of another, eternal life . . .[233]

Christ is risen, trampling down death and raising the dead; O people, rejoice![234]

Christ is the new Pascha, the living Sacrifice, the Lamb of God that takes away the sin of the world.[235]

Today all creation is glad and rejoices, for Christ is risen and Hades has been taken captive.[236]

Today the Master has taken Hades captive, raising the fettered, whom it had held from the ages in bitter bondage.[237]

According to the Eastern Christian interpretation of St Paul's teaching, creation "was subjected to futility, not willingly," but as a result of the fall. Together with mankind creation "groans and labours with birth pangs until now," but awaits its liberation "from the bondage of corruption into the glorious liberty of the children of God."[238] Elaborating on these words, John Chrysostom says: "What does 'creation was subjected to futility' mean? It means that it became susceptible to corruption. Because of whom and why? Because of you, O man. For since you received a corruptible body susceptible to passions, the world became cursed. . . . But it . . . will be freed from the slavery of corruption, that is, it will not be corruptible any more, but will conform to the beauty of your body."[239] Creation will become

---

[232]Easter matins. Kontakion (J-BB). This *kontakion*, like the *oikos* that follows it in the *Pentecostarion* ("the Sun that was before the sun and who had once set in the tomb"), is nothing other than the first part of the 40th *kontakion* of St Romanos the Melodist.

[233]Easter matins. Can. O7 (J-BB).

[234]Easter matins. Can. Refrains of the 9th ode (BB).

[235]Easter matins. Can. Refrains of the 9th ode (J-BB).

[236]Easter matins. Can. Refrains of the 9th ode (BB).

[237]Easter matins. Can. Refrains of the 9th ode (J-BB).

[238]Rom 8.19–22.

[239]*Fourteenth Homily on the Epistle to the Romans.*

incorruptible when man becomes incorruptible, but man's hope in incorruption is based on Christ. He died and was buried but did not undergo decay, opening the path of incorruption to all mankind and therefore to all creation. Christ's redemption of man has significance for the fate of the whole created world.

The paschal canon's author invites not only the material, "visible" world but also the spiritual, "invisible" world. From the moment when the devil and his demons fell away from God, the invisible world was divided into the area of God's presence and the area of the devil's power. Although his power over souls is limited, it nevertheless remains a real power. In the Old Testament, hell was seen as a place of God's absence: "Sheol"—a "land of oblivion" and "place of corruption" populated by the dead whom God does not remember, from whom he hides his face, where his mercy and Truth[240] are not announced, and where he is not remembered at all.[241] After Christ's descent into Hades there came a turning point, a crisis in the destiny of hell: Christ filled it with his presence, which was salvific for all who believed in him and fatal for all who opposed him, especially the devil and demons. Now hell is no more a place of oblivion and abandonment by God but a place where he is present in his love just as he is in paradise. God's love, however, a fount of joy and exultation for those who have attained the kingdom of heaven, becomes a source of never-ending torment for those in hell. In the seventh century this understanding of hell (Gehenna) was expressed with special clarity by St Isaac the Syrian: "The idea that sinners in hell are deprived of God's love is not considered inappropriate by anyone. . . . But love by its power acts in two ways: it torments sinners . . . but it intoxicates the souls of sons of the heavens with its consolations."[242]

The core the Easter matins is a text that, in the East, is traditionally linked with the name of John Chrysostom, "The Catechetical Homily on Holy Easter."[243] In this work Christ's victory

[240]Ps 87.5–15.

[241]Ps 6.6.

[242]*Homily* 27, quoted in: Mar Isaacus Ninevita, *De perfectione religiosa*, ed. P. Bedjan (Lipsiae, 1909), pp. 201–202.

[243]This homily was already an integral part of the Easter service during the time

over hell is depicted with special poetic intensity and theological conviction:

> Let no one fear death: for the Saviour's death has freed us. By enduring it he quenched it. He who descended into hell has despoiled hell. He embittered it when it tasted his flesh as Isaiah proclaimed in prophecy, "Death," he said, "was embittered when it met you there below."[244] Embittered, for it was destroyed. Embittered, for it was mocked. Embittered, for it was slain. Embittered for it was wiped out. Embittered, for it was bound fast. It received a body, and came face to face with God. It received earth, and met heaven. It received what it saw, and fell through what it did not see. Death, where is your sting? Hell, where is your victory?[245] Christ has risen and you are abolished! Christ has risen and the demons have fallen! Christ has risen, and Angels rejoice! Christ has risen, and life has found freedom! Christ has risen, and there is not a single corpse in the grave![246]

As in the *synaxarion* reading for Great Saturday, this "Catechetical Homily" contains several key ideas that are of direct significance to our theme of Christ's descent into Hades: First, in this sermon we cannot but notice vestiges of the "divine deceit" theory expressed by St Gregory of Nyssa. Secondly, it contains the idea of hell's final defeat and the fall of the demons, already observed several times in the liturgical texts. Finally, we also find the notion that after Christ's resurrection *not a single* mortal was left in the grave. This point is already familiar to us from the *kontakia* of Romanos the Melodist and from the liturgical texts that speak of the total "emptying" of hell by the risen Christ.

The theme of the descent is one of the leitmotifs throughout the entire cycle of the paschal hymns. It is also expressed with special

---

of St Theodore the Studite (8th c.); cf.: I. Mansvetov, *Tserkovniy ustav*, p. 105. In Migne's *Patrologiae cursus completus* this homily is listed among the *spuria*: PG 59:721–724. For the origin of this homily cf: *Repertorium pseudochrysostomicum*, collegit J. A. de Aldama (Paris, 1965), pp. 34–35.

[244]Isa 14.9.

[245]Hos 13.14.

[246]Cf. *The Gospel of Nicodemus* 23 ("not a single mortal was left near me").

force in the services of Bright Week, as well as in the services of the Sundays of Thomas, the Myrrh-bearing Women, and the Paralytic. It also infuses the cycle of *triodia* composed by St Joseph the Hymnographer, found at the end of the *pentecostarion* and intended for reading at compline throughout the period from Pascha to Pentecost.

Pentecost itself marks the end of the path along which the church leads its faithful over the course of several months. Beginning with the remembrance of Christ's birth (Nativity), followed by his preaching (Epiphany), the path continues through Great Lent, Holy Week, the day of holy resurrection (Pascha), and the feast of the Lord's Ascension. Pentecost, the day of the Holy Spirit's descent on the apostles, the "birthday of the church," is the endpoint of the journey. It completes the dispensation of man's salvation accomplished by Christ. The cornerstone of the church is Christ himself, and the "gates of hell" cannot overcome it.[247]

Founded by Christ on earth, the church is called to continue his work of human salvation. Moreover, as the Body of Christ,[248] each redeemed person becomes its member. The uniting of redeemed people with the One, Holy, Catholic, and Apostolic Church became possible thanks to the incarnation, suffering, death, and resurrection of the Savior. Because the redemptive sacrifice of Christ extends to all mankind and not only to the chosen, the church has a universal dimension. According to Fr John Meyendorff, "God the Word takes on *our* nature in order to save *all*. . . . Identifying himself with the poor, the weak, the persecuted, in other words, with all of fallen mankind, he leads them to life and joy. . . . The result of his Resurrection is the Catholic Church, which *gathers all* into his risen Body."[249]

Universal and all-encompassing, Christ's church embraces with love and remembrance not only its members but also all those beyond its boundaries. As God himself, who leaves none outside his love, not even those in hell, the church remembers all mankind through its love and prayers. For the church, all are active; no person is erased from its

---

[247]Matt 16.18.

[248]Cf. Eph 1.23; 4.12; Col 1.18, and others.

[249]J. Meyendorff, "Chelovechestvo Christa: Paschal'naya Tayna," *The Theological Journal of St Tikhon's Orthodox Theological Institute* 5 (2000), p. 41.

memory. This is why special kneeling prayers are read on Pentecost "for the captive in hell":

> Christ our God, who ... tore apart the indissoluble bonds of death and the bars of hell, trampling down multitudes of evil spirits ... you descended into hell, smashed the everlasting bars, and showed the way up to those who sat below. With a bait of divine wisdom you hooked the author of evil, the dragon of the deep, bound him with chains of darkness in Tartarus and secured him with the unquench-able fire. ... O Master of all, Lord our God ... who have also been pleased on this most perfect and saving Feast to receive suppliant prayers of atonement for those who are immured in hell ... hear us, lowly and wretched, who entreat you, and give rest to the souls of your servants who have fallen asleep before us in a place of light, a place of green pasture, a place of refreshment, from which all grief, sorrow and sighing have fled away, and establish their spirits in the dwellings of the righteous and count them worthy of peace and repose. Because the dead will not praise you, O Lord, nor do those in hell have the freedom to offer you Thanksgiving.[250]

In praying for "those immured in hell," the church bases its action on the fact that God, who "desires that all people should be saved,"[251] can change the fate of those in hell, just as he did when he descended there and led out the dead. For the mercy of God there are no obsta-cles other than man's free will. In the end it is God himself who "takes away and gives life, brings down into the nethermost parts and raises up";[252] therefore he can lead out from hell those held therein. The church places its faith in this possibility above all through the paschal message of Christ's victory over death and hell, which permeates like a *cantus firmus* all of the liturgical books of the Orthodox Church.

---

[250]Pentecost. Ves. Kneeling prayers 3 (EL-BB).
[251]I Tim 2.4.
[252]I Kgdms 2.6.

The Theological Significance of Christ's Descent into Hades

This book has focused almost entirely on surveying and analyz-
ing primary sources. It has examined works of early Christian
literature and poetry, the writings of the fathers and teachers of the
church, and liturgical texts. It examined the Western tradition but
emphasized the Eastern Christian tradition, expressed most fully and
completely in the liturgical poetry of the Orthodox Church. This epi-
logue will attempt to synthesize the material in order to form a theological understanding.

SOME CONCLUSIONS

Based on the preceding survey of sources, certain conclusions and
general observations can be made regarding an understanding of the
doctrine of the descent into Hades in the Christian tradition.

The teaching on Christ's descent is an inseparable part of the
dogmatic tradition of the church. It was shared by all members of
the ancient church as reflected in the New Testament, the works of
the early Christian apologists, fathers and teachers of the church,
ancient and later writers of both the East and West, as well as in the
baptismal creeds, eucharistic services, and liturgical texts. "It seems
that the descent of Christ into hell was by itself not contested either
in Gaulle, nor in North Africa, nor in Italy, nor in Palestine, nor in
Alexandria, nor in Syria, nor in Armenia," writes R. Gounelle.
According to him, "in the period in question no Christian could pos-

sibly reject the descent of Christ into hell without putting into question the notion which was an integral part of church faith and therefore without joining the side of the opponents of Christianity."[1]

While the fact that the descent was not itself questioned by the representatives of church tradition, there existed various interpretations of this event. Many writers maintained that Christ freed all who were held captive in hell, others thought that only the Old Testament righteous were liberated, and another group believed that only those who came to believe in Christ and followed him were saved. Finally, others held that Christ freed only those who had lived in faith and piety during their earthly lives. The first interpretation is most widely reflected in the liturgical texts of the Orthodox Church: that Christ "emptied" hell and "not a single mortal" remained. The first and second opinions were endowed with equal authority in the Eastern Christian patristic tradition, but with the passing of the centuries the first gradually gave way to the second. In the Western tradition after Augustine, the second and fourth views were given preference.

Christ's preaching in hell, mentioned in 1 Peter 3.18–21, has also been interpreted in different ways. Some writers allowed the possibility that those who did not believe in Christ during their lifetimes could have come to believe in him after their death. Others, mainly Western theologians, rejected this possibility. Some insisted on a literal interpretation: that Christ preached only to the unrepentant sinners from Noah's time. Others interpreted it in a wider sense: that Christ's preaching in hell reached all who were held there. Augustine and later Western writers did not consider the Petrine text to refer to the descent into Hades and did not, therefore, believe it should be understood in an allegorical sense. This view does not correspond to any early or Eastern Christian understandings of the passage.

What is universally endorsed is the teaching that Christ mortified death and destroyed hell. This is, however, understood in different ways. The Eastern liturgical texts and many of the fathers speak of a total destruction of death and hell. Others are more specific, saying that death and hell continue to exist but only inasmuch as peo-

---

[1]R. Gounelle, *La descente du Christ aux Enfers*, p. 141.

ple's evil wills encourage its existence. In the Western tradition the view that Christ's death harmed hell but did not mortify it came into dominance.

The soteriological significance of the descent into Hades has been evaluated in a variety of ways. In the West, some maintained that the descent into Hades was a "one-time" event that had significance only for those who were in hell when it happened. Certain Western writers even considered that the "memory" of Christ's descent into Hades was not retained there. This is a perception that is entirely foreign to the Eastern tradition, in which the descent is seen as an event of universal significance. A great number of Eastern authors perceived Christ's descent into Hades as an event of universal significance, and some extended its saving action not only to past generations but also to all those who followed. The idea that all the dead received the opportunity to be saved is quite widespread among Eastern Christian writers, and it was only in the West where some authors labeled it heretical.[2]

General Church Doctrine and Personal Opinion

Personal opinions (*theologoumena*) of individual church writers, however respected they may be, are not always representative of church doctrine. This section attempts to distinguish which parts of the examined texts belong to the general doctrine of the Orthodox Church and which parts are personal opinions. In order to do this, it is necessary to first establish which sources should be considered more authoritative for Orthodox Christians and which are less significant.

The New Testament is an unconditional and indisputable doctrinal authority for all Christians. In Orthodox tradition, however, sacred Scripture is not seen as something primary in relation to church tradition. Scripture grew out of tradition and composes an inseparable part of it. Scripture is interpreted not spontaneously but from the perspective of tradition. Personal interpretations are allowed

---

[2]Cf. R. Gounelle, *La descente du Christ aux Enfers*, pp. 74, 87.

only as private opinions. Following St Paul's statement that the "veil" lying on the Old Testament was removed by Christ,[3] the Old Testament is seen as a herald of the New Testament. Thus the Hebrew Scripture is interpreted through the prism of the New Testament. Both Old and New Testaments are interpreted in the light of tradition, as reflected in the liturgical life and in writings of the fathers and teachers of the church.

Liturgical tradition of the early church should also be granted unconditional and indisputable authority. Liturgical texts are not simply works of eminent theologians and poets but are part of the liturgical experience of many generations of Christians. The authority enjoyed by the liturgical texts in the Orthodox Church is based on a process of acceptance that occurred over the course of many centuries.[4] Certain works of church fathers can contain disputable or even incorrect opinions. This cannot be said about the canonical liturgical texts, for church tradition throughout many centuries weeds out any such opinions. Therefore, if we were to create a certain hierarchy of authorities, the liturgical texts would come in second place after Scripture.

The dogmatic statements of the ecumenical and local councils, which have also undergone the same process of acceptance, also enjoy the same authority, though it must be remembered that council decisions ought not to be examined outside of the context in which they were written. Each council responded to the challenges of its times, therefore not everything that was decided by the councils is of equal significance for the contemporary Christian. Moreover, the church has the authority to return to the decisions of its councils and, if necessary, modify them.[5]

---

[3] 2 Cor 3.14–16.

[4] This does not include liturgical texts that appeared at a much later time, e.g., the many akathists written in the 17th–19th c., when the dogmatic consciousness of many members of the Orthodox Church was in a state of decline. The theological standard of the authors of these works was far from sufficient. Moreover, these texts have not received the necessary, long-term ratification by the church, which would give them the corresponding authority.

[5] In a separate paper I have attempted to examine the question of the acceptance of Councils. See: "Ecumenical Councils: A Contribution to the Dialogue between

Next in significance after Scripture, liturgy, and councils are the writings of the church fathers on doctrinal questions. In examining patristic works one should differentiate between those written on behalf of the church, which express general church teaching, and those reflecting personal theological opinion. Personal opinion is not sanctified by a general church acceptance and therefore cannot be placed on the same level with opinions that have wide-ranging acceptance. They should also not be eliminated in the attempt to construct a simplified "*summa theologica*" or to find a certain "common denominator" of Orthodox dogma. The authority of personal opinion is based on the fact that the authors are recognized by the church as fathers or teachers. If personal opinions are expressed by a father of the church and not condemned by a church council, they are considered to be within the boundaries of what is allowed and possible. They cannot, however, be regarded as obligatory for the Orthodox faithful.

Among the works that compose the patristic legacy, the writings of the church fathers are to be given priority, especially those of Eastern fathers who exerted a decisive influence on the formation of Orthodox dogma. The opinions of Western fathers that agree with the teachings of the Eastern Church are organically assimilated into Orthodox tradition, comprising the Eastern and Western theological legacy. The opinions of Western fathers that clearly contradict the teaching of the Eastern Church, however, are not authoritative for Orthodox Christians.

Together with the patristic contribution, there exist works by those called "teachers" of the church—theologians who influenced the formation of church doctrine but who, for various reasons, have not been raised to the rank of "fathers." Their opinions are authoritative only inasmuch as they correspond to the teaching of the church.

From apocryphal literature, only those works accepted by the church—either directly or indirectly—are considered authoritative. They include texts that have been reflected in the liturgical life or in

Eastern Orthodox and Oriental Orthodox Churches," in H. Alfeyev, *Orthodox Witness Today* (Geneva: WCC Publications, 2006), pp. 11–24.

hagiographic literature. Apocrypha rejected by the church do not have any standing for the Orthodox believer.

Finally, numerous theological works of both ancient and contemporary church authors, which clarify aspects of doctrine, may also be considered authoritative. Although the dogmatic teaching of the church is unchangeable for all time, it has required fresh explanations in different periods of church history. The Orthodox Church does not limit the "patristic age" to any particular period in church history: this "age" continues over the entire course of history; for as long as Christ's church stands; and for as long as the Holy Spirit, who enlightens and inspires people to theological creativity, works within it. There exists, however, a clear criterion, by which Orthodox theological positions of any period can be "tested" for dogmatic accuracy. For the Orthodox mind the criterion is faithfulness to church tradition.

Having established priorities and thus cleared the way for further investigation, we may attempt to separate what in the dogma of Christ's descent into Hades belongs to the teaching of the entire church from that which belongs to the realm of personal theological opinion.

First of all, belief in Christ's descent into Hades and his preaching to the dead is not a *theologoumenon*,[6] but belongs to the realm of general church doctrine. This belief is based on the New Testament, works of the church fathers, and liturgical texts. It is, therefore, as significant for today's Orthodox Church as it was for the Christian church of early centuries. The teaching that Christ granted to *all* the possibility of salvation and opened for *all* the doors to paradise should also be considered general church doctrine. This teaching is confirmed by the vast majority of liturgical texts referring to the subject, as well as by works of many church fathers.

Did all or only some follow Christ? Answers to this question belong to the realm of *theologoumena*. The doctrine on salvation formulated by the eastern fathers, particularly by St Maximus the Confessor and St John Damascene, can serve as a key to answering this

---

[6]In this we disagree with R. Gounelle, who calls it "notre théologoumène" throughout his study.

question. According to this doctrine, all are called to salvation but not everyone responds. The only hindrance to salvation is one's free will to resist God's call. Such an understanding radically differs from the doctrine of predestination formed in the Western Augustinian tradition.

The entire church also supports the belief that Christ liberated the Old Testament righteous from the bonds of hell. This doctrine is based on the works of the fathers, liturgical texts, and certain ancient apocrypha that became accepted by the church. However, the opinion that *only* the righteous of the Old Testament were saved and that everyone else remained in hell for eternal torment should be considered a personal opinion. In any case, it is no more authoritative than the Eastern Christian belief that Christ led out the Old Testament righteous.

The teaching that Christ trampled on death by his death, abolished the power of the devil, and destroyed hell—a teaching based on the New Testament, liturgical texts, and works of the church fathers—is general church doctrine. The devil, death, and hell continue to exist, but their power over people is neither unconditional nor unlimited, for hell "reigns," but "not for ever," over the race of mortals. The opinion that Christ only "wounded" hell but did not mortify it should be considered a personal interpretation without authority for the entire church.

Statements and judgments in this book may be disputed not only by Western Christians but also by certain members of the Orthodox Church. Some may say that a "hierarchy of authorities" should not be constructed, since all of the above-mentioned sources are of equal authority for the Christian. The aim of this book, however, is not to marginalize certain dogmatic writings but to point to the significance of liturgical sources. Very often "professional" theologians, including those belonging to the Orthodox Church, underestimate the role of liturgical tradition. Some forget that the church's *lex credendi* is based on its *lex orandi* and that Orthodox services are an organic and adequate expression of the church's dogmatic teaching. The fact that liturgical texts are in second place after the New Testament while other sources are placed below them is conditioned by the desire to restore justice. Historically, even the New Testament Scriptures are secondary relative to the liturgical tradition, since the Christian community grew out from the Eucharist and from the liturgy in a wider sense (i.e., from the *leitourgia*, the "common affair," the common life of prayer, and the services). Christians celebrated liturgical services long before the appearance of the New Testament writings and their compilation into one generally accepted canon.

The Descent into Hades and Theodicy

The theological significance of the doctrine of the descent has great significance for theodicy—the justification of God in the face of the accusing human mind.[7] Why does God permit suffering and evil? Why does he condemn people to the pains of hell? To what extent is God responsible for what happens on earth? In the Bible, why does God appear as a cruel and unmerciful judge, "repenting" of his actions and punishing people for mistakes that he knew of beforehand and that he could have prevented? These and other similar questions have been posed throughout history.

At the outset, it may be said that the doctrine of the descent raises the veil over the mystery that envelops the relationship between God and the devil. The history of this relationship goes back to the time of creation. According to common church teaching, the devil was created as a good and perfect creature, but he fell away from God because of his pride. The drama of the personal relationship between God and the devil, however, did not end here. After his falling away, the devil began to oppose divine goodness and love by every means, doing all he could to prevent salvation. The devil, however, is not all-powerful— his might is restricted by God, and he can operate only within the limits permitted by God. This last statement is confirmed by the opening lines of the Book of Job, where the devil appears as a creature having personal relations with God and being fully subjected to him.

In creating human beings and placing them in a situation where they choose between good and evil, God assumed responsibility for

---

[7]The term "theodicy" (literally "the justification of God") was invented by Leibniz in the early 18th century.

their further destiny. God did not leave humans alone to face the devil but entered into the struggle for humanity's spiritual survival. To this end he sent prophets and teachers; and then he became a man, suffered on the cross, died, descended into hell, and was raised from the dead in order to share human fate. By descending into Hades, Christ did not destroy the devil as a personal, living creature but abolished the power of the devil, depriving the devil of the authority and power that he stole. When he rebelled against God, the devil set himself the task of creating his own autonomous kingdom where he would be the master, winning back from God a space where God's presence could not, in any way, be felt. In Old Testament understanding, this place was Sheol. After Christ's descent, Sheol became a place of divine presence.

This presence is felt by all in paradise as a source of joy and bliss, but for those in hell it is a wellspring of suffering. After Christ, hell is no longer the place where the devil reigns and people suffer but is a prison for the devil himself as well as for those who have voluntarily decided to stay with him and share his fate. Christ abolished the sting of death, and the walls of hell were destroyed. But "death even without its sting is still powerful for us. . . . Hell with its walls destroyed and its gates abolished is still filled with those who, having left the narrow royal path of the cross leading to paradise, follow the broad way all their lives."[8]

Christ descended into hell not as the devil's victim but as Conqueror. He descended in order to "bind up the powerful" and to "plunder his vessels." According to patristic teaching, the devil did not recognize in Christ the incarnate God. He took him for an ordinary man and, rising to the "bait" of the flesh, swallowed the "hook" of the Deity. However, the presence of Christ in hell became the poison that began to gradually ruin hell from within.[9] Hell's final destruction and the ultimate victory over the devil will happen at Christ's second coming when "the last enemy to be destroyed is

---

[8]Innocent, Archbishop of Cherson and Tauria, *Works*, vol. V (St Petersburg–Moscow, 1870), p. 289 (Homily on Great Saturday).

[9]*Demonstration* 22, 4–5, in *The Homilies of Aphraates, the Persian Sage*, ed. W. Wright, pp. 420–421.

death," when everything will be subjected to Christ, and when God will become "all in all."[10]

The doctrine of the descent is important for an understanding of God's action in human history, as reflected in the Old Testament. The biblical account of the flood, which destroyed all humanity, is a stumbling block for many who wish to believe in a merciful God but cannot reconcile themselves with a God who "repents" of his own deed. The teaching on the descent into Hades, as set forth in 1 Peter 3.18–21, however, brings an entirely new perspective into our understanding of the mystery of salvation. The death sentence passed by God does not mean that human beings are deprived of hope for salvation because, failing to turn to God during their lifetimes, people could turn to him in the afterlife, having heard Christ's preaching in hell. While committing those he created to death, God did not destroy them but merely transferred them to a different state in which they could hear the preaching of Christ, believe him, and follow him.

Christ's descent into Hades is significant not only for human destiny but also for the destiny of all creation. God's light entered the realm that it had never before penetrated and enlightened not only heaven and earth but also the netherworld. It was noted in the discussion on the paschal canon of St John Damascene that the entire created world underwent corruption and death as a result of humanity's fall. Therefore all creation needs the redemptive sacrifice of Christ, the vanquisher of death. The deed begun by Christ on earth:

> was completed in hell. While nobody over the course of so many centuries forced death to free its captives, "The Master of Angels, descending" into this dark dungeon, forced death to free all of them! And "having bound the strong tyrant," he "stole" its weapon! The shining Divinity of the Sun of Righteousness "shone" on the dark lair of hell, emptied it and spread everywhere the unfading light of his most glorious Resurrection. The most pure body of the Lord was placed into the earth as a bright beacon, and his unstoppable radiance and mighty splendor drove out the darkness that had reigned

---

[10]1 Cor 15.26–28.

in hell and enlightened the ends of the earth. . . . Shining unto the ends of the earth, the striking radiance of the Divinity mortified death and hell. . . . And now everything: heaven, earth, and the nethermost parts have received the light of the serene glory of the Most Holy Trinity. By the warmth of this Divine Light is man, the world, and all creation quickened, celebrating and rejoicing with inexpressible exultation.[11]

THE SOTERIOLOGICAL IMPLICATIONS OF THE DOCTRINE OF THE DESCENT INTO HADES

The doctrine of Christ's descent into Hades is an integral part of Orthodox soteriology. The implications, however, depend on the way in which the preaching of Christ in hell and its salutary impact on people is understood.[12] Were the preaching addressed only to the Old Testament righteous, the soteriological implications of the doctrine would be minimal, but were it addressed to all in hell, its significance would be considerably increased. There seem to be enough grounds to argue, following Greek Orthodox theologian I. Karmires, that "according to the teaching of *almost* all the Eastern fathers, the preaching of the Saviour was extended to all without exception and salvation was offered to all the souls who passed away from the beginning of time, whether Jews or Greeks, righteous or unrighteous."[13] At the same time, the preaching of Christ in hell was of good and joyful news of deliverance and salvation, not only for the righteous but also for the unrighteous. It was not preaching "to condemn for unbelief and wickedness," as it seemed to Thomas Aquinas. The entire text of the First Letter of St Peter relating to the preaching of Christ in hell speaks against its understanding in terms of accusation and damnation.[14]

---

[11]N. Vasiliadis, *Tainstvo smerti*, p. 182.

[12]Cf. I. N. Karmirēs, *Hē eis haidou kathodos Christou* (Athens, 1939), p. 107.

[13]Ibid., p. 119.

[14]Bishop Gregory (Yaroshevsky), *An Interpretation of the Most Difficult Passages in the First Letter of St Peter* (Simferopol, 1902), p. 10.

Whether all or only some responded to the call of Christ and were delivered from hell remains an open question. If we accept the point of view of those Western church writers who maintain that Christ delivered only the Old Testament righteous, then Christ's salutary action is reduced merely to the restoration of justice. The Old Testament righteous suffered in hell undeservedly, not for their personal sins but because of the general sinfulness of human nature, and therefore their deliverance from hell was a "duty" that God was obliged to undertake. Such an act could scarcely constitute a miracle, earning the praise of church hymns or making the angels tremble.

Unlike the West, Christian consciousness in the East admits the opportunity for salvation not only for those who believe during their lifetime but also for those who were not given to believe but pleased God with their good works. In one of his hymns John Damascene develops the idea that salvation was not only for those who confessed the right faith, not only for the Old Testament righteous, but also for those heathens who distinguished themselves by a lofty morality:

> Some say that [Christ delivered from hell] only the
>   believers,[15]
> such as fathers and prophets,
> judges and together with them kings, local rulers
> and some others from the Hebrew people,
> not numerous and known to all.
> But we shall reply to those who think so
> that there is nothing undeserved,
> nothing miraculous and nothing strange
> in that Christ should save the believers,
> for he remains only the fair Judge,
> and everyone who believes in him will not perish.
> So they all ought to have been saved
> and delivered from the bonds of hell
> by the descent of God and Master—
> that same happened by his Disposition.

---

[15]I.e., those who believed in their lifetime.

Whereas those who were saved only through [God's]
    love of men
were, as I think, all those
who had the purest life
and did all kinds of good works,
living in modesty, temperance, and virtue,
but the pure and divine faith
they did not conceive because they were not instructed in it
and remained altogether unlearnt.
They were those whom the Steward and Master of all
drew, captured in the divine nets
and persuaded to believe in Him,
illuminating them with the divine rays
and showing them the true light.[16]

This approach renders the descent into Hades exceptional in its soteriological implications. According to the Damascene, those who were not taught the true faith during their lifetime can come to believe when in hell. By their good works and ascetic life they prepared themselves for encountering Christ. These are the same people about whom St Paul says that, having no law, they "do by nature things contained in the law," for "the work of the law is written in their hearts."[17] Those who live by the law of natural morality but do not share the true faith can hope, by virtue of their righteousness, that in a face-to-face encounter with God, they will recognize in him the One they "ignorantly worshipped."[18]

Does this have anything to do with those who died outside the Christian faith after the descent of Christ into hell? It does not if we accept the Western teaching that the descent into Hades was a "one-time" event and that the recollection of Christ did not survive in hell. But it does if we proceed from the assumption that after Christ hell was no longer like the Old Testament *sheol*, but a place of divine presence. In addition, as Archpriest Serge Bulgakov writes:

---

[16]*Concerning Those Who Died in Faith* (PG 95:257ac).
[17]Rom 2.14–15.
[18]Acts 17.23.

all events in the life of Christ, which happen in time, have timeless, abiding significance. Therefore, the so-called "preaching in hell," which is the faith of the Church, is a revelation of Christ to those who in their earthly life could not see or know Christ. There are no grounds for limiting this event . . . to the Old Testament saints alone, as Catholic theology does. Rather, the power of this preaching should be extended to all time for those who during their life on earth did not and could not know Christ but meet him in the afterlife.[19]

According to the teaching of the Orthodox Church, all people, whether believers or non-believers, appear before God after their death. Therefore, even for those who did not believe during their lifetime, there is hope that after death they will recognize God as their Savior and Redeemer, if their previous life on earth prepared them for this recognition.

The hymn of John Damascene clearly states that the virtuous heathens were not "taught" the true faith. This is a clear allusion to the words of Christ: "Go ye, therefore, and teach all nations, baptizing them in the name of the Father, and of the Son, and of the Holy Ghost"[20] and "He that believeth and is baptized shall be saved; but that believeth not shall be damned."[21] Damnation is extended only to those who were taught Christian faith but did not believe. But if a person were deprived of teaching, if he in his real life did not encounter the preaching of the gospel and did not have an opportunity to respond to it, can he be damned for it? This question disturbed ancient authors such as Clement of Alexandria.

Is it at all possible that the fate of a person can be changed after his death? Is death that border beyond which some unchangeable static existence comes? Does the development of the human person not stop after death? It is impossible for one to actively repent in hell; it is impossible to rectify the evil deeds one committed by appropriate good works. It may, however, be possible for one to repent through a "change of heart," a review of one's values. One of the testimonies

---

[19]Serge Bulgakov, *Agnets Bozhiy* [The Lamb of God] (Moscow, 2000), p. 394.
[20]Matt 28.19.
[21]Mark 16.16.

to this is the rich man of the Gospel. He realized the gravity of his situation as soon as found himself in hell. Indeed, in his lifetime he was focused on earthly pursuits and forgot God, but once in hell he realized that God was his only hope for salvation.[22] Besides, according to the teaching of the Orthodox Church, the fate of a person after death can be changed through the prayer of the church. Thus existence after death has its own dynamics. On the basis of what has been said above, it may be said that after death the development of the human person does not cease, for existence after death is not a transfer from a dynamic into a static being, but rather a continuation on a new level of that road which a person followed in his or her lifetime.

* * *

As the last stage in Christ's divine descent (*katabasis*) and self-emptying (*kenosis*), his descent into Hades became the starting point of humanity's ascent toward deification (*theosis*).[23] Since this descent, the path to paradise is opened for both the living and the dead, a path followed by those whom Christ delivered from hell. The destination point for all humanity and every individual is the fullness of deification in which God becomes "all in all."[24] It is for this deification that God first created man and then, when "the time had fully come,"[25] became man, suffered, died, descended to Hades, and was raised from the dead.

The liturgy of St Basil the Great, celebrated in the Orthodox Church ten times a year, including Great and Holy Saturday, when the church commemorates Christ's descent into Hades, renders this in the following way:

> Though he was God before the ages, yet he appeared on earth and lived among men, becoming incarnate of a holy Virgin; he emptied himself, taking the form of a servant, conforming himself to the body of our lowliness, that he might conform us to the image of his

---

[22]Luke 16.20–31.
[23]Cf. J. Daniélou, *The Theology of Jewish Christianity*, pp. 233–234.
[24]1 Cor 15.28.
[25]Gal 4.4.

glory. For since by man sin entered into the world, and through sin death, so it pleased thine only-begotten Son, who was in the bosom of thee, the God and Father . . . to condemn sin in his flesh, that those who are dying in Adam might be made alive in thy Christ himself. He lived in this world and gave us commandments of salvation, releasing us from the delusions of idolatry, he brought us to knowledge of thee, the true God and Father. He obtained us for his chosen people, a royal priesthood, a holy nation. Having cleansed us in water, and sanctified us with the Holy Spirit, he gave himself as a ransom to death, in which we were held captive, sold under sin. Descending through the Cross into hell that he might fill all things with himself, he loosed the pangs of death. He arose on the third day, having made for all flesh a path to the resurrection from the dead, since it was not possible for the Author of life to be conquered by corruption. So he became the first-fruits of those who have fallen asleep, the first-born from the dead, that he might be himself the first in all things.[26]

We do not know if everyone followed Christ when he rose from hell, nor do we know if everyone will follow him to the eschatological heavenly kingdom when he will become "all in all." We do know that, since Christ's descent, the way to resurrection has been opened for "all flesh," salvation has been granted to every human being, and the gates of paradise have been opened for all who wish to enter through them. This is the faith of the early church, inherited from the first generation of Christians and cherished by Orthodox tradition. This is the never-extinguished hope of all those who believe in Christ, who once and for all conquered death, destroyed hell, and granted resurrection to the entire human race.

---

[26] *The Divine Liturgy of St Basil the Great* (London, 2001), pp. 46–48.

Selected Bibliography

Every effort has been made by the author to make this Bibliography as complete and accurate as possible. However not all information was available, therefore this Bibliography should be used as a guide rather than an ultimate source.

1. Abbot, E.A. "The Original Language of the Odes of Solomon." *Journal of Theological Studies* 14 (1913): 313ff.
2. Acerbi, A. *L'Ascensione di Isaia: Cristologia e profetismo in Siria nei primi decenni del II Secolo.* Milan, 1989.
3. *Acta Apostolorum Apocrypha.* Partis alterius volumen alterium. Edited by R.A. Lipsius and M. Bonnet. Hildesheim, 1959.
4. Alfeyev, H. "Le dialogue avec les préchalcédoniennes et la réception des Conciles. A propos de la réception des Conciles dans l'Eglise ancienne." *Service orthodoxe de presse*, Supplement no. 217, pp. 1–14. Paris, April 1997.
5. Alfeyev, H. *The Spiritual World of Isaac the Syrian.* Kalamazoo, Michigan: Cistercian Publications, 2000.
6. Ambrose of Milan. *Hymnes*, edited and translated by J. Fontaine et al. Paris: Cerf, 1992.
7. Amphilochius of Iconium. *Amphilochii Iconiensis Opera*, edited by C. Datema. CCSG 3. Louvain: Brepols, 1978.
8. Aphrahat. *Aphraatis sapientis persae demonstrationes.* Textum syriacum vocalium signis instruxit, latine vertit, notis illustravit D. Joannes Parisot. Patrologia Syriaca 1–2. Paris, 1894–1907.
9. Aphrahat. *The Homilies of Aphraates, the Persian Sage.* Edited by W. Wright. London-Edinburgh, 1869.
10. Arranz, M. *Le Typicon du Monastère du Saint Sauveur à Messine.* OrChrAn 185. Rome: Pontificium Institutum Orientalium Studiorum, 1969.
11. *Ascensio Isaiae.* Commentarius, edited by E. Norelli. CCSA 8. Turnhout: Brepols, 1995.
12. *Ascensio Isaiae.* Textus, edited by P. Pettiolo, A.G. Kossova, C. Leonardi, E. Norelli, L. Perrone. CCSA 7. Tournhout: Brepols, 1995.
13. Assemani, J.S. *Bibliotheca orientalis* III, 1. Rome, 1725.

14. Athanasius of Alexandria. *Athanasius Werke* II/1, edited by H.-G. Opitz. Berlin: W. De Gruyter, 1940–1941.

15. Augustine. *Sancti Aurelii Augustini De civitate Dei,* Libri XI–XXII. CCSL 48. Louvain: Brepols, 1955.

16. Aulén, G. *Christus victor: La notion chrétienne de rédemption.* Paris: Aubier, 1949.

17. Averintsev, S. *Poetika rannevizantiiskoi literatury* [Poetics of Early Byzantine Literature]. Moscow, 1997.

18. Balthasar, H. U. von, and A. Grillmeyer. *Le mystère pascal.* Paris: Aubier, 1972.

19. Bauckham, R. *The Fate of the Dead: Studies on the Jewish and Chrisitian Apocalypses.* Supplement to *Novum Testamentum* 3. Leiden-Boston-Cologne: E.J. Brill, 1998.

20. Beck, H.G. *Kirche und theologische Literatur im byzantinischen Reich.* Munich, 1959.

21. Bevan, A.A. *The Hymn of the Soul, Contained in the Syriac Acts of St Thomas.* Cambridge University Press, 1897.

22. Bieder, W. *Die Vorstellung von der Höllenschaft Jesu Christi: Beitrag zur Entstehungsgeschichte der Vorstellung vom sogenannten Descensus ad inferos.* Abhandlungen zur Theologie des Alten und Neuen Testaments 19. Zürich: Zwingli-Verlag, 1949.

23. Bonwetsch, N. "Die apokryphen Fragen des Bartolomäus." Pages 1–42 in *Nachrichten der Gesellschaft der Wissenschaften zu Göttingen.* Göttingen, 1897.

24. Bornkamm, G. *Mythos und Legende in den apokryphen Thomas-Akten.* Göttingen: Vandenhoeck and Ruprecht, 1933.

25. Bouman, C.A. "He Descended into Hell." *Worship* 33, no. 44 (1959): 194–203.

26. Bousset, W. "Zur Hadesfahrt Christi." *Zeitschrift für die neutesta-mentliche Wissenschaft und die Kunde der älteren Kirche* 19 (1919–1920): 50–66.

27. Bousset, W. *Kyrios Christos: Geschichte des Christusglaubens von den Anfängen des Christentums bis Irenaeus.* Göttingen, 1921.

28. Bradcock, F.J. *The History of the Creeds.* London: SPCK, 1930.

29. Brock, S. "Baptismal Themes in the Writings of Jacob of Serugh." *Symposium Syriacum.* OrChrAn 205:335–347. Rome: Pontificium Institutum Orientalium Studiorum, 1976.

30. Brock, S. "From Ephrem to Romanos." Pages 139–151 in *Studia Patristica,* vol. 20, edited by E.A. Livingstone. Louvain: Brepols, 1989.

31. Brock, S. "The Christology of the Church of the East." *Traditsii i nasledie Khristianskogo Vostoka,* edited by D.E. Afinogenov and A.V. Murav'ev. Moscow: Indrik, 1996.

32. Brock, S. *A Brief Outline of Syriac Literature*. Kottayam: St. Ephrem Ecumenical Research Institute, 1997.

33. Brock, S. *Spirituality in Syriac Tradition*. Kottayam: St. Ephrem Ecumenical Research Institute, 2005.

34. Brock, S. *The Luminous Eye: The Spiritual World Vision of St Ephrem the Syrian*. Kalamazoo, Michigan: Cisercian Publications, 1985.

35. Bruns, H.D. *Canones Apostolorum et Conciliorum Veterum Selecti*, vol. I. Berlin: 1839.

36. Bruston, C. *La descent aux Enfers d'après les Apôtres et d'après l'Eglise*. Paris: Fischbacher, 1897.

37. Budge, E.A. *Coptic Homilies in the Dialect of Upper Egypt Edited from the Papyrus Codex Oriental 5001 in the British Museum*. London, 1910.

38. Bulgakov, S. *Agnets Bozhiy* [The Lamb of God]. Moscow, 2000.

39. Bumazhnov, D. *Der Mensch als Gottes Bild im christlichen Ägypten*. Studien und Texte zu Antike und Christentum 34. Tübingen: Mohr Siebeck, 2006.

40. Burkitt, F.C. *Saint Ephrem's Quotations from the Gospels*. Cambridge University Press, 1901.

41. Burn, A.E. *The Apostles' Creed*. London: Rivingtons, 1906.

42. Burn, A.E. *The Athanasian Creed and Its Early Commentaries*. Texts and Studies 4. Cambridge University Press, 1896.

43. Cabaniss, A. "The Harrowing of Hell, Psalm 24 and Pliny the Younger." *Vigiliae christianae* 7 (1953): 65–74.

44. Cabrol, F. "Descente du Christ aux Enfers d'après la liturgie." *Dictionnaire d'archéologie chrétienne et la liturgie*, vol. IV, cols. 682–693. Paris: Letouzey et Ané, 1920.

45. Canévet, M. "La mort du Christ et le mystère de sa personne humano-divine dans la théologie du IVe siècle."*Les quatre fleuves: Cahiers de recherche et de réflexion religieuses* 15–16: pp. 71–92. Paris: Beauchesne, 1982.

46. Chadwick, H. "Some Reflections on the Character and Theology of the Odes of Solomon." In *Kyriakon: Festschrift Johannes Quasten*, vol. I. Münster: Aschendorff, 1970.

47. Chaine, J. "Descente du Christ aux enfers." *Dictionnaire de la Bible, Supplément*, vol. II:397–403. Paris: Letouzey et Ané, 1934.

48. Charles, R.H., ed. *The Greek Versions of the Testament of the Twelve Patriarchs*. Oxford: Clarendon Press, 1908.

49. Charlesworth, J.H. "The Odes of Solomon, Not Gnostic." *Catholic Biblical Quarterly* 31 (1969): 357–369.

50. Charlesworth, J.H., ed. *The Old Testament Pseudepigrapha*, vol. 1 (New York: Doubleday, 1985).

51. Charlesworth, J.H., ed. and trans. *The Odes of Solomon*. Oxford: Claren-
     don Press, 1973.
52. Christou, P. Ἑλληνικὴ πατρολογία. Vol. 2. Thessalonika, 1991.
53. Christou, P. Ἑλληνικὴ πατρολογία. Vol. 3. Thessalonika, 1987.
54. Clemen, C. *Niederfahren zu den Toten: Ein Beitrag zur Würdigung des
     Apostolikums*. Giessen: J. Ricker'sche Verlagsbuchhandlung, 1900.
55. Clement of Alexandria. *Clemens Alexandrinus*, Band II: *Stromata* I–VI,
     edited by O. Stählin, L. Früchtel, U. Treu. GCS 52. Berlin–Leipzig,
     1960.
56. Clement of Alexandria. *Clemens Alexandrinus*, Band III: *Stromata*
     VII–VIII, edited by O. Stählin, L. Früchtel, U. Treu.In GCS 17:3–102.
     Berlin-Leipzig, 1970.
57. Connolly, R.H. "Greek the Original Language of the Odes of
     Solomon." *Journal of Theological Studies* 14 (1913): 530ff.
58. Connolly, R.H. *The So-called Egyptian Church Order and Derived Doc-
     uments*. Cambridge: Cambridge University Press, 1916.
59. Cooper, A. "Ps 24:7–10: Mythology and Exegesis." *Journal of Biblical
     Literature* 102, no. 1 (1983): 37–60.
60. Cross, F.L., ed. *Oxford Dictionary of the Christian Church*. Third edition
     by E.A. Livingstone. Oxford: Oxford University Press, 1997.
61. Crouzel, H. "L'Hadès et la Géhenne selon Origène." Pages 291–331 in
     Gregorianum 59. Rome: Pontificia Università Gregoriana, 1978.
62. Dalton, W.J. *Christ's Proclamation to the Spirits: A Study of 1 Peter
     3:18–4:6*. Analecta Biblica 23. Rome: Pontifical Biblical Institute, 1965.
63. Daniélou, J. *Théologie du Judéo-Christianisme*. Paris-Tournai: Desclée
     de Brouwer, 1958.
64. Dante Alighieri. *La divina commedia*. Città del Vaticano, 1965.
65. de Aldama, J.A., compiler. *Repertorium pseudochrysostomicum*. Paris:
     Editions du CNRS, 1965.
66. Der Nessesian, S. "An Armenian Version of the Homilies on the Har-
     rowing of Hell." *Dumbarton Oaks Papers* 8 (1954).
67. Diekamp, F., ed. *Doctrina Patrum de incarnatione Verbi*. Münster, 1909.
68. Dix, G., ed. *The Treatise on the Apostolic Tradition of St Hippolytus of
     Rome*. London: SPCK, 1937.
69. Dmitrievsky, A. *Bogosluzheniye strastnoy i paskhalnoy sedmits vo sv.
     Ierusalime IX–X v.* [The services of Passion week and Easter week in
     the Holy City of Jerusalem in the 9th and 10th centuries]. Kazan, 1894.
70. Dmitrievsky, A. *Opisanie slavyanskikh rukopisey v bibliotekakh
     pravoslavnogo Vostoka* [The description of the Slavonic manuscripts in
     the libraries of the Orthodox East]. Vols. I–III. Kiev-St Petersburg,
     1895–1917.

71. Dörries, H. *Die Theologie des Makarios/Symeon*. Göttingen: Vandenhoeck and Ruprecht, 1978.

72. Dörries, H. *Symeon von Mesopotamien: Die Überlieferung der messalianischen "Makarios"-Schriften*. Leipzig: J.C. Hinrichs, 1941.

73. Elliott, J.K. *The Apocryphal New Testament*. Oxford: Oxford University Press, 1993.

74. Emerau, C. *Saint Ephrem le Syrien, son oeuvre littérarie grecque*. Paris, 1919.

75. Emerton, S.A. "Some Problems of Text and Language in the Odes of Solomon." *Journal of Theological Studies* 18 (1967): 372–406.

76. Ephrem of Syria. *Commentaire de l'Évangile concordant*, edited by L. Leloir. CSCO 137. Scriptores armeniaci 1. Louvain: Brepols, 1953.

77. Ephrem of Syria. *Der heiligen Ephraem der Syrers Carmina Nisibena*, edited by E. Beck. Vols. I–II. CSCO 218, 240. Scriptores Syri 92, 102. Louvain: Brepols, 1961, 1963.

78. Ephrem of Syria. *Der heiligen Ephraem der Syrers Sermo de Domino nostro*, edited by E. Beck. CSCO 270. Scriptores Syri 116. Louvain: Brepols, 1966.

79. Ephrem of Syria. *Der heiligen Ephraem der Syrers Sermones* II, edited by E. Beck. CSCO 311. Scriptores Syri 124. Louvain: Brepols, 1970.

80. Ephrem of Syria. *Patris nostri Ephraem Syri Opera*, edited by J. Assemani. Vol. 4. Rome, 1746.

81. Ephrem of Syria. *Sancti Ephraem Syri Opera Omnia*, vol. III, edited by Stephano Evodio Assemani. 6 vols. Rome, 1744.

82. Florovsky, G. *Vizantiyskie Otsy V–VIII vekov* [Byzantine Fathers of the fifth to eighth centuries]. Paris: YMCA Press, 1933.

83. Franzmann, M. *The Odes of Solomon: An Analysis of the Poetical Structure and Form*. Göttingen: Vandenhoeck and Ruprecht, 1991.

84. Friedman, J. "Christ's Descent into Hell and Redemption through Evil: A Radical Reformation Perspective." *Archiv für Reformationsgeschichte* 76 (1985): 217–230.

85. Funk, F.X., and K. Bihlmeyer. *Die apostolischen Väter*. Tübingen: J.C.B. Mohr, 1924.

86. Garitte, G. "Homélie d'Éphrem, 'Sur la Mort et le Diable.' Version géorgienne et version arabe." *Le Muséon* 77:123–163. Louvain, 1969.

87. Geerard, M., ed. *Clavis patrum graecorum*, vol. II. Louvain: Brepols, 1974.

88. Geerard, M., ed. *Clavis Apocryphorum Novi Testamenti*. Louvain: Brepols, 1992.

89. Gregory of Nyssa. Γρηγορίου Νύσσης ἅπαντατὰ ἔργα. Vol. 10. Ἕλληνες Πατέρες τῆς ἐκκλησίας 103. Thessalonica, 1990.

90. Gregory the Great. *Sancti Gregorii Magni Opera, Registrum epistularum*, Libri I–VII. Edited by D. Norberg. CCSL 140. Louvain: Brepols, 1982.

91. Grelot, P. "La descente aux Enfers et la prédication aux morts." Pages 231–236, in *Etudes sur la première Lettre du Pierr*. Paris: Cerf, 1980.

92. Grenfell, B., and A. Hunt. *The Amherst Papyri*, vol. I. London: H. Frowde, 1900.

93. Grillmeier, A. "Der Gottensohn im Totenreich: Soteriologische und christologische Motivierung der Descensuslehre in der älteren christlichen Überlieferung." *Zeitschrift für Katholische Theologie* 71 (1941): 4–5.

94. Grillmeier, A. *Christ in Christian Tradition*, vol. 1. Atlanta: John Knox Press, 1975.

95. Grosdidier de Matons, J. *Romanos le Mélode: et les origines de la poésie religieuse à Byzance*. Paris: Beauchesne, 1977.

96. Gounelle, R. *La descente du Christ aux Enfers: Institutionnalisation d'une croyance*. Etudes augustiennes, Serie antiquité 162. Paris: Institut d'Études augustiniennes, 2000.

97. Grudem, W. "He Did Not Descend into Hell: A Plea for Following Scripture instead of the Apostles' Creed." *Journal of the Evangelical Theological Society* 34, no. 1 (1991): 103–113.

98. Gschwind, K. *Die Niederfahrt Christi in der Unterwelt: Ein Beitrag zum Exegese des Neuen Testaments und zum Geschichte der Taufsymbols*. Münster: Ascendorff, 1911.

99. Güder, E. *Die Lehre von der Erscheinung Jesu Christi unter den Todten in ihrem Zusammenhange mit dem Lehre von dem letzten Dingen*. Bern: Jent und Reinert, 1853.

100. Guerrier, L. *Le testament en Galilée de Notre-Séigneur Jésus-Christ: Texte éthiopien édité et traduit avec le concours de S. Grébaut*. Paris: Firmin-Didot, 1913.

101. Gumilevsky, Philaret. *Istoricheskiy obzor pesnopevtsev I pesnopeniya Grecheskoy Tserkvi* [Historical Survey of Hymnographers and Hymns of the Greek Church]. Chernigov, 1864.

102. Hahn, G., and G.L. Hahn. *Bibliothek der Symbole und Glaubensregeln der Alten Kirche*. Breslau: E. Morgenstern, 1897.

103. Harris, J.R. "Ephrem's Use of the Odes of Solomon." *The Expositor*, series 8, vol. 3 (1912): 113–119.

104. Harris, W.H. *The Descent of Christ: Ephesians 4:7–11 and Traditional Hebrew Imagery*. Leiden-New York-Cologne: E.J. Brill, 1996.

105. Hennecke, J. *New Testament Apocrypha*, vol. 1. London: Butterworth Press, 1963.

106. Herzog, M. *Descensus ad inferos: Eine religions-philosophische Untersuchung der Motive und Interpretationen mit besondere Berücksichtigung*

der monigraphischen Literatur seit dem 16. Jahrhundert. Frankfurter Theologische Studien 53. Frankfurt-am-Main: J. Krecht, 1997.

107. Hoffman, R.J. "Confluence in Early Christian and Gnostic Literature: The Descensus Christi ad Inferos (Acta Pilati xvii–xviii)." *Journal of New Testament Studies* 10 (1981): 42–60.

108. Hornschuh, M. *Studien zur Epistula Apostolorum.* PTS 5. Berlin-New York: De Gruyter, 1965.

109. Huidekoper, F. *The Belief of the First Three Centuries concerning Christ's Mission to the Underworld.* New York: D.J. Francis, 1876.

110. Innocent, Abp of Cherson and Tauria. *Tvoreniya* [Works], vol. V. St Petersburg-Moscow, 1870.

111. Isaac of Nineveh. *De perfectione religiosa,* edited by Paul Bedjan. Leipzig: O. Harrossowitz, 1909.

112. Izydorczyk, Z., ed. *The Medieval Gospel of Nicodemus: Texts, Intertexts and Contexts in Western Europe.* Medieval and Renaissance Texts and Studies 158. Tempe, Arizona: Arizona Center for Medieval and Renaissance Studies, 1997.

113. Jacquemont, P. "La descente aux Enfers dans la tradition orientale." *Lumière et vie* 17, no. 87 (1968): 31–44.

114. Jaeger, W. *Two Rediscovered Works of Ancient Christian Literature: Gregory of Nyssa and Macarius.* Leiden: Brill, 1954.

115. Jefford, C.N. "Acts of Pilate." Pages 371–372 in vol. 5, *The Anchor Bible Dictionary.* New York: Doubleday, 1992.

116. Jeremias, J. *New Testament Theology,* vol. I, *The Proclamation of Jesus.* London: SCM Press, 1972.

117. Jerome. *Sancti Hieronymi Presbyteri Opera,* Pars I, 6. CCSL 76. Louvain: Brepols, 1969.

118. Justin Martyr. *Dialogue avec Tryphon,* vol. I, ed. and trans. G. Archambault. Paris: Picard, 1909.

119. Kaestli, J.-D. "Où en est l'étude de l' 'Évangile de Barthélemy'?" *Revue biblique* 95 (1988): 5–33.

120. Karabinov, I. *Postnaya Triod'* [The Lenten Triodion]. St Petersburg, 1910.

121. Karmires, I.N. " Ἡ Χριστολογικὴ ἑτεροδιδασκαλία τοῦ ΙΣΤ′ αἰωνος καὶ εἰς ἄδου κάθοδος τοῦ Χριστοῦ." *Νέα Σίων* 30 (1935): 11–26, 65–81, 154–165.

122. Karmires, I.N. *Ἡ εἰς ἄδου κάθοδος Χριστοῦ.* Athens, 1939.

123. Kartsonis, A.D. *Anastasis: The Making of an Image.* Princeton, New Jersey: Princeton University Press, 1986.

124. Kelly, J.N.D. *Early Christian Creeds.* Essex: Longman, 1950.

125. Kelly, J.N.D. *The Athanasian Creed.* London: A. and C. Black, 1964.

126. Klijn, A.F.J. *The Acts of Thomas.* Leiden: Brill, 1962.

127. Köenig, J.L. *Die Lehre von Christi Höllenfahrt nach der Heilige Schrift, der ältesten Kirche, der Christlichen Symbolen, und nach ihrer vielumfassenden Bedeutung.* Frankfurt-am-Main: H. Zimmer, 1842.

128. Kroll, J. *Gott und Hölle: Der Mythos vom Descensuskampfe.* Studien der Bibliothek Warburg 20. Leipzig-Berlin: B.G. Teubner, 1932.

129. Lampe, G.W.H. *A Patristic Greek Lexicon.* Oxford: Oxford University Press, 1987.

130. Langgärtner, G. "Der Descensus ad Inferos in dem Osterfestbriefen des Cyrill von Alexandrien." Pages 95–100 in *Wehzeichen: Festgabe zum 60. Geburtstag von Prof. Dr. Hermenegild M. Biedermann OSA.* Würzburg: Augustinus-Verlag, 1971.

131. Larchet, J.-C. *La divinisation de l'homme selon Maxime le Confesseur.* Paris: Cerf, 1996.

132. Lebon, J. "Une ancienne opinion sur la condition du corps du Christ dans la mort." *Revue d'histoire ecclésiastique* 23 (1927): 5–43, 209–241.

133. Lebourlier, J. "A propos de l'état du Christ dans la mort." *Revue des sciences philosophiques et théologiques* 46 (1962): 629–649; 47 (1963): 161–180.

134. Liddell, H.G., and R. Scott. *A Greek-English Lexicon.* Oxford: Oxford University Press, 1989.

135. Lipsius, A. *Die Pilatenakten kritisch untersucht.* Kiel, 1886.

136. Lipsius, R.A., and M. Bonnet. *Acta Apostolorum Apocrypha,* vol. 2. Leipzig: H. Mendelssohn, 1903.

137. Loofs, F. "Descent to Hades." Pages ???–??? in vol. 4 of *Encyclopedia of Religion and Ethics,* edited by James Hastings. 12 vols. New York: Charles Scribner's Sons, 1908–1927.

138. M.-G. Mara, ed. *Evangile de Pierre.* SC 201. Paris: Cerf, 1973.

139. Maas, P. "Das Kontakion." *Byzantinische Zeitschrift* 19 (1910): ???

140. Maas, W. *Gott und die Hölle: Studien zum Descensus Christi.* Sammlung Horizonte N.F. 14. Einsiedeln: J. Verlag, 1979.

141. MacCulloch, J.A. *The Harrowing of Hell: A Comparative Study of an Early Christian Doctrine.* Edinburgh: T. and T. Clark, 1930.

142. Macarius Symeon. *Neue Homilies des Makarius/Symeon,* edited by E. Klostermann and H. Berthold. Berlin: Akademie-Verlag, 1961.

143. Macarius. *Die 50 geistlichen Homilien des Makarios,* edited by H. Dörries, E. Klostermann, M. Kroeger. PTS 4. Berlin-New York: De Gruyter, 1964.

144. Macarius. *Die syrische Überlieferung der Schriften des Makarios.* Vols. I–II, edited by W. Strothmann.Wiesbaden: Harrassowitz, 1981.

145. Macarius. *Macarii Anecdota: Seven Unpublished Homilies of Macarius,* edited by G.L. Marriott. Cambridge, Massachusetts: Harvard University Press, 1918.

146. Magne, G. *Tradition Apostolique sur les Charismes et Diataxeis des saints Apôtres.* Paris, 1975.

147. Mai, A. *Nova patrum bibliotheca.* Rome: Typis Sacri Consilii Propagando Christiano Nomini, 1844.

148. Makarius/Symeon. *Reden und Briefe,* edited by H. Berthold, vols. 1–2. Berlin: Akademie-Verlag, 1973.

149. Macarius/Symeon. *Epistola magna,* edited by R. Staats. Göttingen: Vandenhoeck and Ruprecht, 1984.

150. Mansi, J.D. *Sacrorum Conciliorum Nova et Amplissima Collectio.* Paris-Leipzig: Welter, 1901–1927.

151. Mansvetov, I. *Tserkovniy ustav* [The Church Typicon]. Moscow: Lissnera, 1885.

152. Mateos, J. *Le typicon de la Grande Eglise: Ms. Saint-Croix No. 40, Xe siècle.* 2 vol. OrChrAn 165–166. Rome: Pontificium Institutum Orientalium Studiorum, 1962–1963.

153. Mateos, J. "Un horologion inédit de S. Sabas." *Mélanges E. Tisserant III,* Studi e testi 233: 47–76. Vatican City: Biblioteca apostolic vaticana, 1964.

154. McDonnell, K. *The Baptism of Jesus in the Jordan.* Collegeville, Minnesota: Liturgical Press, 1996.

155. Melito of Sardis. *On Pascha and Fragments.* Texts and translations edited by Stuart George Hall. Oxford: Oxford University Press, 1979.

156. Melito of Sardis. *Sur la Pâque et Fragments.* Introduction, texte critique, traduction et notes par Othmar Perler. SC 123. Paris: Cerf, 1963.

157. Meyendorff, J. "Chelovechestvo Christa: Paschal'naya Tayna" [The Humanity of Christ: A Paschal Mystery]. *The Theological Journal of St Tikhon's Orthodox Theological Institute,* issue 5 (2000): ???.

158. Meyendorff, J. "Vremya Velikoy Subboty" [The Time of Great Saturday]. *Journal of the Moscow Patriarchate* 4 (1992): ???.

159. Meyendorff, J. *Christ in Eastern Christian Thought.* Washington, D.C.: Corpus Books, 1969.

160. Miller, D.L. "The Two Sandals of Christ: Descent into History and into Hell." *Eranos Jahrbuch* 50 (1981): 147–221.

161. Moricca, V. "Un nuovo testo dell' 'Evangelo di Bartolomeo.'" *Revue biblique* 18 (1921): 481–516; 19 (1922): 20–30.

162. Müller, L.G. *The "De Haeresibus" of Saint Augustin: A Translation with an Introduction and Commentary.* Patristic Studies 90. Washington, D.C.: Catholic University of America Press, 1956.

163. Nau, F. "Notes sur diverses homélies pseudépigraphiques." *Revue de l'Orient chrétien* 13 (1908): 433–434.

164. Newbold, R. "The Descent of Christ in the Odes of Solomon." *Journal of Biblical Literature* 31 (1912): 168–209.

165. Nibley, H. "Baptism for the Dead in Ancient Times." *Improvement Era* 51 (1948): 786–788, 836–838; 52 (1949): 24–26, 60, 90–91, 109–110, 112, 146–148, 180–183, 212–214.

166. O'Ceallaigh, G.C. "Dating the Commentaries of Nicodemus." *Harvard Theological Review* 56 (1963): 21–58.

167. *Die Oracula Sibyllina*. Edited by J. Geffken. GCS 8. Leipzig: J.C. Hinrichs, 1902.

168. Peel, M.L. "The Descensus ad Inferos in the Teachings of Silvanus." *Numen* 26, no. 1 (1979): 23–49.

169. Petersen, W.L. "The Dependence of Romanos the Melodist upon the Syriac Ephrem: Its Importance for the Origins of Kontakia." *Vigilia Christiana* 39 (1985): 171–187.

170. Petersen, W.L. *The Diatessaron and Ephraem Syrus as Sources of Romanos the Melodist.* CSCO 475, Subsidia 74. Louvain: Brepols, 1985.

171. Poirier, P.H. "La 'descente aux enfers' dans le cycle pascal byzantin." Pages 354–369 in *Mélanges offerts au cardinal Louis-Albert Vachon*. Quebec: Université Laval, 1989.

172. Poirier, P.H. "La Protennoia triomphe (NH XIII, 1) et la vocabulaire du Descensus ad inferos." *Le Muséon* 96 (1983): 193–204.

173. Prudentius. *Aurelii Prudentii Clementis Carmina*, edited by M.P. Cunningham. CCSL 126. Louvain: Brepols, 1996.

174. Pseudo-Macarius. *Oeuvres spirituelles (Homélies propres à la Collection III)*, edited by V. Despres. SC 275. Paris: Cerf, 1980.

175. Quillet, H. "Descente de Jésus aux enfers." *Dictionaire de théologie catholique* IV/1 (1924), cols. 565–619.

176. Raes, A. "La risurrezione di Gesù nella liturgia Bizantina." *Gregorianum* 39 (1958): 481–493.

177. Rahmani, J.E. *Apocryphi hypomnemata Domini nostri seu Acta Pilati, antiqua versio syriaca.* Studia syriaca II. Sharfa, Lebanon, 1908.

178. Reicke, B. *The Disobedient Spirits and Christian Baptism: A Study of I Pet. 3:19 and Its Context.* Acta Seminarii Neotestamentici Upsaliensis XIII. Copenhagen: E. Munksgaard, 1946.

179. Revillout, E. "Les apocryphes coptes: Première partie: Les évangiles des douze apôtres et de Saint Barthélemy." Patrologia Orientalis 2, fasc. 2. Paris, 1907.

180. Romanos the Melodist. *Hymnes*, vol. IV. SC 128. Paris: Cerf, 1962.

181. Romanos the Melodist. *On the Life of Christ: Kontakia*. Translated by Ephrem Lash. Lanham, Maryland: AltaMira Press, 1996.

182. Romanos the Melodist. *Sancti Romani Melodi Cantica genuina*, edited by P. Maas and C.A. Trypanis. Oxford: Oxford University Press, 1963.

183. Rose, R. " 'Attolite portas, principes uestras . . .': Aperçus sur la lecture chrétienne du Ps. 24 (23) B." *Miscellanea liturgica in onore di Sua Emi-

nenza Cardinale Giacomo Lercaro, arcivescovo di Bologna, I:453–478. Rome: Desclée de Brouwer, 1966.

184. Rousseau, O. "La descente aux enfers dans le cadre des liturgies chrétiennes." *La Maison-Dieu* 43 (1955): 104–123.

185. Rousseau, O. "La descente aux enfers, fondement sotériologique du baptême chrétien." *Recherches de science religieuse* 40 (1950–1951): 283–297.

186. Santos Otero, A. de. *Los Evangelios Apocrifos. Colleción de textos griegos y latinos, versión critica, estudios introductorios, comentarios e ilustraciones.* Madrid Biblioteca de autores cristianos, 1956.

187. Scaer, D.P. "He Did Descend into Hell: In Defense of the Apostles' Creed." *Journal of the Evangelical Theological Society* 35, no. 1 (1922): 91–99.

188. Schmidt, C. *Der descensus ad inferos in der alten Kirche.* TU 43. Leipzig, 1919.

189. Schürer, E. *The History of the Jewish People in the Age of Jesus Christ.* Vol. 3, part 1. Edinburgh: T. and T. Clark, 1986.

190. Schultz, H.-J. "Die 'Höllenfahrt' als 'Anastasis': Eine Untersuchung über Eigenart und dogmengeschichtliche Voraussetzungen byzantinischer Osterfrömmigkeit." *Zeitschrift für katholische Theologie* 81 (1959): 1–66.

191. Schwartz, E. *Über die pseudoapostolischen Kirchenordnungen.* Strassburg, 1910.

192. Sheerin, D. "St John the Baptist in the Lower World." *Vigiliae Christianae* 30 (1976): 1–22.

193. Simonetti, M. "*Praecursor ad inferos*: Una nota sull'interpretazione patristica di Matteo 11,3." *Augustinianum* 20 (1980): 367–382.

194. Skaballanovich, M. *Tolkoviy Typikon* [A Commented Typikon]. Vols. I–II. Kiev, 1913.

195. Smyth, E.C. "Is the 'Descensus' in the Apostles' Creed an 'Interpolation' and Superfluous?" *The Andover Review* 11 (1889): 414–424.

196. Stewart, C. *"Working the Earth of the Heart": The Messalian Controversy in History, Texts, and Language to AD 431.* Oxford: Oxford University Press, 1991.

197. Stölten, W. "Gnostische Parallelen zu den Oden Salomos." *Zeitschrift für die neutestamentliche Wissenschaft und die Kunde der Älteren Kirche* 13 (1912): 29–58.

198. Stroumsa, G.G. "Mystical Descents." Pages 139–154 in *Death, Ecstasy, and Other Worldly Journeys*, edited by J.J. Collins and M. Fishbane. New York: State University of New York Press, 1995.

199. Studer, B. "Der Abstieg Christi in der Unterwelt bei Augustinus von Hippo." Pages 267–274 in *Psallendum: Miscellanea di studi in onore del*

Prof. Jordi Pinell i Pons, O.S., edited by I. Scicolone et al. Rome: S. Paolo, 1992.

200. Studer, B. *Dieu sauveur: La rédemption dans la foi de l'Eglise ancienne.* Collection Théologies. Paris: Cerf, 1989.

201. Swete, H.B. *The Apostles' Creed: Its Relation to Primitive Christianity.* Cambridge University Press, 1894.

202. Swete, H.B. *The Gospel of Peter.* New York: Macmillan, 1893.

203. Taft, R. *The Liturgy of the Hours in East and West.* Collegeville, Minnesota: Liturgical Press, 1986.

204. Teixidor, J. "Le thème de la descente aux enfers chez saint Éphrem." *L'Orient syrien* 6 (1961): 25–40.

205. Therry, N. "Le thème de la descent du Christ aux enfers en Cappadoce." *Δελτίον τῆς χριστιανικῆς θεολογικῆς ἑταιρίας* 4 (1993–1994): 59–66.

206. Thomas Aquinas. *Summa Theologiae: Latin Text with English Translation.* London-New York: Blackfriars and McGraw-Hill,, 1965.

207. Tischendorff, C. *Evangelia apocrypha.* Leipzig, 1876.

208. Tisserant, E. *Ascension d'Isaie.*Paris: Letouzey, 1909.

209. Trisoglio, F. *San Gregorio di Nazianzo e il Christus patiens: Il problema dell'autenticità gregoriana del drama.* Filologia, Testi e Studi 7. Florence: Casa Editrice Le Lettere, 1996.

210. Tuilier, A., ed. and trans. Introduction to *Grégoire de Nazianze, La passion du Christ: Tragedie.* SC 149. Paris: Cerf, 1969.

211. Turmel, J. "Etude historique sur la descent du Christ aux enfers." *Annales de philosophie chrétienne*, 3e serie, 1 (1902–1903): 508–533.

212. Turmel, J. *La descente du Christ aux enfers.* Paris: Bloud et Cie, 1905.

213. Turner, R.V. "*Descendit ad Inferos*: Medieval Views on Christ's Descent into Hell and the Salvation of Ancient Justs." *Journal of the History of Ideas* 27 (1966): 173–194.

214. Uspensky, N. "Chin vsenoshchnogo bdeniya na pravoslavnom Vostoke i v Russkoy Tserkvi" [The order of the all-night vigil in the Orthodox East and in the Russian Church]. *Bogoslovskiye Trudy* 18 (1978): 5–117.

215. Vaillant, A. "L'homélie d'Épiphane sur l'ensevelissement du Christ." *Radovi staroslovenskog instituta* 3. Zagreb, 1958.

216. Vasiliadis, N. *Tainstvo smerti* [The mystery of death]. Sergiev Posad: Holy Trinity-St Sergius Lavra, 1998.

217. Villette, J. *La Résurrection du Christ dans l'art chrétien du IIe au VIIe siècle.* Paris: H. Laurens, 1957.

218. Vitti, A.M. "Descensus Christi ad Inferos iuxta Apocrypha." *Verbum Domini* 7 (1927): 138–144, 171–181.

219. Vogels, H.G. *Christi Abstieg in Totenreich und das Läuterungsgericht an den Toten: Eine bibeltheologisch-dogmatische Untersuchung zum Glauben-*

sartikel "descendit ad inferos." Freiburger Theologische Studien 102. Freiburg-Basel-Vienna: Herder, 1976.

220. Ware, Kallistos. "The Meaning of the Great Fast." In *The Lenten Triodion.* London: Faber and Faber, 1977.

221. Wellesz, E. *A History of Byzantine Music and Hymnography.* 2nd Edition. Oxford: Clarendon Press, 1961.

222. Wellesz, E. *The Akathistos Hymn.* Copenhagen: Munksgaard, 1957.

223. Wensinck, A.J. "Ephrem's Hymns on Epiphany and the Odes of Solomon." *The Expositor,* series 8, vol. 3 (1912): 108–112.

224. Wilmart, A., and E. Tisserant. "Fragments grecs et latins de l'Evangile de Barthélemy." *Revue biblique* 10 (1913): 185–190.

225. Winling, R. "La résurrection du Christ dans l'*Antirrheticus adversus Appolinarem* de Grégoire de Nysse." *Revue des Etudes augustiniennes* 35 (1989): 12–43.

226. Winling, R. "Mort et résurrection du Christ dans les traités *Contre Eunome* de Grégoire de Nysse." *Revue des sciences religieuses* 64 (1990): 251–269.

227. Winling, R. "La résurrection du Christ dans les traités Pseudo-Athanasiens *Contra Apollinarium.*" *Revue des sciences religieuses* 62, no. 1 (1988): 27–41; 62, nos. 2–3 (1988): 101–110.

228. Wright, W. *Apocryphal Acts of the Apostles,* vol. 1. London: Williams and Norgate, 1871.

229. Yaroshevsky, Gregory. *Izyasnenie trudneischih mest iz 1-go Poslaniya sv. Petra* [An interpretation of the most difficult passages in the first letter of St Paul]. Simferopol, 1902.

230. Yates, J. "'He Descended into Hell': Creed, Article and Scripture." *Churchman* 102, nos. 3–4 (1988): 240–250, 303–315.

231. Zahn, Th. *Das apostolische Symbolum: Eine Skizze seiner Geschichte und eine Prüfung seines Inhalts.* Erlangen-Leipzig: A. Deichert, 1893.

232. Zahn, Th. *Das Evangelium des Petrus.* Erlangen: Deichert, 1893.

233. Zeno of Verona. *Zenonis Veronensis Tractatus,* edited by B. Löfstedt. CCSL 22. Louvain: Brepols, 1971.

234. Zwaan, J. de. "The Edessene Origin of the Odes of Solomon." Pages 285–302 in *Quantalacunque: Studies Presented to K. Lake.* London, 1937.